FAIR GIRLS AND
GREY HORSES

THE AUTHORS

Josephine, Diana and Christine Pullein-Thompson
have been household names to generations of
children since they published their first pony book
back in 1946, *It Began with Picotee.*

FAIR GIRLS AND AND GREY HORSES

Memories of a country childhood

Josephine, Diana and Christine Pullein-Thompson

This edition published in Great Britain in 1997 by
Allison & Busby Ltd
114 New Cavendish Street
London W1M 7FD

First published in Great Britain in 1996 by
Allison & Busby Ltd

A catalogue record for this book is available from the
British Library

ISBN 0 74900 385 5

Typeset by CBS
Felixstowe, Suffolk

Printed and bound in Great Britain by
WBC Book Manufacturers Ltd
Bridgend, Mid Glamorgan

Fair Girls and Gray Horses! A toast to you
Who never went wide of a fence or a kiss.

Will H. Ogilvie

Prologue

What made all four of us become writers? Was it in our genes or caused by an unorthodox childhood with little formal education?

Our elder brother Denis, a playwright, was conventionally educated and, being older, spent far less time at The Grove - which suggests it was genetic. But though our clutch of first cousins yielded a composer, an actor and a publisher, there were no writers among them. And, so far, the next generation has written text and academic books, but little fiction.

We, Josephine, Diana and Christine, all knew that one day we would write about our childhood. And when a film production company approached one of us and asked, 'Are the Pullein-Thompsons still alive?' and the B.B.C. made radio and television programmes about us, we knew that it was time to start.

Our first book, *It Began with Picotee*, published fifty years ago, was a joint effort, which emerged slowly as we argued over every word. But now we are veteran authors with our own styles, such close co-operation has become impossible.

We decided to tell our story in three different voices and, at first, we avoided too much discussion as we wanted to see what would surface and to keep the independence and freshness of our individual recollections. We found that many memories were shared, and to avoid boring repetition it was necessary to divide up some of the material. We agreed, where possible, to start the chapters in turn, and that the last writer, who was sometimes left with a dearth of material, should be first in the following chapter.

There have been disagreements. When it was possible we checked the facts; where this was impossible we voted and, as in childhood, 'two against one' settled the matter, but where anyone has wished to rebut or add to a sister's contribution, this has been allowed.

Journeys back into childhood are not made without poignancy and we have all suffered a little as we re-lived the sharpness of its sorrows and joys and struggled to recall the parents - Mamma and Cappy - as we saw them then.

As well as our own story, we have told of the animals and people around us, the South Oxfordshire of the 'thirties and a way of life that ended with the Second World War.

Chapter One

Diana writes:-

It all began in 1917 at Magdalen Gate House, Oxford, whose front door opens at the side on the High, opposite Magdalen College, but whose façade looks with Georgian grace across the front of the Botanical Gardens.

Harold James Pullein-Thompson, an infantry captain, who had been through the retreat from Mons and much else on the Western Front, was invited to dinner by the Cannans, while he was stationed in Oxford training officer cadets. All three Cannan girls were at home, but Joanna, the youngest, made a late entrance. Five feet three inches tall, pretty, with honey-gold hair and an aquiline nose, she took her place at the table, pulled out her lorgnette and examined the guest with her grey-green eyes. And Pullein-Thompson, six feet two inches tall, with raven-black hair, hooded dark blue eyes and a neat moustache, fell in love. We four – Denis, Josephine, Diana and Christine – were the result of that love.

It is easy to speculate about where our various interests came from. The Cannans were great scribblers; long letters and poems passed between our Cannan forebears. Books were essential to their lives. Our mother's father, Charles Cannan, a classicist, was Dean of Trinity College, Oxford, before becoming in 1898 Secretary to the Delegates (Chief Executive) of the Oxford University Press. His wife Mary, née Wedderburn – the only grandparent we knew – was a fine letter writer. Charles's brother Edwin Cannan (Uncle Teddy), the economist, wrote extensively on his subject. Aunt May became a poet. Our mother wrote forty-eight books.

Love of the theatre was in our genes, too. Great-great-uncle James Cannan was a Manchester drama critic and his grandson Gilbert Cannan became an avant-garde novelist, poet and playwright. On the other side of the family towered Stanley Houghton, the dramatist, my father's first cousin. As if this were not enough, our paternal grandfather James Pullein Thompson, a vicar, exercised his passion for the theatre by staging amateur productions of Gilbert and Sullivan's works, with the Bishop of London; two of our father's plays were performed at fringe theatres and one of his scripts was turned into a silent film.

Both our parents liked riding, but the love of horses probably came mainly from the Wedderburns. Granny, a keen horsewoman in her youth, hunted the carriage horses when her father Andrew came home from India on inheriting Glenlair, the Ayrshire estate of his cousin, the physicist James Clerk Maxwell. She kept a pony and governess cart in Oxford and her aunt, the painter Jemima Blackburn, and her brother's son, John Wedderburn, loved riding all their lives. Some of our aptitude for handling difficult horses surely came also from the Reverend Pullein Thompson's father, hard-drinking John Thompson, an illiterate farrier and blacksmith – in the days when farriers were also horse doctors. John Thompson married Mary Owthwaite (or Outhwaite), a descendent of the Pulleyns of Scotton Hall near Harrogate, where Guy Fawkes, who was taught by a John Pulleyn at the Grammar School in York, lived for a time shortly before trying to blow up the Houses of Parliament.

In 1852 James, the Thompsons' seventh and last child, was born, like the others, in the small village of Crayke near Easingwold. He alone was given the second name of Pullein, probably in honour of his maternal grandmother Mary Pullein. Records of James's youth and education have not survived, but we know he became teetotal, probably in response to a drunken father. In his twenties he studied to become a Methodist minister, before switching to the Church of England when the Manchester girl he loved, comely high-browed Emily Darbyshire, declared she could not marry a man who was 'chapel'. As family legend has it, he was helped to make the change by his mother's kinsman, John James Pulleine, who later became Suffragan Bishop of Richmond, Yorkshire. James passed the Preliminary Cambridge University Theological Examination, probably as an external student, and in 1876 he married Emily Darbyshire and was appointed a *literate* deacon at Salford, Manchester. Four years later, after ordination, he became curate at St Mary's, Manningham, Bradford. In 1883 he moved to London to become

Associate Secretary of the Colonial and Continental Church Society, and in 1886 he was appointed vicar of St Stephen's, Bow. His five children, Muriel, Harold, Edgar, Basil and Eric, were all born in London. Muriel was conscientious and musically talented. Basil died in infancy and Eric was of limited intelligence, but Harold and Edgar were tall and healthy with strong features. Meanwhile Emily's sister Lucy had married a man in the cloth business and produced Stanley Houghton, whose play *Hindle Wakes* would ensure him lasting fame. While he was at Bow, Pullein Thompson's friendship with the Bishop of London blossomed and contributed, I suspect, to his move to Chelsea, where his popularity has long been commemorated by a plaque in the church. The women liked him. 'His voice was so beautiful,' an old lady told me years later, 'and when he pronounced the blessing – it was unforgettable.'

Pullein Thompson's work for the blind and the alcoholic led to a friendship with wealthy, sightless Mrs Graham of Kingston, whose son and daughter he cured of a drink problem. Fortuitously the daughter, fat, cleft-palated Isabella, fell in love with her mentor and moved with her maid into the Chelsea vicarage. Here she took three rooms at an exorbitant rent which financed Edgar's education at Marlborough College, while our bitterly envious father remained a day boy at the less prestigious Merchant Taylors'.

An opportunist, James Pullein Thompson had informally used his second name in conjunction with the first after abandoning the Methodists, but the linkage was not cemented for the next generation until our father and Edgar formally joined the two names together with a hyphen, a necessary change if a double-barrelled name is to be used in the army.

In February 1913 Emily Pullein Thompson died in a Wimbledon nursing home, not far from King's College School where our father taught. In later years their marriage had been soured by sexual strife, after Emily, for reasons best known to herself, had rejected James's advances. Then, Muriel told her son, Emily would flee to spend the night with her, pursued by James who would hammer on his daughter's door vainly demanding that his wife should return to the conjugal bed.

On St Valentine's Day in the year after Emily's death, James Pullein Thompson married Ruby Eastwood, a chorister and parishioner in her twenties – instead of Isabella Graham, as expected. Their daughter Daphne, our indomitable step-aunt, was born in 1916, although we did not meet her until middle age. The same year Pullein Thompson became rector of Luddenham, Kent. He and his wife were soon joined by Isabella, who again rented rooms from them and paid Daphne's school fees, a generous act continued after Pullein Thompson's death in 1924.

Our father disapproved of the second marriage and, although his inheritance (pictures of Scotton Hall and Samuel Pulleyn, and much Pullein silver) came into our teenage lives, we knew little or nothing of the Thompsons. Three years or so after Daphne's birth, our parents settled in Wimbledon, first in 12 Crescent Road and later at 8 (now 4) Marryat Road, which runs between the Common and the tennis courts. Here we three girls were born. Number 8 was (and still is) a grey roughcast-stuccoed house, with a matching addition built on by Granny Cannan, rather French-looking with tile-hung mansards and a large garden by today's standards. It had a tennis court and a huge cedar tree overlooking the night nursery which Christine and I shared with Nana, a coachman's daughter, who had come to work for the Cannans when our Aunt Dorothea was born in 1892. The cedar, jagged and dark against the evening sky, was the first tree I loved, not only for its beauty but also because it was the cause of night-time parties in thunderstorms. Then Mamma, afraid that lightning would strike the tree and send it crashing on the night nursery, wrapped us in eiderdowns and carried us to her bedroom. Our father and Josephine were there, too; and Denis, if he were home, tried to take photographs by lightning. Nana made tea and brought milk and biscuits for us; there was a sense of warmth and excitement, which returns to me even now when thunder wakens me at night.

Our first mount was a rocking horse who lived on the balcony. He had once been dappled but was by then a dirty grey. There was a hole where his saddle had been, into which we later stuffed lumps of sugar which encouraged mice to nest in his belly and led to his destruction. We called him Dobbin, or sometimes Starlight, and rode him constantly. Christine and I also had pretty wheeled horses, with stiff manes and tails, which we pushed around the garden. One night we dreamt at the same moment that we had fallen off Dobbin and woke together with a leap in bed. And then there was Jack, whom Christine will describe.

Identical twins do not bond as closely with their mothers at an early age as single children do, because of their preoccupation with and allegiance to each other. We talked twin language and with our short hair, wide faces and somewhat hooded eyes (mine became more hooded than Christine's), we were oddities.

'Are your twins normal?' asked a Wimbledon neighbour. And our mother, who knew that talent often lies deeply hidden behind eccentricity, replied 'Good God, I hope not.' Later she had her own answer to the difference between the twins, who stumbled and fumbled through life, and her elder daughter, who was so much more at home in the world. Josephine, she said, was an old soul, the twins new.

At three, still only able to converse with each other, habitually car-sick, sometimes train-sick, hyper-active and clumsy, Christine and I were not children of whom intellectual parents could be proud. Mamma was staunch in our defence; our father, trying to be fair, could not love us as much as Josephine. Unplanned, we added to financial problems during a difficult time. In photographs we often look farouche, whereas Josephine, pretty and blonde, smiles confidently into the lens as she poses delightfully on garden steps, garden seats and beside cars. She travelled sometimes with the parents – a recipe for jealousy, I suspect, for one day we beat her over the head with a beaded bag given to Christine by an ancient godmother. Then our father, a man of action, laid us over his knee and smacked our bare bottoms. And afterwards we couldn't stop crying. My sobs took over my whole body and Mamma kept saying 'Do stop, do stop!' while our father said, 'Never, never fight two against one,' and thereafter we never did. It was, I believe, the only time he smacked us. I admired him for a time, but never loved him. He had, like his father (by whom he was frequently caned), a quick temper and he was not a man to snuggle up against. Although he played with us I do not remember ever sitting on his knee or being led by his hand and later I envied girls who had enjoyed a warm relationship with their fathers.

Although brought down sometimes for visitors to see, Christine and I and were definitely nursery children dominated by our adoring Victorian Nana, who was proud of our plump bodies and rosy cheeks. Having grown up poor, she was also extremely frugal. So from our earliest days we saw that nothing should be wasted: brown paper was smoothed and parcel string unknotted for future use. Vegetable peelings and tea leaves were boiled and fed to the hens, whose surplus spring eggs were stored in water-glass for winter days.

Fishcakes were my favourite breakfast – is it significant that a row over fishcakes, which were served lukewarm once again to Cappy's fury, precipitated my birth? But Nana favoured milky rice puddings for small children, soft-boiled eggs and in winter oranges with a lump of sugar in the middle. You did not usually ask for things. My longing for a hard-boiled egg was only expressed in a whispered prayer no one heard when I was taken downstairs to wish as I stirred the Christmas pudding. She knitted us beautiful sweaters; in winter we slept under six blankets, well tucked in, and an eiderdown, our feet cosy in the long white bedsocks she had made us. In the daytime we wore combinations (known as Cossiaggers in twin language) as well as woolly vests, and Granny's old fur coat was cut down and turned into little waistcoats (woofies, we called them) for us to wear under our overcoats. Nana had a stockpile of remedies, among them: Homoceia, an ointment for bruises and aches and pains; and Hazeline Cream, which was antiseptic. Her poultices were legendary within the family. Her linseed variety had saved Aunt Dorothea's baby, Charles, from dying of whooping cough to the astonishment of the doctor treating him.

Our twinny, deep-rooted togetherness defied loneliness. We didn't suck our thumbs or need corners of blankets to finger to help us adjust to our limited way of life. Rarely hungry and constantly warm, with space in which to enjoy ourselves and a nurse who did not often grant requests, we rarely tried to communicate with the grown-ups. But eventually Mamma, despite her insistence that we were normal, became worried about our poor speech and decided to part us. Christine remained in Wimbledon with Nana, whose favourite she was, and I went with Mamma to stay in Oxford with Aunt Dorothea where, traumatised by separation, I sank into lethargy and silence, while at home Christine uttered not a word. Alarmed, Mamma accepted that the experiment had not worked and took me back to my twin.

Nana dug out the Crown Books from which Mamma and her sisters had learned to read. '*I am up on my ox*' began the first lesson in Volume One, and in the second volume: '*Winter days are jolly. The days are long, the nights are short, there is not time for all the things we have to do.*' I soon learned the stories by heart and, pretending to read, recited them when asked, stumbling over the pronunciation. From now on broken English became my second language. But at first I loved books' pictures best. *Struwwelpeter's* were horribly fascinating, the art nouveau illustrations in *A Treasury of Verse for Little Children* a total delight, and the little history I learned came entirely from two history picture books. Then the rhythm and imagery of poetry read aloud by Mamma captured us all. Robert Louis Stevenson's:

> *Up into the cherry tree*
> *Who should climb but little me?*
> *I held the trunk with both my hands*
> *And looked abroad on foreign lands.*

Also Eugene Field's 'Wynken, Blynken and Nod' with its enchanting illustration of three blue-clad figures sailing in a green sabot called Daisy watched by a man-faced moon:

> *Wynken, Blynken and Nod one night*
> *Sailed off in a wooden shoe –*
> *Sailed on a river of crystal light,*
> *Into a sea of dew.*
> *"Where are you going and what do you wish?"*
> *The old moon asked the three.*
> *"We have come to fish for the herring fish*
> *That live in the beautiful sea.*
> *Nets of silver and gold have we!"*
> *Said Wynken, Blynken and Nod.*

And, of course, we Pullein-Thompson girls felt we *were* the three.

What pictures these words conjured up, along with Lear's 'The Owl and the Pussy Cat' and, of course Carroll's 'The Walrus and the Carpenter'. And on winter nights who could resist Robert Louis Stevenson's 'The Lamplighter'?

> *Now Tom would be a driver and Maria go to sea.*
> *And my Papa's a banker and as rich as he can be.*
> *But I, when I am stronger and can choose what I'm to do,*
> *O Leerie, I'll go round at night and light the lamps with you.*

Poor Nana, trying so hard to turn us into little ladies, skilful with needle and thread, was unable to compete with poetry read by a much-loved mother, who was, without knowing it, nurturing the germ of a vocation. I now believe my love of the English language began with *A Treasury of Verse for Little Children,* my first, to use a contemporary phrase, tingle factor. Before we left Wimbledon, there was one unpleasant experience, which lurks at the back of my memory. Christine and I, with our identical genetic inheritance, both suffered from rotten baby teeth, perhaps because Mamma, who had suffered from rickets as a child, was unable to provide us with enough calcium in the womb. Extraction under chloroform was recommended to our parents but nothing was said to us, although Nana's ardent scrubbing of the nursery deal table with Sunlight soap – she could trust no one else to do it properly – filled me with unease. 'Must be clean for the dentist,' she said. I suppose we met the dentist, and Christine says the doctor was there too, but I only remember coming round after the chloroform and spitting blood. We were not expected to be upset and we didn't cry; we were, after all, in our own minds the sort of people who sail fearlessly away in shoes. Unknown to us, Denis's tonsils were earlier snipped under chloroform on the same table. Astonished to be wakened from a night's sleep by a uniformed nurse, he had been given a lump of sugar and led to meet his surgeon, so avoiding pre-operation nerves.

We learned at Wimbledon never to leave strangers alone anywhere in one's property, after our parents put Number Eight on the market and a middle-aged viewer became faint in their bedroom. 'Please, water,' she gasped and Mamma, ever-helpful at such times, rushed to the kitchen to fill a glass. Soon revived, the woman left and in the evening Mamma noticed all the jewellery on her dressing table had gone. 'Oh that's mad Annie,' the police said, on hearing the thief described. The jewellery was soon recovered, and our trust in human nature sensibly diminished.

Although I grew to love my mother more than anyone else in the world, my first memories are of Nana in the night nursery at first light, a short, stout figure, pulling strong lisle stockings up thick thighs criss-crossed with mulberry red veins, dropping vest and petticoat over her head, buttoning blouse and cardigan, fixing a skirt and, lastly, winding her long greying hair into a bun, which she pinned firmly on top of her head. She was then in her fifties dressing a body that was slipping towards old age.

Obstinate, loyal, deeply prejudiced and very hard-working, Nana made us her life; she cuddled us and crooned over us. She knitted, washed and crocheted for us. Although an agnostic since the First World War, she tried to teach us the Lord's Prayer. She adored Mamma, who had been her favourite of the three Cannan girls, and disliked our father. 'There was none of that shouting at Magdalen Gate House,' she would say. 'Your grandfather was such a quiet man.' She pronounced Magdalen like Mary Magdalen, claiming that to speak as the gentry did would be 'putting on airs'. In theory Nana was a servant, in fact she ruled her roost.

But the afternoons we remember best were those when Mamma left her writing and took us and her Sealyhams across Wimbledon Common to Caesar's Camp, or sometimes to The Windmill, and back. Usually Poppy, who had a weak heart, rode home in the pram with Christine, me and the firewood Mamma had collected, while Josephine stumped along in her beloved red riding hood mackintosh. And when years later I walked in the woods of Washington DC with my own children and a dog, I surprised my neighbours by filling the pram with twigs, too.

Spared many boring domestic problems by Nana, Mamma felt like a thirteen-year-old when she was with us. She loved expeditions and sometimes took Denis on long walks in the Surrey countryside. Once Denis, running away with a knapsack on his back at the age of seven (perhaps traumatised by the arrival of three sisters), was asked, by the policeman who took him home, where he had been going. He was put out by Mamma's giggles at his carefully considered reply, 'The Portsmouth Road'.

Sometimes she sang to us, out of tune but with an infectious merriment, and increasingly, twin-bound and Nana-bonded though I was, I responded to that merriment and started belatedly to move very slowly out of the fog of my early childhood into a sense of my own identity and that of other people.

* * * *

Josephine writes:-

We all had our own birth stories. Denis was born in Oxford in the house of our maternal grandparents in 1919. Cappy, as our father became known, who had survived four years in the trenches, was still a regular soldier and could not be there.

Denis was a large baby and a breech presentation. Our mother,

her twenty-third birthday only two weeks away, was small. After forty-eight hours of pain and anguish he was hauled out in a forceps delivery. During those two long summer days a cuckoo in the Botanical Gardens cuckooed unceasingly. For the rest of her life, Nana could not bear the sound, it reminded her too vividly of those hours when she watched, helplessly, the pain of her favourite child.

The five-year gap between Denis and me was odd, for both parents wanted another child, preferably a daughter, and the powerful sexual attraction, which had brought them together, was as strong as ever; but possibly the trauma of Denis's birth had something to do with it.

Mamma had married for love and rather against her better judgement. She had been educated by governesses and at Wychwood School, Oxford, and then between sixteen and seventeen, refusing to follow her two older sisters to Downe House School, she had been 'finished' at a modest establishment in Paris.

She had attended art classes there and, falling in love with Paris, had become a lifelong Francophile; mimosa, she always insisted, was her favourite flower. At eighteen, she had mapped out her future: she would enrol at the Slade School of Art, then paint in a Parisian garret, and free love, rather than the dreary domesticity of an English marriage, was to be her lot. But it was 1914 and, on the outbreak of the first world war, she became a VAD and later worked at the Oxford University Press.

Mamma always admitted that she was bowled over by Cappy's looks, by his assured manner and his ability to hail taxis and summon head waiters. At thirty-four he was so different from the undergraduates who had previously courted her; and though she refused his first proposal of marriage, when later, on leave from France, he asked her again, she accepted him.

A quiet marriage in 1918 put an end to her ambitions as a painter, but, vowing that she would never sink to being a housewife, she began to breed Sealyham terriers and to write. The dog breeding was successful; Hero, son of Spic and Span, was a reserve champion at Crufts. But the writing proved more enduring. *The Misty Valley* was published in 1923, and a review in the *Daily Express* began '. . . one of the cleverest and most delightfully written first novels I have read for a long time' and ended 'her clarity for a beginner is staggering'.

She was finishing her second novel *Wildberry Wine* as I arrived. Tradition has it that the monthly nurse said 'Put away that scribbling dear, Baby's coming.' Conveniently small and the correct way round, I emerged without drama. It was April 3rd and snowing, but the men who had come to sow the new tennis court worked on.

Diana and Christine, who were not planned, arrived eighteen months later. The realization that it could be twins, sent Cappy scurrying for insurance, but, as there had been twins in the last two generations of Mamma's family, it was not forthcoming.

On October 1st, a breakfast quarrel over the fishcakes – I suspect they were either pallid or tepid, Cappy's two hatreds – precipitated the arrival. It was a Saturday, Dr Newton was fetched from the golf course, but arrived too late; our identical twins had been delivered by the monthly nurse.

It seems that Diana and Christine did look exactly alike, for on a traumatic day when their identifying ribbons fell off, everyone was consulted as to which was which. It is said that Smith, the jobbing gardener and a great dahlia man, made the final decision. But if a fortune had been involved, if the twenty minutes between them had mattered, I think Christine could well have disputed such a doubtful identification.

Denis has always complained that my arrival completely disrupted his life and it was true that up until then he had had the attention of two devoted women. But I was a quiet and unobtrusive baby and, as he was becoming bored with nursery life, he had started school early – the compulsory age at the time was seven. The Study, a private school across the road from our house, was mainly for girls, but took boys up to the age of eight.

My short life was far more upset by the arrival of the twins, for Nana announced, with justifiable firmness, that she could not be expected to care for three children under two – in Granny's day, though almost thirty years younger, she had always had a nursery maid – and I must leave the nursery. She adored babies but I don't think she had ever bonded with me. She liked the large, plump, rosy-cheeked variety; I was pale and thin. On arrival I had instantly expressed my intolerance of cows' milk, sometimes reducing Nana to tears with the look of rejection I gave her proffered bottles. And then, according to Mamma, I sat up and ate everything from cheese to lobster; highly inappropriate behaviour for a baby of those days.

We had all been born into a changing and deeply depressing world. The aftermath of the 1914–18 war weighed heavily and Britain's economic position was appalling. Unemployment, which had earlier been swelled by the returned soldiers and the almost two million surplus women (for whom there was no prospect of marriage), was still rife. The widows and orphans of the three quarters of a million men who had died were struggling to survive, and, while the worst cases among the million incapacitated wounded were hidden away, the number of amputees in society were a constant reminder of the carnage.

Both our parents had fairly expensive tastes. Though the Cannans had prided themselves on plain living and high thinking, Mamma had been brought up to accept many of the good things of life – beautiful houses, Swiss holidays, books and regular meals – without considering the cost; while Cappy's longing for the high life was probably a reaction to his penny-pinching rectory childhood.

As well as a mortgage, they had acquired a car and four children. They had staff to pay: Nana, the little live-in maid, the cleaning woman and the part-time gardener and Cappy felt that membership of a London club and the occasional golfing weekend were essential to his happiness. Mamma had refused to marry him unless he gave up bridge, but they both enjoyed parties, the theatre, the 'flicks', eating out and dancing; when too broke for night clubs, they 'slummed' at the Palais de Danse in Hammersmith. They lost most of their investments in the slump, bills and the overdraft were a constant worry, but while she gradually learned frugality, he remained a spender.

Cappy never told us much about his immediate family. He boasted of being born within the sound of Bow bells and we knew from a drawer full of tasselled caps that he had been successful at Merchant Taylors' School – excelling at rugby and running. He never mentioned his afflicted brothers Eric and Basil, but he admitted that he had never forgiven his parents for sending Uncle Edgar to a grander public school and he acknowledged the injustice of their treatment of Aunt Muriel, the eldest and only daughter – now a war widow – who was taught that she was 'only a girl' and must sacrifice her interests to those of her father and brothers. Their mother had been injured in a carriage accident just before Cappy's twenty-first birthday and never wholly recovered.

At Oxford his life blossomed. The escape from home to Wadham seems to have resulted in a violent reaction to his whole upbringing. He became an agnostic, abandoned theology in favour of geography and teetotalism for the presidency of the college wine society. He also, from his own accounts, became a rugger hearty who smashed up poets' rooms, knocked off policemen's helmets and climbed spires in order to decorate them with chamber pots.

After university he taught at King's College School, Wimbledon, from 1909 until 1914. He was probably a heroic figure to the boys as he had played rugger for Oxford and the Harlequins and, becoming a lieutenant in the Special Reserve, he ran the OTC. He also had a circle of friends with whom he played tennis and bridge. The school magazine of December 1914 states that he was one of the first to sail with the British Expeditionary Force and tells of him visiting the school as a Captain, wounded, and 'suffering from the temporary loss of the use of both arms'.

After the war he had agonized for a long time about staying in the army. Mamma was in favour, she longed to see India, but he said later that it was the likelihood of a posting to Ireland, and the possibility of having to kill his fellow countrymen, that finally made him resign his commission. Of course, at that time he was not aware that his wounds were gradually to disable him. The doctors had patched up his shoulders and arms, broken by bullets at the battle of Aisne in 1914, but the second wound left him with shrapnel in his hip and its removal was beyond the medical expertise of the time. At first it caused no trouble, but with the onset of osteoarthritis various cures seemed to have been tried, including an electrical treatment, which by heating up the shrapnel must have caused unbearable pain; by the time I was old enough to be aware of the problem he had a limp and was dependent on painkillers.

Leaving the army his first job was with a film company and he wrote scripts for silent films, but when the company failed, as so many did at that time, he took various jobs to support the family and wrote plays in the evenings and at weekends.

Mamma's sister, May Wedderburn Cannan, had been the first of the younger generation to be published – slim volumes of her war poems had appeared in 1917 and 1919. Carola Oman, the historian and Mamma's best friend throughout their school days, has told of an occasion in 1919 when she, Joanna, and

Georgette Heyer met in Wimbledon to talk about their writing. The Heyer family were Cappy's friends. George Heyer, the father, had also taught at King's College School and he belonged to the Wimbledon tennis and bridge-playing set.

Georgette was the youngest of the three novelists, but the first to be published. Her *Black Moth* appeared in 1921, Mamma's *Misty Valley* in late 1922, Carola Oman's *The Road Royal* in 1924.

We had two family stories about Georgette. One was that as a teenager she had been in love with Cappy, and the other that when her father lost a large sum of money in the collapsing stock market of 1920 she had written *Black Moth* – an historical romance – to save the family fortunes, and handed him her hundred pound advance. Her first modern novel, *Instead of the Thorn*, published in 1923, contains a very fulsome dedication to Joanna Cannan.

At the same time as realising her own ambitions, Mamma had become an important contributor to the family finances. Her third novel *The Lady of the Heights* appeared the year the twins were born and was followed by a romantic serial in the *Daily Courier*; she also wrote articles for magazines and newspapers.

She worked hard and I must have learned to be undemanding and adaptable. While she wrote I played quietly. When Denis tobogganed, Mamma pulled me along in a home-made sledge; when Cappy wanted her company on a business trip to the north of England and Scotland, Denis and I went too. We stayed in York, where I fell in love with the Minster and throughout the rest of the journey constantly suggested 'Let's go back to the Orchestra (sic).' I was bathed in a wash basin because Scottish hotels charged extra for baths. At Cowdenknowes, where we stayed with Mamma's Hope cousins, Denis rode a grey pony and I was sick at breakfast, but the butler dealt with it calmly, bringing a large sponge.

This trip was described to me so often that I doubt whether I really remember it. I suspect that my first memory was being alone in the garden with Denis perhaps there was a crisis with the twins and he had been told to amuse me. Anyway, he took the wooden cover off a drain and there was the most enormous spider with stick-like legs. We weren't frightened, we stood together marvelling at it.

I was an obstinate child. Told on no account to touch the deck chairs, I experimented the moment the adult backs were turned and almost removed the top joint of one finger. The doctor did his best with it, but it has never matched its pair on the other hand.

I was smacked once, but I can't remember the crime or the punishment, only my terrible tears afterwards. Both parents were there and it seemed that they were as frightened by my terrible choking tears as I was. 'Stop crying,' they demanded, 'stop crying.'

Mamma was not a cosy mother and was often preoccupied – she had once come home from a shopping errand without Denis. When Nana demanded, 'Where's the baby?' she had to rush back and fortunately he was still there, parked in his pram outside the shop. In some ways this lack of conventional motherliness was an advantage, for she saw you as a person, almost an equal. When you were sobbing, aged three, at the indignity of wetting your pants, she consoled you, 'Don't worry, it could happen to anyone.' She was also understanding about my square of silk, my equivalent of the sucky blankets beloved of some children, but not permitted by Nana. I took my square to bed with me, rotating it between my first finger and thumb, and Mamma swore that I could not be fobbed off with the new artificial silk, but insisted on the real thing.

I think we had a good relationship. I liked her wit and she enjoyed my earthier sense of humour. She told a story of finding me performing weird antics and, when asked what I was doing, answering 'Only trying to make God laugh!'

I am not sure that this is as original as it sounds, for the poet and playwright John Drinkwater was a visitor – I can remember sitting on his knee while he drew pictures for me – and one of his poems begins with the immortal line 'God laughed when He made Grafton'.

Mamma's family were Scottish with dashes of French blood. Her father, Charles Cannan – small and undistinguished-looking – was possessed of an excellent brain. A double first, he had become classical tutor, Fellow and Dean of Trinity, Oxford. His mother, Jane Dorothea Claude of a French Huguenot family, died in Madeira when he was eighteen months old, and three weeks after the birth of his brother, Edwin Cannan. Their father, an intelligent but weak man, brought them back to England and, after various vicissitudes, they were reared by an aunt in Clifton.

Mamma's mother, Mary Wedderburn, and her twin brother had been born prematurely on the ship bringing their parents home on leave. Their father served in the Indian Civil Service for thirty-six years and rose to be Collector of Madras. There were three older siblings, unhappy remittance children, farmed out in the Kipling tradition.

Their ancestor, Sir John Wedderburn, who came out in the '45, was captured at Culloden, brought south, imprisoned in Southwark and hanged, drawn and quartered at the Oval in 1746. His eldest surviving son was smuggled out of the country; leaving by Wapping Old Stairs he took ship for the West Indies. A fifteen-year-old younger son, Jamie, rode on his pony from Dundee to London, carrying letters to those whom it was thought might help his father. When no help was forthcoming he visited his father in prison the night before his execution, and later rode back to Scotland, according to family mythology, with Sir John's head in his saddlebag. It was from Jamie that we were descended.

Granny's mother, Joanna Kier, also came from a family that had suffered as a result of the rising in 1745. She was a Macgregor, a descendant of Rob Roy's youngest son who had called himself Kier when the family was proscribed. Her mother was French, her father a physician to the reigning Czar, and she was brought up at the Court of St Petersburg. When her mother died, she went home to Scotland and, in Edinburgh, met and married our great-grandfather.

It was obvious that with so few people in the family having had secure and loving childhoods, the Cannan parents were not altogether to blame for a lack of warmth in their parenting. But the three sisters Dorothea, May and Joanna always felt that they had been neglected and left too much with Nana.

Nana, Ellen Hall, the daughter of a coachman from the north Oxfordshire town of Witney, had been reared by a widowed mother who, despite her poverty, scraped up a penny a week to send her children to Dame school. Ellen was obviously intelligent, she wrote and read well, and she became nursemaid to the children of a local doctor. Later she left home for a post as nurse in Surrey, but we could never persuade her to tell us anything about the children she looked after there.

The Cannans were her third place, she was twenty-four, and Aunt Dorothea, the eldest of the three girls, was one month old. One of Nana's responsibilities was to take the three small girls to stay with their relations in Scotland while their parents climbed in Switzerland. Some of the houses were very formal, especially below stairs, but Roshven was different. A remote house in the

West Highlands, owned by their Wedderburn great-aunt and her retired professor husband, it was the Cannan girls' idea of heaven and they spent several weeks there every summer.

Great-Aunt Jemima had known many of the literary men of her day and had travelled round Iceland in a party with Anthony Trollope: some of her paintings and drawings illustrate his travel book. But it was their cousin Margaret, always known as 'Lady', who was to have a lifelong influence on the three girls – an influence that trickled down to us. Lady turned them from town children into country ones. They rode the donkey and later the Highland ponies, they were taught to swim and row a boat and to fish. They were expected to be strong and resolute and to possess the attribute, which my mother was always to admire, of being 'good on a desert island'.

At eight Denis went as a day boy to King's College School, which he hated. But Cappy, loyal by nature, would not listen to complaints against the school or his old friend Woodhill, the headmaster.

Frustrated, Denis had the machiavellian idea of training me to make his subversive remarks for him. In the privacy of the garden shed he taught me to say 'Silly old Woodhill, silly old Woody,' and to repeat it in Cappy's hearing. I obliged enthusiastically but, to my disappointment, I was ignored.

Denis made objects with Meccano, he fret-sawed, he kept silkworms which ate leaves from the mulberry tree in the garden, and he rolled out peppermint creams on the nursery table. The greyish tinge – from unwashed hands or my doll's cup, which he used as a cutter – put off the adults, who only tasted out of politeness, but we ate them with relish.

The twins grew large and very active. Poor Nana could be heard exhorting them, 'Now if you could sit still, just for one minute . . .'

At that time I had no place in their lives. Speaking only their own language, they viewed me as an outsider. On their third or fourth birthday, the parents had given one a toy wheelbarrow and the other a garden roller. October the first was a fine day and I remember standing on the nursery balcony, with Dobbin the rocking horse, and feeling very alone as I watched the two figures running up and down with their new toys. It was about then that I began to tell people that the tennis court was my twin.

In fact the twins' birthday was always a trial to me when small, for with Denis at school, I seemed to be the only child not getting a present. When my mother noticed my struggles with envious tears, she took to buying me a tiny present as a sop.

Mamma read to us regularly: Beatrix Potter, *Little Black Sambo*, poems from a large fat treasury of children's verse. She suddenly banned *Struwwelpeter*, I imagine that one of us had bad dreams or was frightened by the brutal Scissor Man and, remembering her own horror on being given Foxe's *Book of Martyrs* to read on Sundays when a child, she sympathised. I don't think she approved of our weekly comics, but they were really taken for Nana, who read all three of them avidly. The only strip I can remember had a fat character called Porky boy, who thought only of food and always seemed to be opening hampers of good things, but Diana remembers enjoying one about a shelf of saucepans which came to life.

I have no recollection of actually learning to read, but I remember a scene when Nana, who would have thought it a terrible disgrace if any child had left her nursery unable to read and write, was teaching the twins and I sat, fingers in ears, mouthing each word silently, deep in a Victorian work, *Tales to Read to Myself*.

For Christmas and birthdays I was given books in a series about another Josephine and her dolls, which, no doubt for egoistical reasons of identification, gave me great pleasure. The dolls – Josephine's family – ranged from a pair of Korean females in national dress, to wicked Quackie and one-legged Patrick; I was devoted to them all.

We were not great doll lovers, but we each had a very charming one given to us by Cappy when he worked for Chad Valley; I had named mine Party. I also had two very beautiful Swedish dolls in national dress, which Carola Oman had given me. I named them Sailor – obviously no one explained about national dress – and Sweetest. These elegant dolls lived, with the Solitaire board, in the cupboard of the satinwood bookcase, they were drawing-room toys, only to be played with on Sundays, when Nana shut our toy cupboards and took her afternoon off. I also had a large shabby dog called Rover, a lion called Gilbert, and a small teddy bear, all of whom meant more to me than the grand dolls.

Nana didn't like men – except perhaps Charles Cannan – and as Denis grew older she seemed to transfer her love for him to Christine, while he had begun to find some of her habits irritating.

He most loathed her practice of disturbing us as we sat round a roaring nursery fire and announcing, as she deadened it to a smoking heap with coal slack, 'There, that'll be a nice fire presently!'

Ants brought about the final break. The lower boys at King's College School had discovered that the sun, directed by magnifying glasses, could frizzle ants to death and Mamma hearing this had given Denis a lecture on kindness to insects as well as animals.

A few days later he came home from school and found Nana, in the wild part of the garden where the washing was hung out, pouring boiling water on an ants' nest. I don't know what they said to each other, but it ended with Denis hurling a missile at her, which fortunately missed. I remember Nana rushing indoors, and barricading herself and us in the nursery as though he were in pursuit. Somehow Mamma patched things up, but their relationship had changed, and when he went to boarding school, she always referred to him as 'that poor boy'.

Mamma, reared by an atheist father whom she loved and respected and a worldly mother who had her daughters confirmed 'in case they married bishops', had I think a secret longing for faith. Cappy, though an avowed agnostic, was fiercely patriotic and often took us to Armistice Day services. (He also had an embarrassing habit of knocking the hats off men who failed to remove them for the National Anthem.) So, hamstrung by their religious upbringings, they allowed Nana to be responsible for ours.

She made us say our prayers and encouraged us to learn our favourite hymns. Being an optimist, I chose 'All Things Bright and Beautiful', and it was some time before the birth of a social conscience made me leave out the third verse. Christine chose 'Now Day is Over', which was Nana's favourite, and Diana, to my surprise, for I already hated the brutality of the crucifixion, 'There is a Green Hill Far Away'. I very much disliked singing the verse of 'Once in Royal David's City' – 'Little Children all must be, Mild obedient, good as He.' I didn't particularly wish to be good or mild and certainly not obedient.

I think my loneliness grew at this time with Denis away and Diana and Christine so wrapped up in each other, and no friends provided. On our birthdays we were allowed to choose our favourite food – I always chose pancakes and once managed to eat seven – but no other children were invited. On walks we sometimes met two very attractive little boys called Scudamore. They wore the kilt and their mother told mine that they often fought over me, but for some reason (could it have been Nana?) they were never asked to tea.

Then I suppose my isolation was noticed, because I was provided with a red velvet dress and taken to dancing classes at the Study. I also had a trial run with the Brownies. I was too young to join and had no uniform, but I was put in a six with a leader called Pat. After the pack activities and games we were sent back to our sixes to model in *papier mâché*. At the end of the session we had to clear up and Pat handed me a broom and told me to sweep the floor.

When the same thing happened at the next rally, I rebelled and pointed out that it was someone else's turn to sweep. Pat was furious and, twisting my arm behind my back, demanded that I did as I was told. Equally obstinate, I resisted and eventually it was she who gave way. I don't remember going again and I never acquired the uniform, but I don't think I told anyone why I disliked the Brownies.

At seven I went to school at the Study. I learned to cross the road by myself, watched from an upper window by Nana or Mamma and the twins. For some reason there were two of us who sat apart from the rest of the class. We may have been younger than the others, or possibly our parents had waited for our seventh birthdays, instead of sending us at the beginning of the school year, but, whatever the reason, we seemed out of things and neglected.

My memory, which must be wrong, tells me that I spent my entire time sitting and staring at pages of incomprehensible 'sums'. The figures meant nothing to me. I could count, but no one had taught me how to add and subtract with blocks or beans, and I had almost no experience of handling money. To my fury, my fellow outcast, Beryl, knew the secret. I hated her for this and one day when her mother slammed the car door on her hand, I was shocked to find myself almost happy at her screams and tears.

Julia, aged about ten, gave a Christmas party and asked all the juniors. Cappy drove me there and gave a lift to our pretty young teacher, Miss MacGregor. I can remember the mildly flirtatious atmosphere in the car and a feeling of pride that he actually liked my teacher.

Julia's family were rich and it was a lavish party. At the moment of cake-cutting, artificial snowflakes descended. 'Look, it's snowing!' exclaimed the grown-ups. As I pulled a thick velvet curtain aside and peered outside to check, I heard a saccharine voice saying, 'Oh look at that little girl, she's looking to see if it's *really* snowing. Isn't she sweet!'

Life outside the home seemed full of minor embarrassments and Nana's individualistic vocabulary and euphemisms didn't help. Chamber pots were called 'Articles'. Bedroom slippers became night slippers, you washed your head instead of your hair and worst of all was 'making yourself comfortable'. When visiting a friend of Denis's, probably on the day that the twins had their teeth out, I told Joyce, the elder sister, that I wanted to make myself comfortable. She looked surprised and said, 'Well, do it on that chair.' Being an old soul I sat on the chair for a few tactful minutes, and then tried again. This time I asked for the lavatory.

When I was very small, Cappy and Denis had elicited strange noises from a cat's whisker and crystal set, but as the wireless came into general use, our parents seemed to suspect it of having some sort of malign influence on the young. For most of our childhood Nana owned the only wireless in the house – one of those sets with a rising sun on the façade – and she listened to the bands of Henry Hall and Jack Payne after we had gone to bed.

We listened to Children's Hour occasionally, perhaps when Mamma wasn't there to read to us, and we loved hearing the names of the birthday children read out. There was wild excitement whenever the announcer paused, as though in surprise, to say, 'Hullo, *Twins!*' Once, Diana and Christine's names were sent in, but I think they were awed rather than thrilled to hear themselves mentioned.

The gramophone was considered respectable and we inherited the parents' records – the war songs: 'It's a long way to Tipperary', 'There's a Ship that's Bound for Blighty', 'Pack Up Your Troubles' and 'There's a Long Long Trail A' Winding', and the songs from the 'shows' of their courting days: 'If You Were the Only Girl in the World', 'Maid of the Mountains', 'Tea for Two.'

We didn't have many records of our own. Denis had a treasured one, I think the words went:

I cursed and I swore at my father
I told him his words were a lie,
I packed up my things in a bundle
And went to bid Mother goodbye.

Poor mother she burst out a-crying
She said you are breaking my heart . . .

Cappy bought us 'Alfred and the Lion', recited by Stanley Holloway, which I thought very funny, and a record about a character called Barnacle Bill the Sailor. Barnacle Bill, a male chauvinist, sang:

You moaning woman, you're driving me mad,
you haven't as much sense as I thought you had

along with other insults, and one sensed Cappy's obvious enjoyment and Mamma's disapproval.

Both parents thought it important that children should be brought up with a dog, and Spic, the only remaining Sealyham, had grown old and irritable and liable to snap at us, so they decided against terriers and bought a black cocker spaniel, whom they named Barnacle Bill.

Barney was an unlucky dog and immediately went down with distemper, in those days an almost certain killer. Mamma nursed him and he seemed to get better, but then he began to have fits. I can remember the horror of him lying on the floor, in convulsions, foaming at the mouth and incontinent, but the vet prescribed bromide and again he recovered.

He slept, in a much chewed basket, in the downstairs cloakroom and one morning he was found with his head firmly wedged behind the basin waste pipe. The parents couldn't free him, and finally Cappy fetched a wrench and unscrewed the pipe. Barney was unharmed, but the waste pipe was ruined.

We often watched the Oxford and Cambridge Boat Race, usually from Putney Bridge, but one year Cappy knew an umpire and was invited to follow in an official launch. Denis and I were taken, but the experience was rather lost on me. I was really more interested in the dark blue favours we all wore and very disappointed that we were Oxford; I preferred light blue.

Being taken to watch tennis on the Centre Court at Wimbledon was also rather a waste when one was only five or six, but, being a debenture holder, Cappy had two centre court seats for every day of the championships as well as his own badge. Mamma and Nana had to fill the seats for some of the duller matches, and, because I could sit still, they took me.

Of my mother's fourth novel *Sheila Bothways*, the *Observer* critic wrote: 'The wit is constant and never cheap', which became a family saying. *No Walls of Jasper*, her sixth, was well reviewed and went into a second impression. It seems to have confirmed her reputation and several critics noted that she was a woman who wrote about men.

Mamma once confessed to me in later life that she never felt entirely adult. Some part of her seemed trapped at the age of twelve, and she attributed this to domination by Nana, until she escaped to Paris, and then to marrying a man twelve years older and so much more experienced than herself.

All through the Wimbledon years she had found it almost impossible to satisfy these two dominating presences; both were strong-minded, with decided opinions on everything, both wanted to run her and the household. It is possible that a move from Wimbledon was seen as a chance to escape from Nana, who had now seen them through the worst of their child-rearing, but also the house had grown too small for us. Six bedrooms were not enough when one was assigned as the day nursery, a nurse and a maid had to be housed, and married men still required dressing rooms.

The twins could not go on sharing a bedroom with Nana, and I had always slept in our parents' room until wakened one night by the noise of what was, I realised many years later, an orgasm. A little voice enquiring, 'What's the matter?' must have been unpopular and I soon found myself sleeping on a camp bed in Cappy's dressing room or in Denis's little room while he was away at school.

Times were still hard and I suspect that the overdraft was again out of control. The thought of finding a larger but cheaper house in the country would have influenced Cappy, while my mother, though she loved the house in Marryat Road, had always found Wimbledon suburban and still hankered for the country.

* * * *

Christine writes:-

My sisters asked for ice cream, while I asked for a little cake. Respectably dressed in winter coats, we were sitting at a table in the carpeted upstairs restaurant in Barkers Store in Kensington having travelled there with Nana in an open-topped bus. It was Nana's idea of a treat. I must have been four or five years old and, though I still spoke mostly in twin language, I was able to make myself understood. It is a moment I have never forgotten, because I greatly desired an ice cream rather than the little rather dry cake I ordered, which eventually arrived for me in a pleated case on a small white plate. It was I believe my first small step in wishing to be an individual rather than just one of the twins. This feeling has never totally left me.

As was the fashion in those days, we were dressed alike and often given identical toys. We were expected to share to such an extent that on one never-to-be-forgotten birthday, when our parents must have been particularly hard up, we were given just one book between us entitled *The Ghostly Galleon*. I have it still.

But I am in no doubt that we were much loved and that my mother was proud of having twins and as Josephine was hardly bigger than we were, the three of us were sometimes mistaken for triplets. Diana and I were not easy children. I was, I believe, Nana's favourite just as years before Mamma had been favoured among the Cannan girls. I suspect that Nana favoured Mamma because she was the youngest and also because she had had rickets when small and had had to wear irons to straighten her legs. I was of course only the youngest by twenty minutes, but I was the most backward and had almost died when Diana and I had bronchitis, a killer of babies in those days. I was the worst affected and, as Nana often related later, she hardly slept for a fortnight, using steaming kettles to help our breathing and poultices to clear our congested chests. Because of our illness Diana and I were not christened until we were nine months old, when we are reputed to have pulled down a curtain in the church of St Clement Danes, which was later destroyed by a bomb in the '40s.

We were certainly trying infants. A playpen was bought for us, which we instantly climbed out of, falling screaming on our heads on the other side. I managed to fall off the elephant at London Zoo, surely the only child ever to do so. Definitely the slow one, I was still reading *'I am up on my ox'* while Diana had moved on to *'Winter days are jolly'*.

Nana taught us with immense patience, but her aitches, or lack of, caused problems and it was a long time before I could sort out 'has' from 'as'. Josephine insists that we were still talking twin language at six or seven, but the fact that we were learning to read by then surely proves otherwise.

Nana was loving, but strict. Every morning we remained strapped in our high chairs until we had eaten our breakfasts, which consisted of porridge, bread and butter – often cut into fingers – and a soft-boiled egg. (Hard-boiled eggs were considered bad for children in those days, and breakfast cereals were yet to be produced.)

Sometimes we sat screaming; occasionally Aunt Dorothea or my mother, having also suffered under Nana's rule, would throw our breakfast on the fire when Nana's back was turned; but mostly we ate it all up eventually; and to this day I find it difficult to leave anything on my plate. Nana taught us the Lord's Prayer and our last duty of the day was to kneel by our beds and recite it. But instead of saying 'Hallowed be thy Name', Diana and I recited 'Harold be thy name', believing it to be somehow connected with our own father. Nana thought toys should be locked away on Sundays, but did not insist on the learning of psalms or hymns as she had with my mother and her sisters.

When out with Nana we were not allowed to put our hands in our pockets or eat in the streets, or on buses. If one was cross one had 'a black patch on one's back', or 'had got out of bed on the wrong side', common phrases among nurses of an earlier time. Nana taught us to sew. I remember making little pincushions filled with sawdust and knitting dreadful garters for my father's birthday, which Nana always finished and which I'm sure he never wore. We wore a great many clothes. Nana knitted us long socks and even longer bedsocks. Because we had bronchitis, Diana and I wore even more clothes than other children of our time – combinations, bodices, thick knickers, vests, monkey vests. Diana and I slept with Nana in the night nursery. Briskly tucked in and kissed at six o'clock, we were expected to sleep until next morning. Sometimes it was just too long for me and I disgraced myself. Then my mattress was washed and dried leaning against the brass-topped fender which guarded the nursery fire, and though no one complained I can still recall the rising steam and the shame I felt.

In those far off days, Wimbledon seemed more like a village. The pavements were wide and empty and in autumn rusty with fallen leaves. In the dairy there were large model cows which mooed when you pulled their tails. There was time to talk and often we lingered while my mother stopped to talk to people we met. The bank messenger was one of them – young, tall and handsome and wearing a top hat. We would throw ourselves at him calling out something like, 'Your money or your life'. But best of all there was Jack, surely the last cock horse in Britain. Jack waited with his minder near the bottom of Wimbledon Hill, standing under a tarpaulin beneath often dripping trees, partly fenced by iron railings. He was there to assist other horses pulling carts, mainly coal, up Wimbledon Hill. His minder, small and wearing a cloth cap, had bandy legs, as so many horsemen did in those days; he would talk to Mamma while we gave Jack sugar, remembering to keep our hands flat. He was my first real horse.

I remember too one dreadful day when I dropped a pumice stone I had been asked to carry as a privilege by Mamma, far far below on to the railway lines at Putney Bridge. I can still feel it slipping through my fingers; and I wanted it to go, I wanted to see what happened when it fell on to the rails below; though Mamma assumed it was an accident, as I burst into guilty tears, I knew it wasn't. I knew I had meant it to happen, and my sense of guilt made me cry even more.

Our parents had a car but I do not remember Diana and I travelling in it often; for one thing we were car sick. Because of this, when we went for our annual holiday to Bexhill or Westgate, Diana and I travelled by train mostly just with Nana, complete with pudding bowl, flannel and flask of brandy. I don't think I was ever train sick, but I can still recall the feel of damp flannel tainted by sick and brandy on my face, and to this day I dislike brandy and abhor face flannels.

Years later recalling these holidays, Mamma said that sometimes no holiday was better than a holiday. Certainly Diana and I did not distinguish ourselves on these holidays. Once while Mamma was reading the *Just So Stories* to us, we fought and broke a mirror in a boarding house and poor Mamma had to deal with an irate landlady, while we were promised seven years of bad luck! We refused to go into the sea and on one occasion Diana and I were chased along the beach by Mamma with a slipper in her hand. It was some years before we were able to explain that we had both been afraid of sharks; Mamma was appalled by such a revelation.

'But surely you knew that if there were sharks in the sea, we wouldn't have let you go in?' she said.

But we did not reason that way; small children don't. Besides if we were still talking twin language at that time, we could hardly describe our feelings. I rode my first pony at Bexhill, a little brown Dartmoor, and screamed in terror – not a very propitious start to a life in the saddle spanning more than fifty years!

Cappy joined these holidays at weekends to play golf. I do not remember welcoming his presence. Nana disliked him and as I was very involved with Nana at this time, probably some of this rubbed off on to me. I do remember him bringing buns to us at eleven o'clock with one small piece of Cadbury's chocolate in the middle. Somehow they were always gritty with sand. Afterwards my mother was to say that these holidays had been for Nana.

There are many other things I remember about living in Wimbledon. The long passage with the door at the end leading to the house Granny Cannan built on to ours; a door I never went through. Being sick in Granny's car and an angry chauffeur called Mr Clark (later she was to engage an Italian chauffeur who was never cross). The box where outgrown clothes and toys were put for the poor children. Running one's hands along split oak fences to make them tingle. Jumping the lines on the pavement, because if you stepped on one the lions had you. Pushing toy horses along a garden path. The aroma of oranges sucked slowly with a lump of sugar in the middle. The smell of damp clothes drying in front of a coal fire. I don't remember Granny ever entering the nursery; or talking to me. Nor do I remember anyone preparing me for the move to the country when I was six and a half. I don't recall packing or being excited. I had no idea that it was to be the end of my early years, that Nana was to move out to housekeep for Granny, who, still wanting to be near Mamma, had rented a house less than a hundred yards away from ours. No one told me that there would be a spinney and five acres and a large garden in which to play. Or if they did, I cannot recall it. I think that parents did not explain things to their children as they do today; but Josephine had been with my parents and helped to choose the house. Did she tell me about it? If she did, I cannot remember it either. So I didn't say goodbye to Wimbledon at all.

A few years ago I went back to Wimbledon. Our pretty house and Granny's next door were empty and deserted. And everything looked much smaller; the long passage where I had been smacked was after all but a few yards long; the drawing room was really two rooms with fold-back doors between. The tennis court where my father must have played so often had become a swimming pool. The cedar tree which had worried Mamma so much whenever thunder struck was gone. Wimbledon of course has changed beyond recognition. The trees where Jack stood so patiently are no longer there. The streets are crowded with strangers now; it has become just part of the great sprawl of Greater London and homes and flats are crammed together where gardens existed before.

I wish I could remember more of my years in Wimbledon. Josephine says that Diana and I were self-sufficient and didn't need anyone else. Certainly as long as I had Diana I never felt lonely. I don't think I craved great affection. And I was definitely the slow one. It took me a long time to be dry at night. There were no playgroups in those days, and though Josephine and Denis attended school, I had to wait until I was seven. There were no parties either, or if there were, Diana and I were never invited.

From the beginning we were brought up to be tough. Nana never listened to complaint. If you kept on and on about something as children do, she would give you a good shake, shouting, 'Stop it, you tiresome little thing.' But we *were* expected to be special, just as the Cannan girls had been a generation earlier. Nana wanted to be proud of us. Being special can make it hard to fit in with one's own generation, and being special can soon become being different, which can cause problems. I cannot recall ever addressing a word to my brother or he to me while we were at Wimbledon. He says he cannot either. Nana appeared at this time to be frightened of him, just as she was of many men; and what Nana felt I felt too.

I do remember the journey to the house I was to love all my life. The stop for lunch at Henley-on-Thames at the Red Lion. The search for a kettle on our arrival because my parents could not last another minute without a cup of tea. The wonder of an overgrown orchard; tumbling into nettles off a leaning tree; sitting on a window ledge. Spic, the last of my parents' Sealyhams, blind and trying to find her way, struck me then as incredibly sad. But I must have been very unsettled by the move, because my first night I disgraced myself for the last time and though nothing was said, I felt deeply humiliated. Or maybe it was because I realised that my beloved Nana was no longer sleeping in the night nursery with us. Instead I would be looked after most of the time by Mamma; to me a woman in spectacles I felt I hardly knew.

Chapter Two

Josephine writes:-

Cappy had to live within commuting distance of London, I think he was working for Frigidaire at that time. The Great Western Railway was a reliable line and Reading a convenient station. He knew Henley-on-Thames and he had stayed at Peppard Common with Christine's godmother before the war.

Mamma's childhood knowledge of Oxfordshire had not extended as far south. Brought up among willows and watermeadows, she hadn't been aware of the Chilterns or the beech woods, but, so fierce was her loyalty – she always regarded Berks, Bucks and Surrey as irretrievably inferior – she felt that she was returning home.

They started househunting, they took Denis and me in the holidays; the twins, owing to their travel sickness, were left behind with Nana.

I was undemanding on long journeys. In a tuneless chant I told myself a long confused story about some characters called The Blonker and the Stinging Nettle, The Mousetrap and The Car. The Blonker was, I think, a large female of the arms akimbo variety, the Stinging Nettle a tall, thin, slightly henpecked male, but I can recollect nothing of the Mousetrap. The country was still in deep depression, so there was a buyers' market and plenty of houses for sale. I don't remember much about our search, apart from thinking Nettlebed a terribly funny place name and trying to persuade the parents to buy a house solely because it had a little landing with a small window from which there was a wonderful view.

When we found The Grove in Peppard, Mamma seemed to know at once that this was what she wanted. White washed, with a low, tiled roof, the house had a square simplicity which had been given an endearingly raffish and continental air by the slatted green shutters which were attached to the front five windows.

It had been built as a dower house for the Baskervilles of Crowsley Park, probably at the end of the eighteenth or beginning of the nineteenth century, no one was certain, but the window tax had obviously been a consideration, for there was a distinct lack of windows – the parlour being the only room in the house to have two.

The reigning Baskervilles had evidently not wanted the dowager on their doorstep for The Grove was two miles from the Park, but they had given her stabling for two, a carriage house, a granary and two tiny cottages for her staff. The stable was topped with a weathervane, the granary with a dovecot. The yard and the garden were shaded by magnificent trees, the fields and tall thorn hedges which divided them were gloriously green. A linnet nested in the rose arch over the stable gate.

Mr Dent, the owner, confided that a beloved daughter had died, I think it was of diphtheria, and his wife spent too much of her time at the bathroom window gazing across the fields and wood in the direction of the hidden churchyard on the far side of the valley. As we walked round the fields and spinney, Mrs Dent insisted that she and I picked an armful of bluebells. Not a very acquisitive child, I would have been content to look, and was not pleased at having to take a huge bundle of wilting flowers back to Wimbledon. It seemed very late when we arrived home, the twins were in bed and Nana not about. Mamma and I grumbled companionably as we filled jam jars with water and arranged the sad and drooping bluebells along the nursery window ledge.

* * * *

Christine writes:-

I shall never love another house as I loved The Grove. It had four main bedrooms, plus a fifth along a narrow passage, which Cappy named the bottleneck, leading to a bathroom and separate loo. It had two reception rooms; and a lovely brick-floored dining room with an open hearth, a beam across the ceiling and a large black dresser. Four doors led off this room – to the hall, the dairy, the cellar and wine cellar, and to the kitchen; it was really the heart of the house, where later we were to do so much of our writing. The kitchen was old-fashioned, with a blue painted Dutch dresser, an ancient range and a window around which roses grew. It looked out on to the stables. Beyond the kitchen was a scullery or washhouse. It had a large stone sink with wooden plate-rack above, a pump, a cracked well, and a copper with a grate beneath, for boiling the washing. There was a large scrubbed table in the middle of the kitchen and, near the range, a basket chair with cushions under which dishes were sometimes kept warm. There was a boiler of sorts to heat the water and the two radiators in the house, one on the landing and one in the hall. There was a telephone; and electricity was installed the day after we arrived, but I don't remember electric fires until we were grown up. The room we originally called the drawing room had a small bay window where my mother sat in the mornings writing at her antique desk, first in long hand and then on a small Corona typewriter. The other reception room we called The Nursery. It had an ugly mottled-tiled 'thirties fireplace, which must have replaced an earlier one, and a serving hatch from the dairy. It looked out on to the front of the property. Our books lived there in a large bookcase which ran along one wall, with toy cupboards beneath.

Outside, The Grove was white with green slatted wooden shutters. There were double gates in those days opening on to a gravelled piece in front of the house with a border in the middle. Round the corner from the kitchen was an outside flush loo. Built for servants, it was a great boon to us since our father would often sit for hours in the upstairs one, reading *The Times* and no doubt praying for the motion, which had been so obligatory in his youth.

Greengages and plums grew around the dining room window, loganberries flourished along the brick and flint wall which divided the garden from the two humble cottages which went with the property. There was a whiteheart cherry tree in the orchard as well as Blenheims, pippins, russets, Bramleys and many other varieties of apple, including an unforgettable one called by the locals 'the old Jewsan'. It was a wrinkled, bitter sort of apple which kept longer than all the others. I believe it was actually called 'the old Jew's hand' because of its miserly appearance – a bit of pure racism. There were damson trees too in the paddock and mushrooms in the top meadow. Raspberries, gooseberries and red and black currants grew in the garden, blackberries in the high hedges which fenced the fields. So we were never short of fruit. There were hazelnut trees too, and in the spring the spinney was dazzlingly blue with bluebells.

The stables were as old as the house, with a weathervane in the shape of an arrow on the top. There were just two stalls when we arrived, and a dark, earth-floored harness room with a gig house next door; and what we called the bean hole, because it housed the bean sticks. There was also a large wooden building which had recently been used as a chicken house. My parents were not slow to make changes. The two stalls were quickly converted into loose boxes, the harness room became part of the gig house, which became a garage. But it took longer for our neighbours' cows to leave the fields, and for the hideous dark wallpaper to be stripped from the passages, stairs, hall and landing inside the house. But I've forgotten the Granary, which stood on staddle stones and was entered by a small ladder. Bantams sat on their nests there. Cats had their kittens there. They did not kill each other. So maternal were the bantams that more than once a broody hen moved to sit on mewing kittens to keep them warm, one even taking her chicks with her.

Our first Christmas at The Grove was memorable. Our parents decorated the house as they never did again. On Christmas morning we woke to find it transformed. Cut-outs of Father Christmas and reindeer lined the stairs, decorations and tinsel were everywhere and the dining room was bright with greenery and holly berries. It must have been during our first summer at The Grove that my parents held a party for their London friends. I remember it so well – the Chinese lanterns shining amid the trees as dusk fell, the ice Cappy collected from the fishmongers in Reading, some of which he brought to us to suck in our beds, the laughter and the music which seemed to last for ever, as the night was danced away on the lawn. Sadly they never held such a party again.

Around this time, Josephine was in the habit of sleepwalking. One night when we all still slept in one bedroom she accused me of sleeping in her bed – but first she switched the light on and off exclaiming, 'I've eaten the first chick food.' Off went the light. 'And I've eaten the second chick food.' On went the light, then off again, before she accused me of being in her bed and tried to push me on to the floor. Fortunately I was as big as she and quite capable of looking after myself. In the evenings in those early days at The Grove, Nana came to put us to bed; and we had to be in bed by seven. In winter we wore bedsocks above our knees and spent many a sleepless hour picking the wool off the blankets on our beds and making it into little woolly balls. Often, still full of energy, we rampaged about our bedrooms, acting as characters in the books my mother read to us, and then Nana would call up the stairs, 'If you don't behave, I'll tell your father,' until finally we subsided into our beds, beginning what we called 'an imag'. At first these were about our alarm clocks – mine was blue, Josephine's red, Diana's green – and they had many a strange adventure. Later an imag became far more personal. They lasted well into Diana's and my teens. Often then an imag was frightening and concerned people we knew; but never our parents. Other times I was so tired I cried myself to sleep. Once we had hiccups and Denis appeared in our room to tell us that if we hiccupped more than a hundred times we would die. After that I remember lying in bed counting my hiccups, growing more agitated as the number grew, until finally they reached and passed one hundred. I think that was the last time I totally believed my brother. On another dreadful occasion when we were in bed trying to sleep, Diana and I suddenly faced the nothingness of death. I can still vividly recall the terror and the coldness which stole over me then, which became even worse when my mother appeared to kiss us goodnight, and had no soothing answer to our terror.

Next to our bedroom was Cappy's dressing room and it was here that the cook–general, whichever was in charge, would put a tray with cups of tea on it for our parents at seven each morning before calling on us to wake up. Then, after much grumbling the child whose turn it was would finally leave her bed and take the tea into Mamma and Cappy, who would complain often that it was cold. They had twin beds and sometimes they were each in their own and other times together in one, something which I suppose they did not wish anyone but us innocents to see.

Free of Nana for much of the day now, we enjoyed a civilised breakfast with our parents in the dining room where there was fish or eggs on the sideboard and three kinds of marmalade on the table – Coopers' Oxford Marmalade for my mother, Dundee for my father, Golden Shred with a golliwog on it for us. There were different kinds of sugar too and of course plenty of toast in a silver toast rack. We drank milk out of our silver christening mugs, sitting on chairs which our parents had had made, plus a long table, with wood from local beech woods.

At this time our neighbours' cows – blue and red and white – still grazed our land. The Kews ran a shop and a bakery as well as a small mixed farm. Old Charlie Kew had married his cousin and nearly every one of their children had some defect or other. Will was the worst afflicted. Known as Bumper, he worked in the bakery, kneading the bread in a white coat. I dreamt about him once – my parents were trying to reach heaven, my father was desperately pulling my mother up and over gigantic squares of ice, while Bumper was standing above them in his white coat, and Bumper was God! One brother, Morris, was normal and ran a post office and shop. Art, probably named Arthur, was badly afflicted and unable to talk at all, while poor Daisy could only speak in a whisper, and Polly her sister was very nervous and completely dumb. Sometimes Polly worked for us. Arriving very early in the morning, she would scrub the scullery, the dairy, the kitchen and the dining room before doing anything else, and nobody could stop her. Seeing her looking so careworn on her knees I found a sad sight, I think we all did. Daisy delivered the milk twice a day to us in our early years at The Grove; she also ran the shop. Daisy was quite bright and a young man had wanted to marry her, on condition she could be helped with her speech, either by an operation or therapy. But though she must have been nearly thirty by then, her parents refused to give permission, no doubt believing her state was God's will.

As the years passed, old Charlie Kew grew old and was turned out of the house during the day to sit in a small shed hung with horse brasses. He was allowed back in the evenings, and it was said if you went past the house at a certain time, you could hear him saying his prayers kneeling by his bed. The Kews ate off tin plates, and Fred and Ted, who were normal, delivered the bread; Ted with a cob called Nobby and a cart, Fred with a van. It was Fred who showed my parents how to bridle our first horse. It was Fred who separated Diana and me once when we were fighting, as we often were at that time – the trouble being that we were an even match, so neither ever won. Once the Rector separated us. When Cappy did it, he made us kiss each other, which put me off kissing for a long time.

Josephine says that the Kews had only one pair of spectacles between them. In spite of this, Daisy and her mother had beautiful handwriting. I doubt whether any of them had ever left the area or had a holiday, except for Ted who had joined the Navy; hating

35

it, he had had to be bought out by the rest of the family and now ran a pub with his wife at Greys when he wasn't at the farm. As well as Nobby, the Kews had a bay mare called Jane, whom Charlie would drive in a water cart to Spring Wood each morning to collect water from the well there. Jane had an army brand and was said to have been a gun horse in the war.

The Kews were good neighbours and very honest. The only problem was to make oneself understood; it was said that my mother once asked for a tin of sardines and soon after a load of hay was delivered. They had various dogs chained to kennels and pigs in sties, and milking was, of course done by hand. My mother kept an account with Miss Kew and when we had no money at all, we would buy some cream and book it, then hang it in our dairy in muslin until it turned into cream cheese, which we then sold to our grandmother. It was during those early days at The Grove that we stopped calling our father Daddy. In one of our comics the hero was a sterling character, a Captain called Cappy. I don't think Denis liked the idea, but our father was delighted with the suggestion; he became Cappy and remained so until we were grown up.

Before we had a pony of our own, my mother would take us for walks with the two spaniels, Barney and Dinah. Our favourite walk was when we went to see Fluffy, a small pony which leaned over a fence waiting for us. At least we called him Fluffy because he *was* fluffy, what his real name was we never knew. Fluffy lived alone in a field near The Red House in Sonning Common which was a spread-out village then, without a church or a real centre, but with a scattering of shops and a regular bus service to Reading. On our way to see Fluffy we would pass The Butcher's Arms, a small old pub in those days; and then go past the nearby pond which my mother called Bottomless Pond, because it was said that a coach and horses lay at the bottom of its dark waters, and that when the Council tried to drain it, they came to the topmost branches of an oak tree and gave up. Nowadays it looks safe and respectable. Called Widmore Pond, with a small refined island in the middle, all the mystery has gone. We wanted our parents to buy Fluffy and nagged and nagged until finally my mother contacted his owners and was told that he was definitely *not* for sale.

Our first cook-general was Beatrice who came from a cottage near Neals Farm, Stoke Row. I remember her as a large dark-haired woman. I don't think she liked working for us and soon our parents could stand her no longer for she was forever banging drawers and slamming doors, so she left, to be followed briefly by an unsatisfactory manservant and then by Winnie, who was to be our last living-in cook-general. Winnie had short hair held back by a slide. Like Beatrice she had a lot to do. Cooking three meals a day on a temperamental range, she would never bother much with cooking nice meals unless Cappy was at home. If you asked for something special, it was always impossible because it was 'her flue day', or 'her larder day' or something else. Once Denis put a ferret in her bed; and as she was to relate in later years, he would take her bike and leave it in the orchard and throw down his clothes in the hall the moment he came 'home from college'. It was Winnie who told my mother that she was going to have trouble with Miss Josephine in later years.

Bowles was a jobbing gardener who came three days a week. When we were small he would trundle us round the garden in the wheelbarrow. He seemed to me to be the best-natured person in the world and a mine of information. Bowles, who soon became Bowley, was included in my red exercise book of doggerel with the immortal lines, 'Bowley is little and his nails are brittle'. Jack Bowles to his friends, Bowley was certainly little but I suspect that his nails were only brittle in my ditty for the sake of rhyme. Small, ginger-haired and blue-eyed, it always seemed to me that Bowley could do anything. On wet days in later years he groomed our ponies, making the hissing noise old grooms still made to keep the dust from their throats. Like most of his generation, he had handled working horses from an early age and was a dab hand with a curry comb. I can still see Bowley when a bantam chase was on, outrunning all of us. He was a great wit. Asked how he was, he would usually reply, 'Just able to get about'. And watching us feebly polishing bit or stirrup he would say, 'Pop down to the shop and buy a tin of elbow grease. That'll make it shine.'

Bowley lived with his wife and family by the church. He said once that our voices were so loud that he would hear them when he was at home. It was Bowley who stripped off the depressing wallpaper at The Grove and with my father redecorated the hall and passages. He smoked incessantly, rolling his own cigarettes. In the evening he had tea in the kitchen, always the same – a pot of tea, a boiled egg and bread and butter. (My aunt's gardener was given the same, so I suspect it was the custom then.) After tea

Bowley would saw wood in the garage, leaving for home around six o'clock riding his bicycle up Peppard Hill past the chalk quarry and down Church Lane just as he had at lunch time.

Bowley picked the apples for us, putting them in neat rows in straw in the Granary. He made a clamp in the garden and filled it with vegetables. He did not touch the flower beds which were our parents' terrain. But he helped my father layer the high hedges which grew between the fields and which in later years we would jump on our ponies with such relish. And if boys appeared to steal the apples, it was Bowley who chased them off. I don't remember Bowley ever being cross, though at times, following him around, we must have been a terrible trial. It was often Bowley who gave our bantams collective names and, though he was apt to chase a pony rather than simply catch it, he taught us a tremendous amount about life in the country.

Mrs Pearce was also in my red exercise book, She 'did' upstairs for a time, always with a black beret on her head. She smelt rather. Tiny, she was reputed to take home Oxo cubes in her knickers. She found my red exercise book under my bed and, reading 'Mrs Pearce is Stumpy And Always Grumpy' was not amused. She lived with her husband in one of our cottages. He had been a most talented carpenter and had made and fitted the bookshelves in my parents' drawing room. But Mr Pearce had been terribly wounded in the war and had a metal plate in his head, which became hot in warm weather. He would become deranged then and would accuse us of stealing his nails. We were frightened by Mr Pearce. We made up a poem which we chanted to give us courage, but never loud enough for him to hear. It went like this:

> There's something missing out of my head,
> There's something missing out of my shed,
> If this don't cease, I'll inform the police,
> There's something missing out of my head.

Sadly Mr Pearce grew more demented until his doctor advised Mrs Pearce to move away and they went to live at Tadley, near Reading.

When Winnie left too, Josephine moved into what had been known up to then as the maid's room, which looked out towards the stable. The front bedroom which I now shared only with Diana became 'the twins' bedroom'. Above the nursery, it looked out on an old beech tree where squirrels swung from branch to branch, and plump wood pigeons cooed what was reputed to be 'my toes bleeds Betty'.

Our bedroom wasn't far from the road and in later years I was always the first to hear hoofs go by in the night. Then I would raise the alarm and within seconds we would be outside searching for an escaped horse or pony, often still in our pyjamas. It was from this room one night that I heard my favourite bantam Bluebell shrieking for help. She had been nesting at the back of the herbaceous border near the beech tree when a fox carted her off to eat. By the time I reached the window, all I could see was the glint of his brush disappearing in the moonlight. After that any doubts I had held about the rights and wrongs of foxhunting vanished for a very long time. Our bedroom had a small pretty Georgian basket fireplace in it where a fire was lit when we were ill. Otherwise we had no heat in our room except in really cold weather when an oil heater was lit. Made of black metal it had diamond shaped holes in the top and cast strange shadows on the ceiling.

Denis's room overlooked the lawn and was above the dining room. Sent away to school and without local friends, I suspect he was bored at times. But he was an original and inspiring brother. It was Denis who converted the smart dolls' pram given to Josephine by Georgette Heyer into a fire engine. It carried an oil drum filled with water, a ladder, a length of hose and of course a bell. Usually Josephine or Denis, but once Cappy – to our great surprise – would light a fire and then tear around garden or house shouting, 'Fire! Fire!' Everyone would then rush to the fire engine, putting on scout belts as they ran and seizing the small wooden axes Denis had made for us. Then, ringing the bell loudly, we would push and pull the fire engine down the narrow box-hedged paths which fenced Bowley's vegetable garden and, with much excitement, the fire would be put out. So for a brief time we became arsonists.

Diana's and my large old pram was converted into a chariot with fixed wheels at the back and the ones on a swivel at the front. We played horses constantly with it and it was used to carry hay in later years. It also became a hearse when bantams died. Pulled by spaniels, Dinah and Barney, with the small corpse in a shoe box draped by a black cloth, the slow procession would wend its way to the graveyard at the top of the potato patch. Sometimes my mother read the service trying to keep a straight face. Other times we managed without her, simply saying, 'Ashes to ashes, Dust to dust. If God won't have you, the devil must,' as the corpse was lowered into a prepared grave, after which a cross was erected. More than once the proceedings went disastrously wrong; the spaniels took off and the coffin fell open on the ground. Then the ritual would have to begin all over again. But whatever happened, it was always a sad and serious occasion.

In our first year at The Grove, towards the end of June, the hay was cut in the top meadow by a cutter pulled by Jane. In the evening the Kew men came to turn the hay with caps on their heads and Fred with a watch chain across his waistcoat. Two new five-barred gates were up by then and the hay smelt wonderful. Later, after it had been forked by hand into haycocks, Jane carted the hay away to be put into a stack which would later be thatched.

Those early days at The Grove seem endless to me now. I cannot remember ever being bored. Diana and I were always on the go and fell down so often that Cappy offered us a halfpenny for every day we stayed up. I cannot recall ever earning it. Or maybe we did, and no one noticed; for such payments were generally erratic, and though we were meant to have a few pence a week pocket money, it was too often forgotten.

Chased by Denis in a game I fell down the coal hole and he pulled me up by my hair. I cannot recall why it was open; perhaps because Mr Ledbetter was delivering coal from Josey's the coal merchant in Sonning Common, with his mule. Mr Ledbetter was small, like so many men at that time, but in spite of this immensely strong, put down to the fact that he always ate five beetroots with his tea; to this day, whenever I feel weak I have an overwhelming desire for beetroot. I don't recall ever talking to Mr Ledbetter's mule. I suspect he was too tired, too cross or just too plain mulish to be interested in a scruffy small girl. Or perhaps with good reason he hated people for I seem to recall that he was muzzled.

At seven or eight years old when Diana and I went with my mother to stay with Carola Oman at Bride Hall in Hertfordshire, we were in our best clothes and on our best behaviour. I remember wearing a skirt and sticking cut-outs provided by Carola into a very tidy scrap book and making such a mess of it that the book was ruined. We spent that night in a palatial bedroom – or so it seemed to me then – each in a large impressive bed with a blazing fire in the grate. But soon after eight o'clock, coal fell out of the fire and there was no fire guard, only a beautifully polished brass fender. I remember my heart beating faster and longing to call, 'Fire, fire.' Diana and I looked at each other and, after a short discussion, decided to pull the bell rope near our beds. This brought a butler, who soon put the coals back on the fire, but afterwards my mother was to say that it had taken a long time to settle us that night, and that the dinner party downstairs was badly interrupted. For years after, I felt guilty about this episode. But what should we have done? Were we big enough to put the coals back on the fire? But even if we were, we had been brought up on 'Willy in one of his bright blue sashes, Fell on the fire and was burnt to ashes. The fire died down and the room grows chilly. But we haven't the heart to poke poor Willy.' And Willy had played with fire, so we decided to play safe.

In my book of doggerel I wrote, 'Mummy is right by day and by night'. And I really did believe it – in my eyes she could do no wrong. And though once, offended by something she said, I ran away and hid in Spring Wood, when she hurried by, calling to me in a distracted voice, I coughed loudly, wanting to be found, and was taken home in disgrace and sent to bed. But on the whole punishments were rare at The Grove. My father would occasionally set lines for us, a hangover I suspect from his days as a schoolteacher. *I must shut the door* was something I was told to write one hundred times. After scribbling it one hundred times with different coloured and increasingly blunt crayons in an old exercise book, I handed it to him and then slammed the door after me and was instantly recalled and told to write *I MUST NOT SLAM THE DOOR* fifty times. I don't remember feeling resentful, just a sense of boredom and the thought that it was just Cappy in a bad mood again. And to this day I still don't shut doors after me, though gates are a different matter altogether!

Josephine says that during our first year at The Grove we began to speak proper English instead of twin language. I suspect we had used both for some time, but were sometimes misunderstood. It was about this time too that I wrote a ditty about my large and beloved Teddy Bear whose head was missing. It was surely my first entry in my red exercise book and went as follows: 'Teddy's heady has come off and you can see his guts, they are not nuts.' Hardly an inspired bit of writing – a small beginning, I suppose. But I was still backward. I still existed as a family rather than as a person on my own. For me no one on earth counted for as much as Mamma; her word was law in my eyes and would be for many years to come. I respected Cappy, but did not love him. I fought with Diana, but not with Josephine, whom I respected for being older and maybe wiser. Nana, once so important in my life, was not always obeyed now, nor loved as much as Mamma whom I worshipped. I don't think I talked much to Denis. I admired him and his intellect so much that I felt incapable of holding a conversation with him. Diana had a far better relationship with Denis and on numerous occasions he took her side when Josephine and I teamed up together. Mamma called me Rosie Posie and Cris-Cross, while Diana was Jumbo and Josephine was Jo Jo, particularly to Cappy. Once, when Cappy had been away, he brought us back a scarf each. We were told to choose which we wanted in order of age which meant that I, being the youngest, had no choice at all. (I still have that scarf, a little red silk one with a West Highland terrier on it.) My father always said, 'Eldest first'. My mother, perhaps she had been the youngest but more likely from an inherent sense of fairness, sometimes said, 'Youngest chooses first this time.' So Diana remained in the middle, which wasn't quite fair either.

But mostly we drew lots for things, for there is always something which can be used for lots – blades of grass, torn paper, twigs, hay; even strands of wool held firmly will do. Overall, life at The Grove seemed perfect to me and I only desired that it should stay the same, for I was part of the tribe which lived there and though we were so different from other children in so many ways, it was to me the best tribe in the world.

* * * *

Christine's doggerel:-

> Georgy is big,
> He likes a fig.
>
> Mummy is right,
> By day and by night.
>
> Cappy is large,
> And would like a barge.

Denis is high,
I don't know why.

Nana is niether big or tall,
Nana is niether tiny or small.

Diana is wee
And likes the sea.

Josephine is low,
And very slow.

Christine is midling
And always fiddling.

Bowley is little,
And his nails are brittle.

Mrs Pearce is stumpy
And always grumpy.

Winnie is tall
And comes to the call.

Georgy was Winnie's boy friend, later her husband. In a later edition Mummy becomes 'tiny and always shiny' and the piece is called '*Sizes of People* (Comical)'. I am not sure why Mamma was demoted.

* * * *

Diana writes:-

Which of us fell into the tank of dirty gutter water which stood against the stable's northern brick and flint wall, wearing an emerald green embroidered skirt which we shared? Christine or me? There was a time when we argued about this, but eventually Christine forgot the incident, so perhaps I was the clumsy one, who perched on the tank's narrow edge and slipped.

Predictably, like Christine I deeply loved The Grove, although here and there the emphasis varies. For me the great beech trees that stood sentinel on the south side of the house, their prominent roots covered with pincushions of moss, soft as velvet, were all-important. They were the last thing you saw before the bedroom curtains shut out the night and the first when you flung them back in the morning: immense in the gathering dust, silvered in moonlight, verdant in summer, glorious in autumn and noble still in the bareness of winter, through all the changing seasons a symbol of permanency, of home.

Beyond our fields, the paddock, orchard and top meadow, lay the magic of Spring Wood, owned by Lady Agnes Peel, who lived half a mile down the road at Blount's Court, an elderly and distinguished woman, whose habit of ending every sentence with 'Yes, yes,' we imitated with many giggles. Spring Wood with its glades and hollows, its winding paths and its spring of clear water, under a brick arch decorated with a carved elephant and Latin words no longer readable, was magical. And by the spring was a spot from which you could see in autumn a stretch of plough leading the eye to a line of trees and the curve of a hillside. I like to think now that it was the genes which inspired Jemima Blackburn to paint and my grandfather's Huguenot mother, Jane Dorothea Claude, to draw that made me drink in this landscape. Perhaps I shared then in youth a characteristic with Mamma's largely autobiographical heroine in *The Misty Valley* which caused her to love places better than people, a characteristic which for almost a decade made me loath to leave The Grove and contributed to my hatred of school. When years later, suffering from TB, I was allowed out briefly after six months' bed rest, I went first to see that view.

Soon after our move Granny, who liked to live near Mamma, leased Highclere, an Edwardian villa about a hundred yards away in the more built-up end of Crowsley Park Road, where she installed Nana, now no longer needed full-time by our parents, as housekeeper. Nana hated going; the hurt was deep and for the rest of her long life she resented the way Cappy broke the news. 'He just said "You must go,"' she told us later. 'No thanks for all I had done.' For Mamma, as Josephine says, it meant greater freedom from a stubborn woman who had dominated her childhood; for Cappy the welcome departure of an ever critical presence; for us a closer bonding to a mother who became an abiding influence. But only to a degree, for Nana still turned up every morning. She still knitted us beautiful socks and sweaters, washed our clothes and watered the hens, and sometimes Mamma invited her to meals, especially tea. And, of course, she child-minded whenever asked. She also invited us when Granny was in

France to play in Highclere's huge empty attic, whose barrenness depressed us. Still bent on turning us into young ladies, she continued to buy us sewing things for our Christmas stockings. Lonely, she got herself a puppy, which she named Tiny, but Tiny grew into a big, lively dog and after enduring many hours tied to a kitchen table, he was eventually found a new home by the Kews.

On that first Christmas Day at Peppard which Christine remembers so well, our parents gave us a mate for Barney, whom we called Dinah. They had left finding a spaniel bitch rather late and Dinah was, they said, the runt of the litter. Small and short-legged, she looked more like a Sussex than a cocker spaniel. Of course we loved her too much and she used to jump in a chair and sit behind Mamma to escape our affection.

Mamma took us to Harpsden to buy bantams. Bowley made a hen house and a duck pond was dug. Then Mamma went to a horse dealer, called Sworder, and bought Countess, a broken-down old polo pony recovering from a bout of pneumonia. Dark bay, thin as a rake, Countess towered above us; her head now too large for her wasted body. She was a bad buy, but probably Mamma hoped to nurse her back to health and save her from the knacker's yard. And although she wasn't soft like Fluffy, we loved her because she was ours and I have a picture postcard of puppies I sent Mamma in France, which says I gave Countness [sic] a kiss.

Soon we watched Mamma struggling to bridle Countess. Every time she got the snaffle, which she held with both hands, into Countess's mouth, the bridle slipped down (an event Mamma described graphically in *A Pony For Jean*), until she was rescued by Fred Kew. Our parents always expected us all to learn as we went along and much later typically bought a cow without knowing how to milk her.

Cappy, despite arthritis, ran leading us on Countess, shouting 'Up down, up down.' When Christine, who was frightened of him, failed to rise at the trot at the right moment, he pinched her thighs, and I hated him for pinching. Sometimes, happier without the grown-ups, Christine and I sprang early from our beds and still in our pyjamas slipped a halter on Countess, mounted her by step-ladder and took it in turns to ride and lead her. Countess was the inspiration for Cavalier in *A Pony For Jean* in which the painfully thin pony eventually becomes a prize-winner, a fate which eluded the once beautiful Countess, who, despite

Mamma's efforts, one day lay down for the last time.

We stood outside the locked stable door when the vet shot her. I don't think we saw the corpse, which went to the local hunt kennels to feed hounds, but in the country death was ever present. Sweet fledgling birds were caught by cats or simply fell from their nests. Rabbits were shot by Fred Kew, bantams died. You could not walk far in spring without coming across little bodies, sometimes half-eaten, stiffened or limp in the ditches or hedgerows. Butchers' shops sported graceful dead pheasants hanging by their necks, and huge carcasses of bullocks, sheep or pigs. Later on, when a chicken had to die, you heard its frantic squawks, so like 'help, help,' as Bowley carried it upside down by its legs to a spot behind the outside loo, where he hoped he would not be seen. Lurking, horribly curious, you saw him break its neck and the way its legs went on kicking afterwards. Upset, I tried to explain death in the many stories I wrote about wild animals by saying each time, 'It was nature,' a phrase which was half-mockingly repeated on appropriate occasions by us all, especially Mamma, for many years.

By now formal education had begun for Christine and me, after a school inspector accosted Josephine and Nana walking along the road and wanted to know why the 'little girl' was not at school. 'You must speak to the mother,' Nana said, and, to Josephine's surprise and relief, Mamma told the inspector that we would all be attending Highlands in the autumn.

Highlands, a Parents' National Educational Union (PNEU) school, was run by two genteel sisters, the Miss Coopers, whom we were instructed to call Auntie Christine and Auntie Mary. They lived with and revered their white-haired mother, and there was a strange smooth-faced brother in the background, who didn't work. They were assisted by a more down-to-earth teacher, Miss Vine. The atmosphere was kind, the other children well brought up; but, although we longed to join in, Christine and I felt misfits.

Our inadequate vocabulary, laced with Nana's Victorianisms, was an embarrassment to us both, and being twins who were still uncannily alike, we were noticeably different from the other children. Often unable to tell us apart, our teachers usually addressed us as *the twins*, rather than Christine and Diana, prolonging the identity crisis for us as for so many others, with this short cut.

At first, unused to other children, we enjoyed being chased

round the table by an elder girl, crying 'You goose!' and the drama when a child called Kitty was accused of stealing pennies from coat pockets in the cloak room. We loved shouting at the tops of our voices when Miss Vine asked us to name in French objects and features in the class room – *la fenêtre, la porte,* and so on – perhaps because Mamma loved and romanticised France. But her distrust of teachers and her determination that they should not mould our characters were catching. Her gentle mocking of the Aunties, who were too refined and sentimental for her taste, only confirmed eventually our own feelings about them. Although, thanks to Nana, we could read to ourselves, write in sentences and recite our tables, we were depressed by our backwardness. Our poor speech and inexperience of other children handicapped us. We were gauche and, because our English was still mixed with twin language, Josephine was sometimes called in to interpret, a humiliation we found hard to bear.

Disheartened, we grew naughty, always backing each other up, and when we realised sitting in the cloakroom was the only punishment, we left home with books in our overcoat pockets, preferring to read in disgrace, rather than make fools of ourselves again in front of the class. Christine remembers being sent upstairs alone to an empty room as a punishment, so perhaps the Aunties realised that sending us together to the cloakroom was an easy way out for us both.

Despite our backwardness, Mamma, who believed children should enjoy their childhood, insisted our school days should end at lunch time. Then all three of us left, with Christine or I carrying a small red book in which the English words we must learn to say before next morning had been neatly written; a book which was forgotten as soon as our feet touched the gravel of The Grove's back drive.

We left Highlands after two terms, but our parents didn't tell us why. Josephine thinks they never intended us to stay because they never bought us uniforms. It could be that the school fees were too high for them or that the Aunties were fed-up with us only going mornings. I distinctly remember an Aunty suggesting that Christine and I were educationally sub-normal and should, therefore, go to a special school, which in the 'thirties might have branded us idiots in our own minds for life. Yet it's possible I imagined this explanation, simply because I felt unacceptable and expected rejection. On the other hand, our parents could well have found an establishment they preferred, for our next school, which belongs to the following chapter, was certainly much cheaper. No uniforms were needed and lessons were in the mornings only, so suiting Mamma's philosophy.

Today's children would, of course, have asked, 'Why?' But, reared on 'Curiosity killed the cat,' to which I only learned the answer 'Satisfaction brought it back,' many years later, we remained silent. We were also taught not to whine and to bear set-backs with fortitude. Exhortations, quotes from the Bible and Shakespeare and Latin tags were part of every day life. When we wanted to stop fighting we shouted 'Pax!' And when Cappy offered something which could not be shared, he called 'Quis?' and whoever answered 'Ego!' first got it.

'Never say die', 'There's no such word as *can't*' and 'If at first you don't succeed, try, try again,' were other favourites. 'Don't be feeble,' was a constant cry and, also, if you ventured an un-welcome suggestion, 'Don't teach your grandmother to suck eggs.' When told to do anything, you were expected to leap into action, and 'Do it *now*,' was Cappy's frequent order. Hesitation or delay could be countered with several quotes: 'Procrastination is the thief of time,' or 'He who hesitates is lost, but he who sitteth upon a pin shall rise again,' or, later, more threateningly, 'The road to hell is paved with good intentions.' As we grew older we buoyed ourselves up with quotes we had found for ourselves, some, fittingly, from Whyte Melville or Adam Lindsay Gordon. Poetry was simply part of life. Daisy Kew and her mother Ellen wrote verses in our autograph books, and my mother wrote in mine 'Love many, trust a few, learn to paddle your own canoe,' and drew a lovely picture of me paddling down a river.

Doing good deeds was supposed to be part of life, too. Mamma and her sisters had been brought up to visit sick cottagers at Roshven and to perform plays to amuse the staff, and just down the road was the perfect candidate for us – poor Mr Shea, a middle-aged man, who had lost both legs and one arm when two trains ran over him in India. His creeper-clad cottage was the other side of a gate to Spring Wood and only a few yards from Granny's house, but whereas Highclere was light and charming with pretty furniture and lots of white paint, poor Mr Shea's cottage was dark, damp and cheerless.

His legs had been amputated near the top and he came to the

door on stumps about four inches in length. Once a big man, his head and torso were large and strong and his face, distressingly, on a level with mine.

After bidding us sit down, Mr Shea would pull himself up into a chair with his one arm and then you could see how his short trousers ended in the leather pads on which he walked – or waddled. After his accident he had broken off his engagement to a girl back home and now he seemed without kith or kin; hence Mamma's theory that he would be cheered by a visit from three young girls with a present of eggs.

I can't remember what we talked about, except once or twice when he politely steered the conversation to cricket because Denis had come with us. I suppose we told him about our animals, but, although he offered us sweets and toffees, my abiding memory is of unpleasant smells, embarrassment and horror.

'How does he wash himself?' I asked, after one visit.

'He rubs himself against a cake of soap fixed to the bath,' Mamma said. 'And Mrs Moring cleans his cottage once a week.'

The vision of Mr Shea in the bath stayed in my mind for years, like a maggot in an apple, nibbling at my natural feeling that the world was a happy place. And I suppose I put him in my book *The Boy who Came to Stay*, as an unconscious act of therapy. Meanwhile Barney, in search of titbits, took it upon himself to visit the poor man daily, going via Spring Wood and coming back, to our consternation, by the road.

As we grew older, my cries of 'He 'mells, Mummy, he 'mells,' ended our visits. But by then Mr Shea must have become interested in our life, because he became a familiar figure in our yard, bringing leftovers for the chickens, in a wheelchair he could work with one arm. Much later the unimaginable happened. His old sweetheart, a spectacled woman who was I believe a retired school teacher, found him and they married. A happy ending, we thought, but perhaps she had come in the spirit of a saviour and Mr Shea was not a man to be bossed or pitied. Sadly, we were told, they had a fine capacity to make hell for each other. Rumour has it she died first, but I'm not sure rumour was right.

Meanwhile, Dinah had puppies, our bantams produced chicks, the cats kittens. Sitting in the granary's doorway, which faced south, we dangled our legs in the sun and made plans. We each chose a tree to own and climb, which, in true Robert Louis Stevenson style, became a ship. In the spinney, supervised by

Denis, we made huts and, outside the huts, stockades. Denis ruled we were to use no saws, hatchets, nails or string, so we had to find forked branches, and very often the shape of our buildings was decided by the wood to hand. We roofed the huts with fallen branches from the two beautiful pines which stood at the top end of the spinney. Then when all was ready, loving mock battles, we declared war and stormed each other's stockades, yelling war cries. I was usually on the winning side, because, as Christine and I remember very clearly, Denis had one day announced that since Josephine was Cappy's favourite and Christine was Nana's, I was to be his. It was a very welcome development for me (although I don't think I had noticed I was nobody's favourite), because I rather revered him.

Although small for his age until fifteen, when he grew eight inches in one year, Denis was indeed good-looking, with his forelock of fair hair, blue eyes and general air of self-confidence. He was also a fine painter, a wit, a useful carpenter and very kind to his young sisters. He had strong views, which he expressed so forcefully that I hung on his words, a mistake sometimes because, growing up himself, he was inclined to change his opinions from term to term. Josephine says our spinney games would not have worked anyway, if I had not paired with Denis, because leaders were necessary and I would obey him, but not her, while Christine was willing then to accept her orders. In more peaceful moments, Denis showed us how to make fireplaces out of flints and stones. Matches were allowed; we lit fires and we boiled water to make hot Oxo to drink. It was bliss.

There was, however, one fairly regular event, which ended suddenly and, for Christine and me, inexplicably. It concerned Cappy, who was, I realise now, emotionally insecure. His own childhood had been at times traumatic. His father had not spared the rod and sometimes Cappy had been sent to buy the cane with which he was to be beaten. His parents' marriage had been unhappy, and love, it seems, was scarce in the vicarages where he grew up. Add to this the horror of Flanders and his own stiff-upper-lip attitude and it is clear there were many horrific experiences in his life locked in the *do not enter* part of his mind. Yet in many ways the war was a highlight in his life, and for some months after we moved to The Grove, Cappy occasionally came to our bedroom just before seven to sing us First World War songs: 'Pack Up Your Troubles', 'There's a Long, Long Trail A-Winding', 'Keep The

Home Fires Burning', and so on. An impressive figure standing at the bottom of our beds, he sang in a manly baritone voice, which I enjoyed. Then suddenly he came no more and I, with my tendency for self-blame, suspected it was somehow my fault. Years later Josephine explained that one night when we were all in the parlour, Cappy said, 'Come on, off to bed!' and she refused his kiss. Deeply hurt, he rejected Mamma's explanation that all little girls feel like that sometimes and, without a thought for Christine and me, he never kissed any of us again. I didn't miss the kisses, which I don't even remember – some psychological clue there – only the songs.

Poor Cappy became increasingly critical, an angry father always shouting. But letters he wrote to Mamma when she was away with Granny in the South of France describe how he played Blindman's Buff, Bears and other games with us, events which have entirely slipped my memory, so convinced have I become over the years that our relationship was always unhappy. And sadly, Cappy knew he was for us second-best, for he wrote to Mamma, again in the South of France, that we hung around him because we were missing her. He would have liked to ride with us, too – he had ridden a good deal in the war – but his arthritis prevented him. I remember him sitting on Countess and saying it was no good, it hurt too much. Of course, with his temper, he might have spoiled our riding, too, but nobody explained to us that constant pain shreds nerves. Yet on his good days he often became a practical joker, cushions were balanced to fall on your head when you opened a door; apple pie beds were carefully made, and one April the First he sent a fender bumping down the stairs and, shouting 'Help,' pretended he had fallen. All the same, The Grove became a happier place when he was away and we had our merry-hearted mother to ourselves; a mother who didn't mind untidiness or absent-mindedness, and allowed us to bring tame bantams into the dining room on our shoulders; a mother who climbed up trees to rescue us when we got stuck and giggled when we giggled.

Then we would take it in turns to sleep in Cappy's bed, partly because Mamma hated sleeping alone, having come straight to marriage after sharing a bedroom with her sister Dorothea. At first light the other two of us would pile into *her* bed and quarrel about who should lie next to her; symptoms of a closeness which, I realise now, must have been hard at times for Cappy, still in love, to bear.

If I was asked now who in Peppard, apart from our family and those my parents employed, had the greatest influence on my life, I should answer the Kews. Unlike anyone else we knew, they belonged to a kind we would not meet again. Early every morning Daisy delivered us milk straight from the cow for breakfast – Nana believed in freshness. It came in a can and was ladled into our jugs and I can still remember its creamy warmth. The afternoon milk came just in time for tea and Christine and I each drank at least a pint a day.

Daisy was unfailingly kind to us, a familiar and homely figure behind the shop counter, who addressed us as 'duck' in that hoarse whisper which we quickly learned to understand. On Sundays if Mamma discovered she had run out of a grocery she needed, we went round the back of the small farmhouse and knocked on the door. Daisy came, usually pushing another Kew out of the way, and, without any complaint, found and gave us what we wanted.

One night Fred Kew took us with Denis in his van to hear a nightingale sing on Peppard Common. Josephine remembers the delicious smell of bread as we sat on the van's floor, but I only remember my feeling, shared by my sisters, that the song was overrated and could not compare with the dawn chorus which welcomed the day so dramatically at The Grove, or, for that matter, the haunting evening song of a blackbird.

Sometimes Fred invited us to see his bob-tailed sheepdog jump a five-barred gate. Other times when we went to buy chaff we watched the Kews' mare, Jane, circling as she turned the chaff cutter.

Fred took Denis shooting and one day, hearing that we were to visit Denis at school, caught some fleas off a sow's back, put them in a match box, and said, 'Give him those.' I don't know what Denis's school friends thought of the present, but I think he rather liked the idea of starting a flea circus.

Old Charlie Kew was a raconteur who, while he talked, dug his listener in the ribs with an elbow to punctuate a point. 'That's wot 'tis,' he would say. 'That's wot 'tis.' He brought any forms he found perplexing to Cappy for advice and told us he had had thirteen children and buried two – or was it three? I can't remember. Christine has already mentioned wild-eyed Polly and epileptic Will, who rather frightened me because of his lumbering gait, his rolling eyes and loud voice. But I remember especially how, when we went round the back of the shop, Daisy would shoo Will and Polly away like chickens, if they dared to show their faces. Daisy controlled the family, ran the business, served behind the counter and worked from dawn to dark. Nowadays, mothers might be suspicious of Fred's kindness to us all, but country people then seemed to have a lovely, totally uncalculating way with children, and we felt completely at home with most of those we met.

Cappy, astonished by our frequently grazed knees and hands, offered Christine and me a halfpenny for every day we didn't fall over, a sum rarely earned. Usually we jumped up quickly, but when I tripped over an open tap cover and cut my leg to the bone, I lay still for a moment and the puppies came and licked away my tears.

The doctor, a sober-faced, rather silent man, ordered bed rest and bathing with salt and water twice a day, a boring remedy which brought Nana to the fore. Mamma said I would have an *honourable scar*. Aunt May visited and read me stories and, unknown to Mamma, my sisters, wanting to amuse me, brought some of our animals to see me.

Roly Poly, my bantam was perched on the end of my bed when the doctor called unexpectedly. Looking down at me from a great height, he pulled back the eiderdown – how could I have stopped him? – and found five little black puppies wriggling excitedly. Then, although a bandage and a sheet protected the wound from infection, he was furious. I don't know what he said, and I can't remember which grown-up was with him, but later our parents decided he wasn't a kindred spirit and changed to a woman doctor whose uncle had mountaineered with our grandfather.

Whatever happened Mamma continued writing. Sometimes when we pretended to be horses on the lawn, from where we could see her, she jumped up from her desk and shouted. 'Why must you play just by my window when you've five acres to run in?'

And reluctantly we would move away. Later, when Winnie or Nana pestered her too much she drove off and stopped further down the Crowsley Park Road, where she could write in peace. Other times she continued writing in her Woolworth's exercise book, with chaos around her. My cousin, John Gardner, remembers her writing with an HB pencil while sitting on a laundry basket in the kitchen. By 1931 her three latest novels: *High Table, Ithuriel's Hour* and *No Walls of Jasper*, had established her as a serious and successful novelist. *Snow in Harvest* followed in 1932. *North Wall* was the first novel she wrote completely at The Grove.

* * * *

Josephine writes:-

Apart from the passages, the parents decided to leave the house as it was. They tolerated the wallpapers – large blowsy roses in their bedroom, life-size wistaria flowers in ours – and, though they mocked at the horrid juxtaposition of a 'thirties fireplace beneath a Victorian overmantel in the nursery, they made no effort to change it. In the time of the Depression an air of shabbiness, of peeling paint and faded chintz, was in good taste; the concept of DIY did not yet exist and would not have been well received at a time when providing work was seen as the duty of the better off.

Both parents liked gardening, and as long as you employed a man for the vegetables, this was acceptable. Cappy took on the lawn, the roses, and made plans to change the old ha-ha, between the lawn and the paddock, from two sloping beds on either side of a gravel path to four raised beds with flint walls and flights of cobbled steps in the centre. Mamma undertook to look after the two herbaceous beds, and decided to keep bees.

Mamma's schemes were usually romantic – Virgil had raised bee-keeping to poetic heights; Cappy's were supposed to be practical but, though designed to make or save money, rarely did so.

He decided on a potato patch. The vegetable garden was large, but not large enough for main crop potatoes as well as vegetables and soft fruit. So an area of the orchard, rank with nettles and alongside Spring Wood, was enclosed with split chestnut fencing and laboriously dug over and planted by Bowley. It took Cappy several years to realise that it was cheaper to buy main crop potatoes by the sack than to pay someone to grow them.

The bees were a disaster too. The two hives were placed at the top end of the potato patch, and Nana's neighbour, a Mrs Francis, had a trunkful of bee-keeping equipment for sale. A tall woman with long teeth that clicked, she had heard that Mamma was a writer, and explained, with pride and a formidable click of her teeth, that she never read books, 'the real world left her no time for the world of make believe.' We bought the trunk and giggled for days over 'the world of make believe'.

The swarms were installed and, as Cappy and Nana both fled in terror, I was dressed in white gloves and one of Mrs Francis's large, black-veiled straw hats, and appointed bee-keeping assistant. I wasn't afraid, bees didn't seem to sting me, and I was fascinated by the gloom inside the veiled hat and its powerful smell, a mixture of camphor, beeswax and Mrs Francis. But the whole enterprise began to seem fruitless when Mamma developed qualms about taking the honey and substituting the guilt offering of sugar and water, and this, with the impossibility of making any sort of relationship with individual bees, relieved me of sorrow when the hives succumbed to disease and an invasion by mice.

We had inherited geese from the Dents. Jack the gander was white and aggressive, he pecked our bare knees until we learned to drive him off with Oxfordshire cries of 'Gid 'arn'. Jill, the white goose, had very little character, but Susie, the grey one, was friendly, she would eat out of our hands. Making a down-lined nest in a sunny corner of the paddock she sat with tranquil pleasure, surrounded, in the idiom of the Easter card, by wild violets.

The Dents' hens had been joined by Nana's, which, released from their cramped Wimbledon run, began to develop characters. A motley collection, they slept in a wooden building – probably the old cow byre – with long perches and a row of nest boxes. They roamed over the yard, orchard and sometimes, to Cappy's fury, the garden. On wet days they took dustbaths under the granary.

They went broody and Bowley constructed a row of sitting boxes at the top of the potato patch. Turves had to be removed and the boxes placed on earth, with a floor of wire netting to keep out rats and a door which was wedged with a brick to keep out foxes. For three weeks the broody hen sat on her nest in total darkness. She was let out and fed once a day. At first she would have to be attached to a stake by a string looped round one leg, but most of them quickly developed feelings of responsibility towards their eggs and lost any wish to abandon them.

On fine days feeding the broodies was an enjoyable chore. Having filled their water dishes and given them as much corn as they could eat and, if the weather was dry, sprinkled their eggs with water, you were free to read or think for fifteen minutes. It was a sheltered spot and a suntrap; a profusion of wild flowers bloomed among the ungrazed grass. The only drawback was the enormous turds produced by the hens, who had controlled themselves for twenty-four hours in order not to sully their eggs.

The bantams, far too intelligent to accept human interference, stole their nests away. They regarded the garden and the granary as safe places and imposed an equally strict routine on themselves. It was important to feed them when they appeared, fluffed out and clucking importantly, and sometimes, recognizing their capacity for self-sacrifice, we delivered food to the stolen nest.

The motherly hens adored their chicks and Mother of Millions – a neat brown hen, her neck speckled with yellow – gladly fostered the chicks of less enthusiastic mothers. Mother of the Nakeds – a censorious-looking hen, orange-feathered and flecked with white – had a large family of cockerels who took longer than usual to fledge and ran round the orchard long-legged and pink-fleshed.

Our first human death was that of Mr Tanner, the ancient inhabitant of the smaller cottage, who had fought in the Boer war. He fell ill and one night, when the doctor had announced that the end was near, a deputation appeared to tell Mamma that his last wish was to see an elderly brother who lived in Berkshire. Cappy was staying in London, but our car was at home and Mamma realized that some lingering feudal bond demanded that she coped. She set off into the unknown with a Tanner relation as guide, and I suppose cook-general Beatrice kept an eye on us. Later, when the farewells had been said and a treasured Bible handed over, she drove the brother home; Mr Tanner died next day.

Denis had been provided, rather late in life, with a bicycle. Mamma thought them soulless. In her children's books the ownership of a fairy cycle, especially in conjunction with hair worn in corkscrew curls, was a damning indictment of character. Denis learned to ride with Cappy's assistance and was bicycling round the lawn, showing off his new skill to the family, when he fell into the rosebed and hurt his arm. White and shocked, he was sat on the garden seat. Asked to shake hands – Cappy's test for broken arms – he failed and the parents put him in the car and set off for the doctor's.

The twins and I were left, for what seemed like an age, presumably again in the care of Beatrice. When at last they returned, with Denis's arm in wooden splints and sling and the bad news that it was broken in two places at the elbow, they found us in floods of tears. It transpired that we thought we would have an armless brother for ever. When dolls' arms broke they were thrown away; it hadn't occurred to us that human arms could be mended.

Godparents visited us. Gerald Hankin – who later married Mary Field of the Children's Film Foundation – had put on so much weight that one of the new dining room chairs collapsed under him. Carola Oman sat on the lawn and made clothes for our toys. We had given up dolls, or rather Barney had turned out to be a serial killer and chewed up all our best ones, but Carola obligingly made clothes for Teddies and shapeless garments for rabbits. Georgette Heyer came and was plainly horrified by a nursery lunch; faced with jelly, she announced that she never ate it and demanded cheese.

We were lunched separately when a young publisher came to discuss a book. The menu was roast chicken – a treat in those days – but Barney, an incurable thief, stole the uncooked bird from the kitchen table. It was dragged from his jaws too mauled for roasting and hastily washed, jointed and turned into a stew. Mamma reported that the young publisher had pronounced it delicious, he had recognised a Spanish recipe, and passed his plate for a second helping.

Barney, as accident-prone as ever, had begun country life by putting his nose into a wasps' nest. Covered in stings, his whole head swelled to a gigantic size and, though after a week of misery it went down, his muzzle bore grey, hairless scars for the rest of his life.

Diana has described the awful incompetence of our parents when confronted by a bridle, and Carola Oman kindly sent Mamma a book on stable management for her birthday. Titled *To Whom The Goddess* it was illustrated with photographs of ladies – mostly titled – riding to hounds, sidesaddle in Leicestershire. Bursting with good advice it insisted that a horse should be groomed for forty minutes a day, by a groom who knew his job and always took his coat off. It also explained how to check that the bridle was properly adjusted when the groom had put it on, but not how to get it there.

Jack Bowles, the jobbing gardener, became a central figure in our lives. His wife suffered horribly from bouts of rheumatic fever and with their three children – two girls and a boy – they lived in a council house near the church. Bowley didn't seem to resent Cappy's authoritative manner or his early morning roars of 'Bowles', when he wanted to give orders before leaving for London. Assuming a military stance – he had served in the army at the end of the war – Bowley would reply with a equally loud shout of 'Sir?'

With Mamma he had a very different relationship. They exchanged philosophic observations, gossip and later confidences, while to us he was friend and mentor on everything except horses, of which he insisted, he had little experience.

That autumn Denis went off to Eton, with, he later told me, only half the clothes list and not nearly enough pocket money. Considering the state of the parents' finances, it seemed madness to send him, but it had been our Cannan grandfather's dearest wish. In his days as a don he had come to the conclusion that the tutorial system made Etonians the best-educated of all public school boys, and Cyril Alington, the reigning Headmaster, had been his pupil and his friend. However, Grandfather did nothing about providing school fees and when he died unexpectedly at the age of sixty-one, the greater part of his estate went to Granny.

Always vaguely dissatisfied – in England she hankered for foreign parts, abroad she missed England – Granny tried life in an elegant Kensington house. Then she went round the world twice – in opposite directions – before living next to us at Wimbledon and near us at Peppard. Finally she decided to settle in the south of France; but she offered no help with school fees.

The parents contemplated other public schools for Denis, but at that time most of them placed great emphasis on games and the artistic or eccentric boy was despised. At Eton art was respectable and he could row. Mamma consoled herself that there would be no train fares – it was only twenty miles away – and with her belief that it had fewer extras than other schools.

We found ourselves more modestly at Highlands. In common with Diana and Christine I remember being taught by Miss Vine, who was even more horse-faced than Mrs Francis. In Auntie Christine's class I sat below a shield depicting an ascending skylark with the PNEU motto 'I am – I can – I ought – I will', inscribed round it. I quite approved, at least it was better than being mild and obedient.

I think my chief interest was in the other children. There was Peter, a fat little boy bursting out of his brown corduroy shorts who, always in trouble, would foolishly confess when his mother came to fetch him. Her invariable 'I should be *ashamed*, Peter,' became a family joke.

Then there was Patricia who tiresomely demanded a share of the biscuits you brought to eat in break, especially if they were chocolate. Bored and rather embarrassed, we told Denis and, wise in the ways of prep schools, he provided us with a bar of Ex-Lax – the fashionable chocolate laxative. We could barely control our giggles as we watched Patricia wolf it down. It worked; she never reproached us, but she never bothered us again.

A few of the children were boarders, remittance children, with parents working in India or some other outpost of the Empire. I remember feeling pity for those we left behind on Fridays; when school ended at lunchtime, there was an orphaned air about them as they hovered in the shrubbery or stood on the lower bar of the gate watching the rest of us collected by parents.

Chapter Three

Christine writes:-

The next years were decisive ones. Not only did our mother acquire her own car, not only did we become the proud owners of Milkmaid, but we changed schools. I cannot remember worrying about this, or even talking about it, but I am sure we did. Our new school was very different from Highlands. No one was called Auntie at Miss Fryer's, no one misbehaved. Miss Fryer was a rare person in those days. A female graduate of Cambridge. Small and indomitable with a small curly piece of fair beard sprouting from her chin, she had just opened a school where the better-off would pay and the poor would attend for nothing.

It must have been September when my mother drove us for our first morning at Miss Fryer's in her baby Austin which she had called Bouncing Bertha. No uniforms were necessary which must have pleased Mamma, who hated buying them.

Miss Fryer's school was in a shed attached to a small thatched cottage standing at the end of a lane. The cottage is no doubt gentrified by now; but in those days it was low-ceilinged and small-roomed and I suspect without bathroom or flush loo. Miss Fryer's companion, Bossy, reigned inside, taller than Miss Fryer, with a pinched face, dark drawn-back hair and glasses. I don't think I ever saw her as a real person; for me she was just there, Miss Fryer's companion, another oddity. Other people saw them differently, even as kind little ladies, so perhaps I was prejudiced from the start, for I must admit that I felt not an ounce of affection for either of them.

There was not much room in the shed, and in winter the heat was not allowed to rise above fifty Fahrenheit, so that soon we were wearing a great many clothes to school – zip-up felt bootees, vests, monkey vests, Fair-Isle jerseys, thick skirts, and our woofies. We had small blankets cut out of a Scottish plaid to put over our knees, and, as winter progressed, mittens to put on our hands. But, well wrapped by Nana in infancy, I was still cold.

Miss Fryer was an authoritarian; no one argued with her. There were certain things she disliked intensely; fingers were to be kept flat when writing, elbows off your desks at all times. It was not obstinacy which made me forget these rules so often, rather a certain vagueness which Miss Fryer seemed to relish. A crooked finger gained a sudden and painful rap with a ruler which soon flattened it. An elbow resting on a desk was grabbed from behind, raised and slammed down again. There was no warning. But in spite of sore elbows and a repeatedly bruised first finger I never gave up these habits and to this day I still crook my first finger of my right hand while writing and rest an elbow on the table while paused in thought; so, like my father's lines, Miss Fryer's punishment had no effect whatsoever. I think the simple truth is that at that time only Mamma could have changed me. A word from her meant more than a hundred other words from someone else. She always gave a sensible reason for any criticism which to me was more persuasive than a sudden blow. I soon decided that Miss Fryer's punishment was caused by bad temper, and a bruised elbow and battered finger were just things to be endured.

We made some friends at Miss Fryer's – the Brownlows and the Laidlaws we saw quite often – and we feuded with a family who came later, ambushing them on their way home.

Though we only attended Miss Fryer's in the mornings, there was still time to learn how to cane chairs, and to take part in a never-ending search for the lesser spotted orchid in the open, sweet-smelling land behind Miss Fryer's cottage. Did we ever find it? If we did I cannot recall that triumphant moment. We did however pick flowers and take them home to press in my father's trouser press in his dressing room. I never saw the point of it, preferring to see them wild and free. Miss Fryer would also take us to a pond where she would stand calling, 'Froggies, froggies'. Whether frogs ever surfaced I cannot remember, but it caused much mockery from my brother. Josephine learnt to milk one of Miss Fryer's many goats – Miss Fryer was a goaty person – but Diana and I never gained that privilege, never rising above chair caning, not even when Josephine left to attend boarding school. Obviously we were not considered reliable enough to be trusted with a beloved goat.

Tom lived with Miss Fryer and Bossy. I never discovered what the relationship was between them. He was well into his teens when he was arrested for stealing and an enlightened judge gave him the choice of the Merchant Navy or prison; not surprisingly he chose the Merchant Navy. He was replaced by Edwina who came from London and was occasionally beaten by either Miss Fryer or Bossy in the cottage in the mornings, usually with a hair brush or a slipper, I suspect. I think it was for the sin of vanity, for her long, beautiful, red hair must have made Bossy and Miss Fryer feel like the ugly sisters. I remember how silence fell among us when Edwina screamed. People have asked me since why we did not intervene rather than remain frozen to our chairs. But times were different then and one accepted brutality in a way one wouldn't today. Dogs were beaten, kittens drowned, chickens' necks wrung; these were every-day occurrences, I did not complain about my bruised elbows either; for, picking off the scabs, I knew I would only be told not to grumble or Mamma would say that it was 'another injustice to Ireland', a favourite phrase of hers, which somehow settled the matter, as even then one knew that the Irish and their problems would always be with us.

While at Miss Fryer's, we must have talked a great deal about The Grove, because one freezing night, there was a knock on the front door and we found Edwina outside. To say we were amazed is of course an understatement. Edwina insisted that she had found her way by our descriptions of The Grove. But I suspect she followed the signposts to Peppard, intent on walking the five miles to find us. Apparently Miss Fryer for some reason had turned Edwina out of her cottage and told her to find shelter in a shed. So, very sensibly, Edwina had decided to run away. Of course we rushed her inside the house, gave her tea, persuaded her to have a bath and change into some dry clothes of ours. Then and only then did Mamma tell her to write a letter home explaining what had happened. Meanwhile she contacted either the Laidlaws or the Brownlows and asked them to tell Miss Fryer that Edwina was safe with us. Then she wrote a letter to Edwina's family herself saying that Miss Fryer was not a suitable person to look after such a young girl. I cannot recall Edwina saying much to us. I suspect she was very tired and went straight to bed in the spare room.

The next morning Edwina travelled back to Miss Fryer's with us, only stopping to post the two letters on the way. I'm not sure what Mamma said to Miss Fryer, but predictably Miss Fryer was very annoyed that Edwina had been allowed to write a letter home.

A few days later a shabby car arrived at Miss Fryer's driven by a man in a grey homburg hat the worse for wear, and a tired-looking woman, and Edwina left for ever. After that things seemed to become easier at Miss Fryer's. I do not think she and Bossy ever had another child lodger. I hope not.

Looking back, maybe the beating or beatings were not as bad as they sounded. It's possible that Edwina was the sort of child who screams as soon as she is touched. She may have been an habitual liar as well. Certainly I never saw any bruises on Edwina. But whatever else she was, she must have been a very disturbed child, and what happened to her in that small old-fashioned thatched cottage would never be allowed today.

Armistice Day was still observed at that time, and we would assemble in Miss Fryer's cottage to listen to the service at the Cenotaph on her ancient wireless. At eleven o'clock exactly, even if it was a weekday, everything stopped – including us – to observe the two minutes' silence, followed by the Last Post. None of us moved a muscle as we stood straight and silent in the little thatched cottage nor giggled, for the results of the war were still all around us in the lame and the mad, the blind and the gassed.

Sometimes when Granny was living at Highclere rather than in France, her chauffeur Silvio would drive us to school. Silvio, a handsome Italian man, was extremely good-natured. In Granny's big car, unshaven and collarless, he would drive us at high speed through Gallows Tree Common and Cane End, mostly on the wrong side of the road, only slowing down to point out piglets to us, crying out, 'Look at ze little piggies.' Used to the Kews' piglets we were not much impressed. Silvio's erratic driving was soon observed by an interfering woman, who telephoned Mamma suggesting that she tell her 'man friend' to drive more carefully and on the correct side of the road in future, which made us all laugh, Mamma most of all.

Mamma's Bouncing Bertha was not very reliable. Sometimes even her starting handle failed to get her going and then it was all hands to push – Nana, being heavy, was a much valued pusher. Occasionally as we travelled the doors would fly open and then Mamma would shriek, 'Look! Bouncing Bertha's flying.' I am quite sure that Bouncing Bertha would have failed the present MOT test. With Nana and my mother in front, there wasn't much room for us inside and, when Bouncing Bertha was also loaded with shopping, she would sometimes stop altogether, notably up the Devil's Elbow near Crowsley Park, which really is shaped like an elbow and very narrow. When this happened we would all leap out and push and push, piling in again as Bouncing Bertha reached the top. I don't think Bouncing Bertha had a boot, just a luggage rack on the back. I don't remember her ever stopping when Nana was not on board, so I suspect Nana was the proverbial last straw.

In those days we often shopped in Henley-on-Thames. Mamma would call, 'Anyone for Henley?' Nine times out of ten we wanted to go and would leap into Bouncing Bertha without further ado. Once we realised too late that we were shoeless. It didn't bother us because Henley was quiet and empty then, just a small town which was reputed to have the most pubs per person in the whole of Britain, and, of course, famous for its Regatta. It was easy to park in the market place; sometimes the only other vehicle there was Colonel Noble's phaeton drawn by an imposing horse which interested us greatly, though we kept our distance, awed by the driver who wore some sort of livery.

On one particular day, I remember we wandered barefoot into the almost empty and sparsely stocked Woolworths in Bell Street. Nothing cost more than sixpence in Woolworths in those days and the floor was made of wood and always dusty. Wandering round wondering how to spend the few coins we had in the pockets of our shorts, we forgot about our bare feet, until an elderly lady stopped to inspect us with an expression of pity on her face before slowly opening her bag and taking out her purse. Almost too late we realised that she was about to give us money and fled in confusion, not wishing to be considered needy and given money for shoes of which we had plenty at home. After that I don't think we ever went barefoot in Henley again, though we were often without shoes at home and I can still recall the feeling in hot weather of melting tarmac and the tar which it left behind on my feet.

There were not so many shops in Henley in those days. Hales the baker and Cross and Sons the corn merchants were two shops in the market place. Cross and Sons was full of things like chick food, flaked maize, biscuit meal and biscuits for dogs. There was grit, fed to hens to make their shells strong, and a host of other things which fascinated us. Occasionally in later years we ordered hay from there. It was always very expensive and was delivered by cart pulled by a beautiful shire horse bedecked with shining brasses, his driver walking beside him. There was Boots too in Henley; it had a lending library upstairs which my parents used, ordering books each week for the next, usually crime novels which they read on winter evenings sitting on each side of the fire in the drawing room. There was the Kenton Theatre in New Street and a cinema in Bell Street.

We learnt to swim in Henley in the pool on the Thames along the Wargrave Road. Our parents would not let us go in a boat until we could swim to the boom in the middle of the river and back again. As ever, I was the slowest to learn and Cappy made it worse by swimming behind me and pinching my toes when he considered them too low in the water. Having a cross, six-foot-two man swimming behind me was terrifying enough, to have him pinching my toes made it far worse. I did eventually learn to swim, but to this day I remain a poor swimmer.

Every year Mamma went to France to stay with Granny. I always felt bereaved then, we all did – my father once wrote a letter to her with a drawing of the house gutters crying for her. We all wrote letters. In one I mentioned that Cappy had paid us for the blackberries we had picked, in another that Miss Letchford had managed to make us '3 cootie and is sending them home next week.' (Cootie was twin language for coats.) I signed myself 'love Rosie Posie and love to Granny.'

It must have been a little later that Granny sent us eskimo style coats from Canada. Made out of blanket, with vivid stripes across them and with pockets and red buttons, we wore them into Reading. We must have looked a strange sight and certainly people stopped to look at us. I remember saying afterwards, 'Us different', and we *were* different. I think Mamma wanted us that way.

Reading was quite a small town then. You could park anywhere. Friar Street was my favourite street. GP Male, MRVS and Partners had a large imposing entrance there and Bradbury's the old fashioned saddlery shop was nearby; a little further down the street was Simmonds the brewers' yard from which huge horses emerged pulling drays loaded with barrels of beer. There was always a whiff of horse in Friar Street and it was wide and empty, unlike Broad Street which was busier with a Woolworths and Wellsteeds and a fishmonger's and much else.

When Nana took us to Woolworths, she always headed straight for the biscuit counter. Tipped sideways so that customers could see inside was a row of biscuit tins. Waiting until the assistant's back was turned, Nana would grab two or three chocolate biscuits and, handing them out to us, would hurry us on muttering, 'Go on, eat them up.' I never understood what made Nana, honest through and through, do this; and though the biscuits, half chocolate, half shortbread, were probably delicious, fearful that we would be caught and dismayed by such dishonesty, I never enjoyed eating them.

When my mother had time she took us to the London Road in Reading. Trams still ran up the hill there, which was wide and paved in places. We never rode on one but rushed straight to the two bookshops: William Smith, which catered for the University, but in those days had a secondhand department at the back; and another one which had floor after floor, room after room of secondhand books. The second was a very dusty shop, but we would have gladly stayed all day. We sometimes drove past Huntley and Palmer's biscuit factory and even from the car we could smell the biscuits cooking. Then past Reading gaol with its high barred windows giving on to a view immortalised in Oscar Wilde's 'Ballad of Reading Gaol' as 'that little tent of blue, which prisoners call a sky'. There was a theatre in Reading then, and several cinemas including the brand new Odeon with what seemed then a palatial car park.

Driving into Reading from Peppard we would pass the Reading and Caversham Laundry which constantly telephoned us requesting their account be settled; then over the Thames which separated Oxfordshire from Berkshire. It took me a long time to discover all of Reading: the castle-like County Offices, the Forbury lion stately and forbidding; the shop in the market place which sold milking stools and pails, everything one needed for cow and dairy in those days. But I've forgotten wide and imposing Castle Hill; the rope shops were there. And as well as the Thames, there was the canal with little metal bridges over it and small pubs by the water. Most interesting of all, perhaps, there was the Cattle Market where monthly horse sales were held, our haunt in later years. Nana took us to Reading quite often by bus. In my letters to Mamma I wrote that she took me to buy shoes and another time that she bought us all ices, 'which were very good'.

Poor Nana, it must have been lonely for her in three-storied Highclere, housekeeper to Granny who was hardly ever there. Each evening she listened to her radio and ate the same meal, white bread and Cheddar cheese washed down by beer – I don't think she ever drank water straight from the tap, perhaps because the water in Witney, where she grew up, wasn't safe to drink. We were her family as the Cannan girls had been before and she spent as much time as she could at The Grove, fussing over the chickens' water, helping turn the hay; bossing the helps about (which always came to a head when Mamma was away). Fred Kew would take bets if asked, and Nana always put her money on Gordon Richards, the top jockey of the day. If the National Anthem was played Nana would stand up and sing it in a high, tremulous voice. But because of the horrors of the 1914–18 war, she no longer believed in God.

In later years we weren't very kind to Nana when she sometimes looked after us in the evenings. Once we climbed high into the whiteheart cherry tree and then kicked away the ladder when it was time for bed, leaving Nana to find Bowley to help her put it up again. We romped in our bedroom when she was looking after us and we were meant to sleep, until she called up again and again, 'I'll tell your father when he gets back.' But she never did.

Cappy loved picnics, and each year on my mother's birthday on 27th May we had one on the Wittenham Clumps, near Dorchester in Oxfordshire. One year we knighted Barney there with a tin sword. We knighted him Sir Barnacle Bill the Sailor, for some brave deed none of us can now recall. Another time there was unpleasantness because Mamma had forgotten the sugar for Cappy's tea or coffee. Our early birthdays passed without fuss. I cannot recall having a party, though once Denis had one with rounders in the top meadow. Diana and I were fielders, but I do not remember ever catching a ball, just an increasing sense of boredom. I think the adults enjoyed the game far more than the children. I know there was trouble when a man of around fifty found his team had lost. He grew redder and redder in the face while his wife kept saying, 'It's only a game, Humpers,' a saying which soon became part of family folklore.

One Christmas Lady Agnes invited us to her party for the children of the village, at Blounts Court. We had a large sit-down tea in an impressive dining room, when Diana and I fed the marzipan on the Christmas cake, which we hated, to her Dalmatian dog Otto. Unfortunately he grew tired of it and spat a large lump out on the carpet for all to see. But that was not our only faux pas that day; no one had told Denis that it was not done to win all the prizes at a party, which he now proceeded to do, leaving only the last for me to win. We were never asked again to Lady Agnes's Christmas party. But I did go once more with my parents. On that occasion we played poker and I won, beating all the grown-ups. Impressed, Lady Agnes gave me half a crown and an ivory ink pot.

With poor Countess dead, my parents began looking for another horse. Inexperienced and without expert advice, they soon found Billy. He was around fourteen two, mousey coloured with some white on his face. He was standing in a loose box too low for him, which I suspect made my parents decide straight away that he needed a better home. I cannot remember anyone trying Billy, though I think Josephine may have been led around the yard on him. I can only imagine that our parents, used to being provided with suitable horses to ride, thought that no one would ever offer them anything else. So without more ado, they bought Billy and a few days later he was delivered. I cannot recall the tack he wore, or whether it fitted; but after he had had a day or two to get used to his new home, Mamma mounted him. She did not stay in the saddle long, a few quick bucks and she was on the ground with her spectacles broken. After that my parents sought advice from Mr Smith, who ran a small riding establishment near Nettlebed with stables built against a bank. He diagnosed a cold back and suggested Billy be lunged with his tack on before being ridden. I think he gave our parents a demonstration of lunging and certainly our parents did their best; but it made not an iota of difference. So Billy was sent back and, as they had never thought of having him on trial, they lost quite a lot of money on the deal. But, intrepid as ever, they did not give up the search and quite soon afterwards found the pony we called Milkmaid, who became greatly cherished and enriched all our lives.

* * * *

Diana writes:-

Those first two years at The Grove were only marred by school. Yet going to Miss Fryer's was, for me, rather like a temporary illness, when the pleasure of recovery almost compensates for the horrible experience you've just been through. My heightened joy when Mamma turned up to take us home – 'What's for lunch?' was always the first question, for we were ever hungry – over-rode the morning's experience. I can't now remember how often my tears wetted the newspapers which covered the school's tables, inspired by my own sense of inadequacy, Miss Fryer's cruelty and the hatred of being away from home. Looking back it seems to me that I was constantly crying, and I remember (but my sisters don't, so perhaps I'm wrong) Miss Fryer discussing our tears with Mamma. I remember her saying that perhaps we twins should be allowed to run wild for a time and come back when we were more mature. But in my heart I know that if Miss Fryer had been young and dashing, we would have tried harder, and also that she knew our conduct was partly motivated by bloody-mindedness. I, for one, would not work hard for someone I despised. Nevertheless, unlike Christine, I learned after many a whack to keep my finger flat on the long-handled pens we used, and subsequently could never handle an ordinary fountain pen without getting inky, so ball-points are now a blessing.

Tom and Edwina suffered in the cottage, but I never saw anyone except us hit in school, so why did Miss Fryer vent her anger on Christine and me? At least one pupil was a slower learner than we were. Irritated by our clumsiness and lack of enthusiasm, did she convince herself – if she thought about it at all – that she was whacking us into shape? If so, it is sad that no punishments were ever countered for us by praise or encouragement. One summer holiday we tried to show our mettle after being asked to embark on a holiday project. While Miss Fryer with her passion for botany probably hoped we would return in September with an immaculate book of pressed flowers, we learned a long ballad by heart and recited it together in front of the school. We chose 'The Burial March of Dundee', by Aytoun, which begins:

Sound the fife and cry the slogan –
Let the pibroch shake the air
With its wild triumphal music,
Worthy of the freight we bear . . .

and three pages later, we declaimed fervently words which are with me still:

On the heights of Killicrankie
Yestermourn our army lay:
Slowly rose the mists in columns
From the river's broken way.

Five and a half pages of resounding words rolled off our tongues: romance, tragedy, colour and imagery were all there, in glorious contrast to Miss Fryer's school room and the poor, dead pressed flowers she treasured. We sat down. We had done it. But no one said a word, no one even understood. Miss Fryer, a Sassenach and probably a pacifist, seemed unmoved. Our enthusiasms would never be hers and vice versa. We felt peculiar again, *different*. Then we were told to get down to work. We dipped our pens in the inkwells and struggled again with sums, or Latin, which I rather liked because it was logical, or, best of all, essays, which sadly I always spoilt with blots. Mamma knew we didn't like school, Cappy said we never would, because our home life was so happy, but they wanted for financial reasons to believe it was all right, so we told neither how awful it was. Instead we became stoics.

My sisters have already mentioned the Laidlaws and Brownlows, both impoverished gentry, who no doubt found Miss Fryer's establishment conveniently cheap. Commander Laidlaw and Major Brownlow, like Cappy, had fought in the war and returned jobless to civilian life; but unlike Cappy, they had small private incomes on which they frugally survived, with the help of a little farming. Lunch at the Brownlows, with Colin and Neville, was enlivened after those boring rests by games of 'sardines,' and 'hide and seek'. Their dilapidated farmhouse had a plethora of small bedrooms where we hid in cupboards, full of clothes whose fusty smell, common in the days before widespread dry cleaning, I still vividly remember. When a couple of years later they bought a cream pony, called Bubbles, Mrs Brownlow rang Mamma up.

'Would you girls come and try him? I don't want the boys to be hurt,' she said. And suddenly we were experts of a sort, and if things went wrong at least Christine and I knew how to fall.

But the road to that level of expertise had not been easy. There had come a day in our second year at The Grove when Milky bucked us all off and Denis lay once again in a darkened room saying over and over again, 'Is it Monday or Tuesday?' And Mamma decided we must have riding lessons. The choice of school was not difficult, because at the recent Woodcote Show we had seen Miss Lawrence's pupils carry off most of the juvenile prizes. In particular Claudia Severn had performed brilliantly in the Junior Jumping Class on her pony, Little Fellow. If only we could ride like her. Such an achievement seemed almost impossible.

At Miss Lawrence's Moulsford stables a week or so later, Mamma said, 'My children keep falling off.' 'Oh we never let them fall off here,' Miss Lawrence, thin and short with straight fair hair and a lined face, smiled kindly. She was very different from most horsy woman of her age. Indeed some of her pupils parents described her as 'a saint'. And in keeping with her gentleness, she had the gentlest of dogs, a Bedlington terrier.

'Diana,' she said, 'you will ride Dickie and Christine Celandine.' We mounted a grey Welsh gelding and a dark bay Dartmoor mare, both under twelve hands, and were told to trot down to the bottom of a field, circle round a copse and canter back. Dickie felt very small and narrow after Countess and Milky, but we reached the copse, a clump of trees fenced with iron railings, without difficulty. Then, as we turned for home, well hidden from Miss Lawrence and Mamma, the little ponies swerved violently, unseating us easily, and cantered back with empty saddles. While we walked back sheepishly, a mortified Miss Lawrence told Mamma that neither pony had ever done anything like that before. Meanwhile Josephine, the old soul, had ridden a mealy brown pony, called Billie Boy, without mishap.

Then Mamma booked us lessons and on the way home stopped in Streatley to buy a delicious mocha cake for tea, a ritual which continued for several years.

Miss Lawrence and, later, her dashing assistant, Christina Edwards-Jones, became important figures in our lives. The stars at the school were Claudia and her brother Guy Severn, two large, well-built, very self-confident children who, unlike us, knew their right hands from their left and were always well turned-out. Their tall, widowed mother, Lady Severn, was the first on the scene when any of us fell off. While Mamma sat writing or knitting in Bouncing Bertha, this kind woman would gather up her over-long grey or black skirts and run, like a full-breasted and distraught bird, to pick up and comfort us. Not wishing to be gathered up in her maternal arms and hating any fuss over yet another fall, we would try always to be on our feet before she reached us. Only once was this endeavour thwarted, when my stomach hit the ground first and I lay for a moment prostrate, ashamed of the long groan which left my winded body, before I could leap to my feet and say the usual, 'I'm all right, thank you.' This habit of remounting immediately after a fall became so automatic that when in my late teens I broke two vertebrae in my neck, I was so quickly back in the saddle that my companion, who had cantered on ahead, was not aware I had fallen off.

As time went on, Christine and I found our métier at Miss Lawrence's by volunteering at busy times to ride the ponies no one else wanted, usually Daisy and Jennie. They were both considered almost unjumpable, so every time we got them over an obstacle, there were cries of 'Well *done*. Did you see, Jennie's jumped a hurdle?' and so on, achievements which stood us in good stead later in life when we schooled and broke-in difficult and discarded ponies. Meanwhile, Josephine, always a little ahead of us, progressed to riding a large mare called Darkie, and on Saturdays in the term-time she rode Little Fellow and other superior ponies while their owners were away at boarding school – a step-up which, like milking Miss Fryer's goats, Christine and I never achieved. The previous year we had been luckier than Josephine at a gymkhana where she struggled in vain to thread a needle, because, being by nature both a quick eater and dresser, I came first in the Costume Race and second in the Bun Race, and Christine won, as usual, the Apple and Bucket Race. But to Cappy's disgust we were always the first out at every gymkhana in Musical Chairs.

Oxfordshire in the 'thirties seemed awash with ponies bought for children who couldn't ride them in term-time, so now we were rarely short of mounts. Ida, who stayed with us a whole summer, was a special favourite: compact, bay and plump, with a wide blaze and white socks, she had a splendid firm rump, on which Christine and I practised cantering standing up like circus riders, vying with each other as to how many times we fell off – one hundred and ten falls by the time we reached eleven.

Encouraged to run topless and barefoot, we were hardly aware of our bodies and when one day our parents asked, after a trip to Reading, what we had been doing we told them truthfully and without shame that we had been riding Ida in the top meadow with nothing on.

By now Christine and I were moving closer to Josephine – or she would say beginning to pester her – but until we were eleven or twelve she was still the elder sister, who knew our frailties. Unlike her we were both terrified, as Christine has said, of death, so she only had to say, 'You're going to *die*' and we would cover our ears with our hands and shout, 'No'. When the kitchen was empty she would sometimes call us to the big blue cupboard in the corner and take out groceries: tea leaves, perhaps, or spices or curry. 'Try this, it's good,' she would say, holding out a spoonful of her choice, and Christine and I always fell for the trick and then frantically tried to get rid of the lacerating taste on our tongues. The 'elephant trick' was another minor humiliation. We drank a great deal of milk in great gulps at tea-time and if anyone made a joke at the right moment the milk would come rushing down our noses instead of our throats, a failing Josephine knew just how to exploit. Cappy would be annoyed if he were there, but Mamma only giggled too. Spilt milk was, she said, easily washed off the table or aertex shirts and, having been strictly controlled by Nana at Magdalen Gate House, she loved to see us free and happy.

Sometimes we played murders in the dark, which could be frightening, but courage was expected of us and the fear of being thought a coward over-rode all our terrors. The Pullein-Thompsons were *brave*. Any divergence from this accepted fact let the whole family down and was *feeble*. We taught ourselves to jump into nettles without flinching, to walk up the spinney in the pitch dark, and to recite poetry silently to stop ourselves crying out when the dentist drilled holes in our cavity-ridden teeth, in the days before a local anaesthetic was administered. Only Winnie's boy friend George, with his quiff of oiled hair, undermined this conceit, when, wearing a townee's shiny blue suit, he came to the top meadow where Christine and I were pretending to be horses and urged us to leap over higher jumps than we could possibly manage.

Mamma, proud, although she would never admit it, of our courage, and now confident of our riding, readily accepted an invitation from Mrs Greenwell, whose daughters rode correctly but carefully at Miss Lawrence's, to try a pony she had bought. The Greenwells lived in an Edwardian house in Goring-on-Thames, a house so beautifully kept that in contrast The Grove seemed terribly shabby. The garden had terraces and gravel paths, along which it was suggested I should ride the pony, who must have been known to be difficult, because Mrs Greenwell, like Mrs Brownlow, said she didn't want her children hurt. I was, for some reason, expected to ride first. The pony was well-rounded and almost too small for the elder, long-legged Greenwell girl, who was older and taller than us. And there was *no* saddle, presumably because the Greenwells did not want to buy one unless the pony proved suitable. Later, as a mother myself, I think I would have said 'No, not bareback,' but Mamma's confidence in our skill seemed absolute. One of my sisters gave me a leg-up; I squeezed the pony's sides with my calves; and the next moment he reared up and, before I could grab hold of his mane, I was sliding down his back; then I hit the gravel path hard, landing on my coccyx. Although I felt rather faraway, I was, seconds later it seemed, in Mrs Greenwell's very feminine bedroom with cold cream being smeared on my bottom, But for me a quarter of an hour had gone missing, for I learned on the way home that after my fall we had been shown white mice with pink eyes. 'Surely you *must* remember them?' my sisters said, but, although I had walked across the garden, round the house and up the stairs, the shock of the fall had for a time rendered me unconscious of my surroundings – a useful experience for a future pony book.

Rearers we learned to reject, unless they could be broken to harness; at first because the owner of a Peppard Common livery stables was killed when his rearing horse fell over backwards and crushed him against a tree; later because we knew they were usually incurable.

Most of our cautionary tales came like this from our everyday life. We always drank carefully in summer, because a man had died after swallowing a wasp with his beer at the Woodcote Show, and, although Christine and I were for ever turning somersaults, we bore in mind that an acrobat, again at the Woodcote Show, had broken his neck fatally during a demonstration. Mamma, trying to teach us to be ready for every eventuality, told us never to go on expeditions or walks without a knife, a piece of string and sixpence. We were usually armed anyway with the sort of sheath knives, which are unlawful today, and there was plenty of string around, but how could we find sixpences when our tuppence a week pocket money rarely materialised? This was an example of our parents' sometimes paradoxical behaviour, which we would never dream of mentioning.

* * * *

Josephine writes:-

Cappy kept his pre-marriage promise to Mamma to give up bridge, but he taught us to play *vingt-et-un* and poker. I preferred acting charades and the paper games we played on birthdays. Consequences was popular with everyone, giving scope for bizarre meetings and snatches of dialogue, rather than the display of knowledge. Mamma was inclined to opt out of cards and, as Denis grew older, he began to resist family games altogether.

As the twins have written, it became obvious that I was Cappy's favourite child and '*You* ask him, *you're* his favourite' was used as a taunt. I didn't want to be a favourite, I rated it as a nuisance, on a level with the nose-bleeds which now afflicted me, or the constant toothache as my adult teeth appeared, for some reason, full of holes.

Cappy's ferocity in protecting me could also be embarrassing. On a summer afternoon as we walked along the towpath looking for a picnic spot, a rowing coach on a bicycle – shouting at his eight through a megaphone – ran into me. I wasn't hurt, but the paper bag I was carrying burst and twelve penny buns scattered. Cappy raged with noisy fury and refused to be mollified until the apologising coach had picked up every bun. I was deeply embarrassed and the crew, resting on their oars, watched with interest.

We were taught to swim in the Thames – it was before the days of polio epidemics and no one bothered about sewage. I enjoyed the roped-off pool at Henley, even though it was unheated and one emerged blue with cold and trying to control chattering teeth, but I resented being made to practise on the floor at home. For some reason our generation was not taught to crawl; at Eton, Denis learned to dive, but still swam with a solemn breast stroke. He taught us all to do honeypots, jumping in with your knees tucked under your chin and your arms embracing them.

Cappy enjoyed picnics, and when we could swim, trips to the river at Shiplake became a regular Sunday afternoon entertainment. He tried to overcome Mamma's dislike of cutting sandwiches and filling Thermoses by presenting her with an elegant picnic set. It was known as Little Boy Blue and included a special container for his constantly forgotten sugar.

I was finding the twins far too energetic. Now that they accepted me as a playmate they demanded that I raced and chased with them all day long. Mamma said, later, that I held my own and developed a lot of low cunning, and I suppose fishing was an example of this. There were no anglers in the family, but I must have observed that it was a solitary pursuit for I bought a rod and, sitting on the river bank, could tell the twins to go away, they were frightening the fish.

When the parents had recovered from the episode of Billy, they decided that though Mr Sworder had cheated them over Countess's age and health, he had been honest in selling her as a suitable mount for 'the kiddies', and they decided to give him a second chance.

This time we all drove to Crowthorne, and Mr Sworder, square, watch-chained and wearing the sort of loud check suit favoured by bookies, produced bananas for 'the kiddies' and then showed us two grey ponies in his paddock. The taller one, with the high action of a harness pony, was, he said, too lively for us, the other – a thirteen-hand grey mare called Sylvia – was a ride and drive pony. She had drawn a phaeton, but was safe with 'kiddies', and, aged seven (Mr Sworder's ponies were always seven, the age of equine maturity), was priced at twenty guineas complete with saddle and bridle.

I stood with Denis, as Mamma rode Sylvia round the bare, wire-fenced paddock and, sensing his disapproval, asked, 'Don't you like her?' 'She's already much too small for me,' he pointed out. And it began to dawn on me that one pony couldn't suit us all; we needed two.

The parents bought Sylvia and in the car on the way home we agreed that as Mr Sworder obviously thought up names for his ponies on the spur of the moment, no bad luck would be involved in changing them, and somehow Milkmaid was decided upon – Milky for short.

Having been a harness pony, Milky's favourite pace was a fast trot, she preferred roads to woods and fields and had her fair share of obstinacy. When she didn't wish to leave the yard she ran backwards, and when otherwise thwarted she would try to get her own way with slow-motion, but not particularly unseating, bucks. Mamma and Denis took her out hacking on their own, but the twins and I went for walking rides, along the bridleways and through beechwoods, riding in turn while the other two walked with Mamma and the dogs.

The discovery of Ginger changed this. His owner kept him, a quiet but obliging chestnut cob, at Blount's Court Farm and would hire him for a small sum, which meant that we could take it in turn to go for proper hacks with Mamma. In the holidays turns became fewer because Denis would ride Ginger and Mamma Milky, so we were always longing to ride and we fantasized about the day when we could have a pony apiece.

A complete riding outfit was purchased – we had been riding hatless and in our uniform of aertex shirts and grey flannel shorts. Mamma was quite firm: as there was only one pony, only one set of riding clothes was needed and we must share. We were approximately the same size, so there was no problem about fitting, except for the cap; brown velvet, cork-lined and bought from Harrods, it was the first of the modern hard hats to appear, and must have fitted Christine, whose head was always larger than mine.

We were entered for our first gymkhana, an experience that should have put me off them for life. Not only was there the struggle of getting into and out of the jointly owned jodhpurs in the back of the car, but the parents had entered me for a thread needle race without a trial run. Though Cappy suffered from an astigmatism and read with spectacles or a monocle and Mamma was short-sighted, it hadn't occurred to them that their children – apart from Denis being colour blind – might have less than perfect eyesight. Severely astigmatic, I was quite incapable of threading anything but the largest darning needle.

I cantered down the ring, dismounted and then stayed struggling with my needle while all the other competitors remounted and raced back; at last a kindly steward told me I could give up. The parents greeted me with sarcastic references to 'The boy stood on the burning-deck,' and the twin waiting to compete began to drag the riding clothes from me.

A much greater pleasure was provided by Dinah's puppies. Five tiny black sausages, with blunt noses, floppy ears, and mostly with Barney's white waistcoat, they had the delicious smell of young animals, which reaches its highest form in puppies and foals. We loved teaching them to lap and spent hours in puppy games. The only horror was the visit of the vet to dock their tails, a necessary horror, we were told, if they were to find happy homes; no one wanted spaniels with long waving tails.

A new generation of bantams was growing up. I remember three speckled hens named Lucy and The Screamers and we each tamed our own chick – mine, Piebald Jimmy (a misnomer – she turned out to be a hen), Diana's Roly Poly and Christine's Fi Fi. We trained them to ride on our shoulders and Mamma allowed them into tea, when they perched on the backs of our chairs and were fed on cake.

Though no one but Nana cared if we looked like ragamuffins, the parents did insist on their own brand of social graces. We were taught to speak loudly and clearly – on the grounds that older people were often deaf – and to look people firmly in the eye. My father was also passionate about handshakes, he was convinced that they demonstrated a person's character and immediately invalidated his theory by making us practise. We all had to shake hands with him exerting exactly the right pressure, though a painfully firm grip was considered less heinous than a limp or, worst of all, a clammy handshake.

We were taught to be polite to servants; it was permissible to insult your peers, to cheek your superiors, but to be rude to an employee, who risked losing a livelihood if he or she answered back, counted as a deadly sin.

Mamma believed that the custom of servants addressing the children of their employers as Master and Miss was demeaning for the adults and bad for the children and she did her best to discourage it. The maids obliged, except when answering the door to strangers; then their knowledge of what was proper overcame them and in mincing tones they would offer to see if Miss Josephine was at home.

Bowley had no problem, he accepted us as equals and informed Mamma that though Denis and I enjoyed a racy conversation, 'the twins leave the orchard when the talk gets coarse.'

Fred Kew also clung to prefixes for a time. He had been invited to shoot over our fields and would wander round with a gun after work. He took Denis rabbiting, provided him with a ferret and, and when he came home after his first half at Eton, observed dryly to Mamma, 'How Master Denis's language has come on this term.'

We had a copy of *The Three Little Pigs* which we enacted with great vigour. The twins insisted that I was the sensible pig who built his house of stone, Diana was the one who built with sticks and Christine was happy to be the silliest one who built in straw. I also saw myself as the sensible pig, but was surprised that they gave me the part so readily, though it was hardly a compliment for, at that time Christine, in particular, equated sense with tedium.

We liked rousing poetry, preferably Scottish, and rather despised poems about babbling brooks and flowers. Young Lochinvar coming out of the west and all the laments of the displaced and exiled Scots; I could recite 'The Fighting Téméraire' and 'Fidele's Grassy Tomb' – we were learning and writing poetry for fun.

We each adopted a Scottish character: Diana was Cameron of Lochiel, Christine Cluny Macpherson, and I, hankering for the high life, settled for Walter Scott, Duke of Buccleuch. Armed to the teeth with toy guns and swords we jumped out on Sid Pearce, walking in Spring Wood with his 'young lady', and demanded 'Cavalier or Roundhead?' He was not pleased and plainly had no views on the English Civil War. At that time we were always being someone; if you wished to change character, you were required to turn round twice.

As soon as I could read, I had devoured *Black Beauty* eight times, sobbing over Ginger and the hardness of human life. At The Grove I embarked on the books, outgrown by the Cannan girls and Denis, which filled the nursery shelves. There was *Little Lord Fauntleroy, Misunderstood* and *The Crofton Boys* – in which the youthful hero has his crushed foot amputated without an anaesthetic. *The Fairchild Family* – ours was the expurgated Edwardian edition without the gibbet, but still full of awful warnings.

I had no time for E. Nesbit's magic stories, but I took the Bastables to my heart. Oswald, Dora, Dickie, Noel, Alice and H.O. were absolutely real to me and became close friends. Sibling tensions and jealousies I understood and I always identified with the feelings of an older child, threatened by the ambitions of the next one down. Oswald had trouble with Dickie, and Sam – in *The Stokesley Secret* – had even greater difficulties with his younger brother, Hal. I think I recognised that Diana and I were locked in the same sort of unspoken rivalry.

I read Henty. In the company of complacent, clean-limbed, clear-eyed and insensitive young Britons I shot the Fuzzie-Wuzzies and outwitted cunning yellow Chinamen. *The Young Franc-Tireurs*, a story of the Franco-Prussian war, made a great impression on me. For though the French brothers compare unfavourably with the two British boys – slightly effeminate, they do not play manly games – they all join the guerrillas and fight bravely against the Germans, only to *lose*. It was the first time I realised that wrong could triumph.

And there was *Knights at Bay*, in which the Christian hero, wounded and captured, is nursed back to health by a Turkish infidel, a most civilized enemy who provides cooling sherbet. This endorsed my innate optimism that all infidels were not devils nor all Chinamen cunning. A more practical part of me loved what we called 'hammety-bang books', in which the battle is for survival: *Out on the Pampas*, another Henty, in which a female character is capable of shooting as well as cooking; *The Children of the New Forest*, in which I identified with Humphrey, who caught and domesticated the wild ponies and cattle, rather than with the older and more political Edward. And in so many children's classics, the girls' roles – truthfully mirroring their times – were drearily inferior. Jo March in *Little Women* was a great improvement, but I resisted all adult attempts to identify me with her because I hated to be called Jo. When I was very small I had answered to Jo-Jo, but as soon as I could speak, I insisted on Josephine.

At ten I read *Jane Eyre* and fell in love with Mr Rochester, though I did feel doubtful about marriage when Jane found him blind and covered in egg stains. Another heroine, Daphne Vereker in Ian Hay's *A Safety Match*, increased my doubt about the female role, for when she escapes the self-sacrificing life of the rectory by marrying the successful Juggernaut, her life of luxury makes her tiresomely unhappy. It is only when her husband is blinded – in a pit accident – and needs her to deal with the egg stains etc, that she too becomes fulfilled. This vital connection between blind heroes and true love seemed thoroughly unsatisfactory to me.

I took to deathbeds. In *The Green Graves of Balgowrie* the two heroines, brought up in isolation in a freezing Scottish house, both die of TB. Little Paul in *Dombey and Son*; Charlotte M. Yonge's families, doubly decimated by scarlet fever, carriage accidents and more TB. Yonge's sorrowing orphans, suffering invalids and a trial for murder were strong stuff and I wept happily.

In comparison the children's books of the 'thirties appeared tame. The adventures in *Swallows and Amazons* seemed feeble and the fact that the children established a naval hierarchy and obeyed without discussion amazed us. Though Denis, when at home, was indisputably our leader, we often argued with him and would not fag for him without bribes; we would never have said 'Aye, aye, sir.' My leadership role was even more precarious. 'Don't you tell us what to do,' was the twins' threatening response to anything resembling an order.

The first pony books – *Moorland Mousie, Skewbald, the Story of a Pony* and others – were in the *Black Beauty* mould, but though the pony was rounded up from the wild, broken in, stolen by gipsies and cruelly treated by uncaring owners, Anna Sewell's acknowledgement of the human predicament was missing. Seeking a diet of Victorian melodrama, I began to buy the works of Nat Gould at sixpence a time. His racing novels, full of gambling and nobbling and the horse whippings of cads on the steps of London clubs, also had a emotional storyline: wrongly accused jockeys would be cleared on the final page, while supposedly orphaned stable boys were reunited with long-lost mothers of noble blood.

Realizing that I didn't know enough of the world to write about deathbeds and battles, I joined the twins in starting endless works about ponies. They all began, 'The sun was shining when I was born' and went on to describe the foal's first meeting with 'Man'. Sometimes they reached the breaking-in stage before petering out.

Though Denis was making model theatres – a new and improved one appeared every holidays – he still played with us. On wet days we fortified the bottle-neck passage with a mattress, propped up by his prep school tuck box, and built it into a wall with blankets and eiderdowns. Two of us would defend the bathroom end of the passage, two attack from the landing and when the attackers managed to scale the fortification, we changed places and the battle began again. Our weapons were blackjacks made, on Denis's instructions, by putting a tight ball of rolled-up socks inside a large one, which could then be wielded as a bludgeon.

Mamma began to make regular visits to Granny, who had settled in the south of France, and Denis, now a teenager, was invited too. Nana would move into the spare room to look after us and Cappy would spend the weekday nights at his club in London and appear at weekends. This arrangement enabled Mamma to make up for Denis's banishment to school and gave Cappy a taste of bachelor high life: Dover soles and fillet steak at his club and the occasional night at the theatre. It pleased Nana too, giving her the opportunity for endless warfare with the maids, her ammunition varying from implications of waste to the discovery of dust. We became wicked, ignoring her constant threat, 'I'll put on my hat and go straight home.' At tea I had only to look at the twins in a certain way for them to do the 'elephant trick' and at bedtime we would disappear into the orchard and climb into a

81

distant apple tree, aware that poor Nana, loath to walk through the wet grass in her 'night slippers', would only call plaintively from the garden gate.

I missed Mamma and, before one of her departures, I took my available wealth – sixpence – and searched Woolworth's for a parting present. I chose a large china sabot of unbelievably bad taste: it was a mottled dun colour and scattered with horrid little flowers and figures in Dutch national costume. She recognised it as a love offering and carted it in her suitcase to France. For years afterwards she kept it in a prominent position on her dressing table and I was well into my twenties when I at last persuaded her to throw it out. Our other love offerings were little posies carefully picked and put in water on her dressing table for her return.

Cappy measured us all at regular intervals against the white wall of the dairy – a book over your head and then your name and the date against the pencilled line – and it became apparent that I wasn't growing. Mamma fixed her hopes on the new dentist's calcium tablets, which had to be taken in conjunction with a delicious malt extract. She also provided me with packets of raisins on the grounds that mountaineers carried them as iron rations.

Cappy, convinced that beer would do the trick, betted me sixpence that I couldn't drink half a pint. I did, but I hated it and, as no more sixpences were offered, my beer-drinking ended.

We lived in cherry country. Wild cherries grew on the edges of beech woods and, flowering early, made their ghostly presence known before the woods leafed. Then the cherry orchards of Kingwood and Stoke Row, Highmoor and Checkendon became bridal with blossom and, in fine springs, the car owners of Reading drove out to view them. Mamma quoted Housman, 'Loveliest of trees, the cherry now,' as we walked or rode by.

One of the many joys of The Grove was the whiteheart cherry tree. Whoever planted our ancient orchard had put in a wild cherry, taller even than the Blenheim apple, with a great silver-grey girth that exuded blops of fascinating gum. Intended for the birds, the wild cherry was left unprotected, while the whiteheart had various frighteners attached, including a bell that previous owners had been able to ring from the bathroom window. Bowley would pick a basket of cherries for the house and then tie the ladder in to make it safe for us. I spent perfect half hours eating the sweet, sun-warmed cherries and contemplating life from among the leafy boughs, while Bowley, who had confessed a lifetime ambition to drive along in a car spitting cherry stones out of the window, was provided with a licence, Bertha and the cherries by Mamma and sent off to realize it.

I don't think that either of our parents had read Rousseau, but some of his theories – the dignity of labour and the feeling that there should be no drones (whatever your class you must learn to produce something) were fed to us. It was confusing, for though we were to be feminists, free, educated, in possession of the vote, and to avoid household drudgery, we were to embrace the nobility of labour when it concerned gardening, the mucking out of stables and the care of chickens.

I suspect that abandoning our education to Miss Fryer was part of this confused thinking. They heard she was a good educationalist and that her pupils came from all walks of life. There was no afternoon school, no uniform and it only cost five shillings per week per child; milking goats and caning chairs were included in the curriculum. The parents thought it sounded ideal, but one look at Miss Fryer should have made them think again.

Like the twins, I found her very unattractive. Her shapeless figure was dressed in drooping fustian, her whiskered face had never known make-up, and her greasy hair was cut once a year – in a pudding basin style, by Bossy her female companion. In those days two women could live together without any suggestion of lesbianism, since the post-war problem of surplus women had made all-female households a fact of life, but the tensions and quarrels that drifted into the schoolroom suggested a highly emotional relationship, if not a sexual one.

Our school fellows were interesting: Catherine and Christopher Kennington – children of Eric Kennington, the painter and sculptor; the Brownlow boys, whose father, a wartime major, was now trying to make a living from a smallholding and chickens; the Laidlaw girls, whose father, a wartime naval commander, was trying to make a living from sheep; Jean the daughter of the local postmaster and Bernice whose father was a blacksmith. Other children came and went, but these and the two boarders, Edwina and Tom, are the ones I remember. We learned maths, Latin and geography, which seemed to consist of reciting the counties of England – not Britain – with their principal towns and rivers. 'Berkshire, Reading on the Kennet,' we chanted in unison. Miss Fryer read extracts from Euclid aloud to the assembled class. She taught French grammar, but explained to our parents that her accent wasn't good enough to teach conversation, so we were left to invent our own pronunciation as we mouthed the unsaid words to ourselves.

We wrote essays, witnessed Christopher's asthmatic attacks. Milking the goats and caning the chairs were outside activities and not demanded of us in winter. Botany was another summer pursuit. We despised it and my father would roar with rage when he found his trouser press full of half-pressed wild flowers; but though my memory rejected most of the Latin names, many of the country ones remained with me and have been a source of pleasure.

Mamma formed what she described in a novel as 'the slipshod intimacies of women' with some of the other mothers at Miss Fryer's and this led to invitations. We went to tea with the Laidlaws: their father – the retired naval commander – was a small silent man, their mother large and talkative. Afterwards we argued as to whether we liked Anne or Jean best. A Laidlaw relation had commanded my father's regiment, but I don't think it occurred to our parents to invite the adult Laidlaws to dinner.

The Brownlows asked us to lunch. Their house and farm were less elegant than the Laidlaws', and Mrs Brownlow, careworn and gaunt, boasted that she found the potatoes we were eating discarded on her neighbour's bonfire. (She had, she assured us as we eyed them suspiciously, cut off all the green bits.) After lunch we had to rest on beds in different rooms; we didn't approve – resting was feeble – but I read my first Dr Dolittle book.

The Brownlow pony, Pat, brown with a wild mane and tail, was loaned to us when they were on holiday. Her saddle, apparently designed for non-riders, had a metal bar, arched over the pommel, for the beginner to clutch. A bay pony called Rockie also came on loan; he was broken-winded and so straight-shouldered that his saddle had to be held in position by a crupper, but it was wonderful to have an extra pony to ride.

Mamma made vague attempts to steer our horsemanship into more orthodox channels. There were very few riding schools, but the Pony Club had been founded in 1930, to provide children with instruction in riding and stable management, and she took us to a stable management rally at Stonor Park. I remember glimpses of the clipped horses and ponies resplendent in their elegant rugs, but the stables were Victorian, and the loose boxes had high wooden walls and doors, topped with iron bars. Unless the door was open, there was no way a small child could see into the box, and during the lecture the older children filled the doorway; at the back, I saw and heard nothing.

Then we attended a mounted rally at Bix. It wasn't my turn to ride so I was a spectator until the groom from a livery stable – sent with a couple of ponies to tout for custom – decided that I was a likely client. I found myself on a clipped, stabled and corn-fed pony over which I had absolutely no control. He took off round the large field and everyone shouted instructions. I think I was dazed rather than frightened, and clung on until eventually the pony slowed down and we rejoined his stable companions.

After that there were no more pony club rallies and Denis assumed control. Armed with pitchforks, we shaped the hedge trimmings from the newly clipped hawthorn hedges into miniature steeplechase fences round the top meadow. Then, acting as starter and using the crack of a hunting whip instead of a pistol, he would send his sisters racing round the field. This caused such a dramatic rise in the falling-off rate that even the twins lost count of their tallies.

Mamma had never been allowed in the kitchen at Magdalen Gate House, and on her war-time honeymoon in a houseboat at Clifton Hampden, she had made her first attempt to cook. Completely baffled by the instruction 'stew the apples' she was forced to consult the lock keeper's wife and this made her determined that her children should not grow up incompetent. So, to her demand that a civilized person should be equally at home in London, Paris and St Petersburg, she added the virtue of 'being good on a desert island', which entailed the possession of basic cooking skills.

On the maid's nights out the twins and I had already begun to assume the characters of James the butler and his two female underlings Edith and Gladys, in which we served and cleared away the parents' dinner. When Denis was at home he had dinner, but helped with the washing-up. There were four roles: Washer-up, Dryer, Helper Dry and Putter Away, but Helper Dry, who also assisted Putter Away, was dropped when there were only three of us. Putter Away ran from the scullery, through the kitchen to the dining room, and to encourage ourselves we all gave loud cries of 'Express!' Meanwhile the parents drank their coffee and smoked their cigarettes and, though there might be the odd complaint afterwards, left us unsupervised.

Our cooking was equally unsupervised. On Winnie's afternoon off Mamma shut us in the kitchen with instructions to cook. At first we made biscuit meal puddings, stirring them up with gravy made from Oxo cubes, and the dogs, being spaniels, ate them with apparent relish. Then we became more ambitious, all poring over the pages of a tattered copy of Mrs Beeton's cookery book, and because the only control on the ancient coal burning range was a damper, and three cooks were using the oven at once, problems soon arose. Diana took years to forgive me for opening the oven to insert my cakes and causing the collapse of her bread rolls, and Cappy caused further offence by referring to them as 'the bullets' when he sampled our efforts at a picnic at Mapledurham. I also remember some appallingly hard rock cakes, but I forget who made them.

There was an active branch of the Oxford Group – later Moral Rearmament – in the neighbourhood and the parents were invited to a meeting. They went a little apprehensively and afterwards told us how the members had risen in turn to explain the ways in which God had changed them. A local Lord told of how he had been too embarrassed to give to beggars until he 'changed', but could now do so easily. Most of the 'changes' seemed mildly absurd and Mamma used it, as she used everything, in a book. The Culme Seymours were leading lights and the twins and I were invited to lunch at Well Place, Ipsden to meet their children. We played in a loft and were rather surprised when Primrose and John retired for their 'Quiet Times' after lunch.

Later they gave a children's fancy dress party, to which we went as pirates. We wore yellow bell-bottom trousers – made by Miss Willis – aertex shirts, red spotted handkerchiefs tied round our heads, and exotic sashes round our waists. We brandished cutlasses made from three-ply by Denis and painted with silver blades and black hilts. It turned out to be a dance and was one of the highlights of my childhood. I was unaware that I didn't dance well, that the other girls were portraying female characters and wearing dresses. I fell in love with John Culme Seymour, who was attired as an eighteenth-century gentleman in black velvet and a powdered wig, and in my recollection we danced every dance. Mamma had, as usual, told us that we must converse at all costs. 'If you can't think of anything else to say, ask "Do you like string?'" she insisted. I can't remember what I talked about, but Diana was reported to have asked her partner, 'Have you read *Treasure Island?*'

We weren't asked again. Perhaps I ruined my reputation by monopolising the host, or it may be that we never asked the Culme Seymours back, or possibly our parents' flight from the embarrassment of Group meetings made us unsuitable friends.

Rashly, I announced my intention of being a poultry farmer when I was grown up – I even wrote an earnest article for *The Grove Magazine* on the subject, in which a line – 'This is called profit' – was immortalized by family mockery. The twins and I went into prize bantams. There were our post office accounts – so carefully built up by Nana – waiting to be raided and I imagine we had made a little money selling eggs and young cockerels to Nana and Granny, though I doubt that my observations on profit took into account the fact that Mamma provided all chicken food and that Bowley killed, plucked, drew and trussed the cockerels in our parents' time.

I bought a pair of Silkies, beautiful fluffy white birds with blue skins and feathered legs. The hen had an elegant blue face and a puff of soft white feathers on her head, the cock's face was apoplectically purple and his crest composed of stiffer feathers. I named them Hero and Star and loved them dearly. I wrote a very bad poem to them, beginning, 'Oh Hero and Star, how lovely you are . . .' which was *not* accepted for *The Grove Magazine*. Diana had bought Frizzles and Christine Japanese bantams. We set them up with houses; I painted mine yellow and bought yellow dishes to match. Christine's house and dishes were blue, Diana's green. The bantams wore rings in our colours, except for the Silkies whose legs were too feathered.

Cappy began to take an interest and despising the collection of mongrel chickens which roamed the yard and orchard, he bought some pure-bred hens – White Wyandottes and Rhode Island Reds – from a golfing friend. As with all his schemes, financial expenditure was necessary: a new hen-house, with divided sleeping quarters and two runs was set up against the orchard and top meadow hedge. I found myself in charge, which was quite demanding as they had to be fed and watered separately from all the other chickens.

A later purchase was an incubator. This was housed in the spare bedroom, the one tidy room in the house; it never recovered.

Fascinated by procreation, I cheerfully carried out the small chores of turning and damping the eggs and, like an intervening midwife, assisting the arrival of the chicks by picking at the outside of the shells once they were pipped from within. I would watch over the chicks as they dried off and then take them out to the brooder, where they spent their motherless infancy.

My mother's acquisition of guinea-fowl – in Oxfordshire they were known as gleanies – was as usual more romantic and less demanding of outlay. Wild and scorning chicken houses, the gleanies roosted in one of the taller apple trees. They laid their eggs, brown, pointed, and slightly smaller than hens' eggs, in communal nests, generally in patches of stinging nettles; with shells so hard that they survived falling from a height, they were perfect for mounted egg-and-spoon races.

We had become indifferent to nettle stings, rarely needing the antidote of a dock leaf, and when eggs ran out we would be sent to search for the gleanie nest. Our largest find was eighty eggs, all reasonably fresh.

The guinea-fowl hens were deplorable mothers. Frequently two of them would sit on one nest and appear with about twenty of the tiny chicks – grey and mouse-like with orange legs. Then they trailed them round in the tall, wet grass until they died from exhaustion. We tried shutting them in runs, but the hens, frantic at captivity, would dash themselves against the wire netting and trample on the chicks. Setting the eggs under bantams seemed the only solution and the grown chicks appeared to have no problems in recognising themselves as guinea-fowl; they would join the flock and roost in the apple tree as soon as they could fly.

Mamma had grown out of her childhood sleepwalking and almost out of nightmares, but she often had amusing dreams. The one I remember was about a guinea-fowl who wrote, applying for the place of cook. Her sole qualification, offered in spiky handwriting: 'I can pour hot water on the dinner.'

When I moved into my own room I was only aware of my sleepwalking if I woke in the middle of a walk. This was frightening, because your sense of direction and ability to find your way in the dark abruptly deserted you and you spent several disoriented minutes crashing into the furniture as you searched for the light switch. Once I woke standing on the bed and clawing at the big sash window and after that I always slept with the lower

Granny

Nana with Denis

Josephine on Rum

Christine on a bay pony

Mamma and Cappy soon after their marriage

From left to right: Denis, Diana, Christine and Josephine

Diana and Christine with their first horses

A day out

Pupils of the Grove Riding School

Sulhamstead Gymkhana. From left to right: Josephine on Rum 1st., Christine on Pilgrim 2nd., and Diana on Tarragona 3rd.

The Three Jumpers. From top to bottom: Christine, Josephine and Diana

Josephine and Diana with Milkmaid

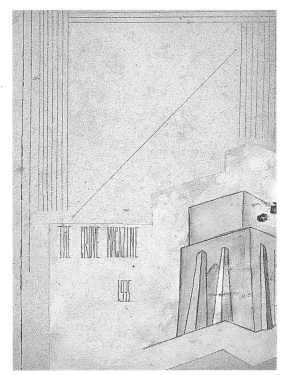

The *Grove* magazine

Playing at horses, with Denis posing as a charioteer

Barney, Pippin and Dinah

half closed, however hot the weather. My plate, or brace, for my teeth, which obviously worried me, would turn up in odd places, once in Cappy's sock drawer, but I had no memory of putting it there.

Chapter Four

Diana writes:-

Most of the visitors to The Grove made little impression on me. Immune to fame, I was more intrigued by the Bride Hall chauffeur/butler, another Bowles, than by Carola Oman herself. The unapproachable Bowles looked so important behind the wheel of the huge black car he drove, in which Carola was a mere passenger. He walked with a dignity which seemed to belie the word '*servant*', and it was difficult to imagine what he and Winnie said to each other when they lunched together in the kitchen.

The most delightful and amusing visitor of all time was Allen Lane, the enterprising publisher who published *High Table* and *No Walls of Jasper* in his new Penguin paperbacks, which were to change the market for ever. Young, lively and rather, I think, in love with Mamma, Allen counted the scars on our knees to see how many we had and how much they had multiplied since he last came. He carried us shrieking to the old bath, which served as a water trough for the Kews' cows and pretended he was about to drop us in; he chased us merrily round the orchard. Once he rang to ask whether he could bring over another young man who was contemplating suicide after being jilted by his girl friend. They came; our parents took them to look over a house which was for sale. Afterwards the tall young man, whom (perhaps wrongly) I think was Allen's brother Richard, regained his spirits and ate vast quantities of lardy cake. Had his state of mind been exaggerated by Allen as an excuse to come? Or was The Grove such a tonic to a worn Londoner that life seemed worth living again? Allen was, he told me many years later, very fond of Mamma, and she was one of the first to hear that he had done a deal with Woolworths, so bringing quality novels at sixpence a copy within the reach of everyone. But, despite her outward cynicism, she was shocked when he complained to her that his mistress spent too much money on butter.

Opposite us in a large red brick turn-of-the-century house lived the Platts, whom Mamma later put in her novel *They Rang Up The Police*: three unmarried sisters, who, like the Miss Coopers, still lived with a revered white-haired mother. Marjorie, the eldest, was the boss; Geraldine, the second one, painted, and Peggy, the youngest, was the underdog. There was another daughter, rarely seen, who had married, moved away and produced pale, well-behaved children, who found us barbaric. The Platts wanted to be friends and good neighbours, but our parents only really liked amusing people. Unpunctual, sensitive Geraldine, the most feminine and the most intelligent, painted in a room above the garage and was frequently summoned to meals by Marjorie's high-pitched voice with always the same prelude, 'Darling, are you in your studio?' with a special emphasis on *dio* – a cry which all of us, including Bowley, imitated from time to time. The poor Platts, despised as three spinsters – although Marjorie was said to have lost a potential husband in the Great War – later became a warning to us of what could happen to three sisters who remained with a beloved mother; an example which was a small persistent irritant at the back of my teenage mind and later an increasing worry to Christine.

We learned to project our own voices, when we were sent upstairs to shout from a window to the others in the top meadow that lunch was ready, and, also, when we drag-hunted on foot with the spaniels, with many calls of 'For'ard away', ''ware rabbit', and other cries familiar to those who hunt. For a while, before the puppies found homes, we had a pack of three and a half couple. We had no horn, but carried hunting whips and tried to dress the part, with the huntsman – we took it in turns to play each role – wearing an old blue blazer left over from Denis's Emscote Lawn Preparatory School days. The quarry set off, with a fifteen-minute start, dragging a chunk of meat on a string, while, locked in a stable, the dogs waited impatiently. The chase always took us through Spring Wood and over the fields beyond, and the quarry dodged and zig-zagged and doubled back to put the spaniels off the scent. I remember hanging the meat on a gate and crouching panting behind a clump of gorse bushes, while my sisters' cries rang across the landscape. The dogs, noses down, ran silently, and we later found they didn't need the meat because our own scent was strong enough for them to follow. We trespassed, of course, but we knew not to run on young cereals or through hay fields, and roads were out of bounds. Later, when the puppies had gone, our pack shrank to Dinah, Barney and Pippin, the only puppy we kept.

Barney travelled with us on two caravanning holidays, when Bowley and his curly-headed children stayed at The Grove to look after the other animals. We didn't like leaving the ponies, but Cappy seemed in his element when he parked the caravan in a field above a cove near Parr Sands, Truro. He dug a latrine and with Denis's help erected a lean-to tent where the males slept. It was cold and wet both holidays. If the rain was torrential, we played cards in the caravan and after supper when everyone was in bed we told stories to the parents. On the second holiday I started on a long novel I was writing about Edwin, an upstanding man, blinded eventually by cataract (like old Mrs Kew), who was destined to walk by mistake into the river at the end. I had been slow to begin this story, because earlier in the year our parents had discussed a libel case during lunch, which had cost an author a great deal of money. As a result I thought my hero's surname had to be unique. So every time one came to mind I went through Cappy's London telephone directories. Each name I chose was there, so what was I to do? Eventually I hit upon Pisspot, which to my intense relief wasn't to be found anywhere. And not for a moment did I associate the name with pee-ing, because Nana called potties *articles*, and *piss* was a word never used in our family.

Confidently I began my story in the lamplit caravan. 'One day Edwin Pisspot . . .' Tactfully my parents listened to the end of the first instalment, before Cappy called from the lean-to. 'Why Pisspot?' I was silent. If they, of all people, didn't know, I must have totally misunderstood the libel laws. And I didn't want to lose face by admitting my mistake. 'I should change it,' Mamma said. Then, thinking I was keen on the letter 'P', Cappy suggested Pespit. This, which was surely in the London telephone directory, seemed far too low-key to follow a fine name like Edwin, but . . . it was no good arguing with grown-ups. So Pespit it was, but somehow the change spoiled the story and I never reached blind Edwin's terrible death by drowning.

Early on the first caravan holiday we were walking along the cliffs above our cove when Barney suddenly vanished and we realised with sudden misery that he had fallen over the edge. We called his name again and again, shouting above the sound of the sea breaking on the rocks below and the heartless cry of the gulls. We ran down a winding cliff path with Denis and Mamma leading the way, and, when we reached the bottom, we heard a distant barking. Looking desperately across a blue-black stretch of rocks, touched here and there with lichen, we wondered how anyone could fall on them without breaking every bone in his body? Would we find a battered, dying dog? Then suddenly we saw a small black hump lying on the only patch of sand below the cliffs big enough to take a dog's body.

Cappy was too lame to clamber over rocks, so Denis and Mamma went and, to our intense relief, returned carrying Barney between them. Miraculously he was alive, and a boy appeared as if from nowhere and said "E fluttered down like a bit of paper.' A sad and anxious little procession, we carried Barney, limp but breathing, back to the car. We took him to a vet in Truro, who pronounced him shocked and very badly bruised, but without any broken bones. The holiday's happiness was saved. For several nights Barney slept on Mamma's bed and she squeezed in the double one with Christine and me.

I suspect that, unknown to our parents, Barney's sight was beginning to fail – a fact disguised by his very sensitive spaniel nose – because on the second caravan holiday he fell into a rectangular reservoir of water when we toured a china clay factory, and Denis dashed down steps and dragged him out, covered in clay. These incidents were, among others, grist to the mill that helped eventually to turn us into writers.

While in Cornwall we went to tea with Sir Arthur Quiller-Couch at the Haven in Fowey, where his kind and loyal daughter, Foy, lent us a rowing boat. Somehow we repaid this generosity inexcusably by breaking an oar. I don't remember whether we or our parents were to blame, only that Mamma was very upset and a sense of guilt spoiled my visit. Q, whose name was for us a household word, had been our grandfather's student and close friend and, when up at Trinity and later, while working on the Oxford anthologies of English and Victorian verse, he was often at Magdalen Gate House. Q's son, Bevil, had been engaged to marry Aunt May when he tragically died in the great 'flu epidemic in 1919. Mamma had read us Q's poem, 'Upon Eckington Bridge, River Avon', which begins 'O pastoral heart of England! like a psalm', and one day we were to read 'Dead Man's Rock', so he was one of our heroes. But at the Haven we found an old man, who was to our young eyes very white, spider-thin and unsteady on his legs. Worse still for us, he was no longer interested in children. The grown-ups ate their tea in the drawing room; we, according to Josephine, were segregated on a balcony – although I only remember the three of us sitting rather forlornly on steps facing the picturesque harbour with the cry of seagulls in my ears.

Much later when I was grown-up, I learned that, although Q was at one time an enthusiastic chairman of the local Cornish education committee, he disapproved of the education of women; consequently Foy never went to school and taught herself to read and write. It was an odd as well as a horribly chauvinistic view in a prolific author who needed large sales to support his life-style – so perhaps we three girls did not miss as much as I imagined.

One afternoon when I was eight or nine I found Mamma crying as she knelt dusting books in the parlour. Afraid to ask why, I fetched a cloth and, without a word, started to pull out books too, banging them together before dusting them and returning them to their places. Neither of us spoke, but gradually Mamma stopped crying and when, after about an hour, all the books were back, she handed me from a shelf, a copy, as a thank you, of *Wild Animals I Have Known* by Ernest Thompson Seton, who soon became, despite the sadness of his stories, one of my favourite authors. Christine, who had no idea Mamma was crying – a matter too private for me to mention to anyone – remembers wishing she had helped, too, and been rewarded with a book.

Emotional problems and deeper feelings were never discussed in our family and 'Don't be personal,' was a reprimand we took seriously. Unlike children today, who may ask why their parents are quarrelling, I listened in anxious silence to the rows on the stairs, which woke me sometimes, as a furious and frustrated Cappy shouted that he was leaving home.

'Oh Nicky, don't be silly. Give me back those car keys! And *do* be quiet. The servants will hear.' I've never forgotten Mamma's pleading, slightly irritated voice on one occasion, but I can't remember what my father shouted in reply – perhaps his words were beyond my comprehension. Mamma's distress was signified more by her inaccuracy – there was only one servant in the house – than by her tone of voice. But she was the youngest in a strong family, and Sir Walter Raleigh, an eminent Oxford don, watching her with her sisters at their beloved father's graveside had noted for posterity, '. . . the girls are splendid metal and don't flinch.' And this was the tradition we were expected to follow. But I was always on Mamma's side, because I loved her unreservedly and she was little and delicate, while Cappy was big, and loud in anger. Denis, older, and more worldly, believed the arguments were over money. He remembers Nana's earlier outraged announcement, at Wimbledon, 'Now he has lost all your mother's money too!' But Nana knew nothing about the financial market in the 'twenties, when wiser men than Cappy lost fortunes on the stock exchange. Anyway, Mamma went to Granny in Wimbledon at the end of that decade and borrowed £2000 from the Cannan Estate. A depressing experience one might think, but she always said worrying about money was bourgeois, and when, following Cappy's death, the Pullein-Thompson overdraft was at last paid off, she declared that she felt for the first time middle-class.

Clearly another financial crisis stared our parents in the face soon after moving to Peppard, because Great-uncle Teddy (Edwin Cannan) came to the rescue and advanced them £1500, against his Will; a sum only three hundred pounds less than The Grove had cost. Wise and clever financially, Uncle Teddy, aged fifteen and still at Clifton College, had insisted on managing his half of a small fortune inherited by Charles and himself – an inheritance which came originally from the Claude relations, who owned coal mines in Chile. Our family was therefore saved twice from bankruptcy, not by our Scottish or by our largely improvident English relations, but by our Huguenot forebears.

Uncle Teddy believed that *if you look after the pennies the pounds look after themselves.* He insisted his wife kept household accounts and found it easier to write a cheque for hundreds of pounds than to part with a penny. His arrival at The Grove to discuss the loan is immortalised for me in a small snapshot taken on a Brownie camera. Impossibly old, white-bearded, small, like many Scots of his generation, he arrived with his shrewish wife, Rita, in a Baby Austin called Lucy. Serious and soft-spoken, both these Cannans paid us scant attention, perhaps because the matter was so important or because their everlasting grief at losing their only son David through measles made it hard for them to relate to other people's children. For years we chiefly remembered this distinguished professor for the way he cut oranges, not in cubes, but sliced round and then divided into squares – and for his habit of killing wasps by cutting them in half with scissors as they flew.

Mamma's nightmares, another nocturnal disturbance, which I do not think ended as quickly as Josephine suggests, sometimes wrenched me from my dreams; her anguished cries against a tormentor tore at my heart, until Cappy's shouts of 'Wake up Janner, wake up' ended her misery. Cappy claimed these nightmares were due to a persecution mania caused by Nana's unkindness to her as a child, a fact not corroborated by our aunts.

Then there was Barney's dream, an eerie howl curdling the blood like the wail of a lost soul. Leaping out of bed we ran to shake him awake where he slept curled in his basket by the passage radiator. Josephine says he was reliving the terror of his fall over the Cornish cliffs, but I have sometimes wondered whether this howl was connected with the meningitis he suffered after his distemper.

Bluebell's end haunted me as well as Christine – her cries as the fox took her and the empty nest next morning among the periwinkles in the garden, those cold eggs. If only we had made her sit indoors . . . So we learned early that our mistakes could lead to death. And that tragedy of all kinds could come at night. I think these experiences may have helped to set Christine and me apart from other children in an England less violent than now. Certainly, behind our slowness and apparent thick-headedness were minds struggling to come to terms with a cruel fate which struck the Mr Sheas and disabled Kews of our world, not to mention a gaunt woman with a huge goitre who stood at her gate most days, staring across the road with large unseeing grey-blue eyes in a face the colour of yellowed paper. In comparison with all this, Miss Fryer's insistence on a straight writing finger was indeed both irritating and insignificant.

By this time Cappy's morning bath ritual was well established and we knew that the passage and the bottleneck, which led to the loo and bathroom, must be free of us by the time Cappy finished his early cup of tea. Our bedroom was unheated, so on cold mornings Christine and I dressed quickly in the bathroom, warming our clothes against the hot water pipes, which led directly from a large unlagged tank, before dragging them on. Absent-mindedly I sometimes then, as now, wore my sweaters inside out – a lucky omen, it was said, so long as you didn't change them before midday – or back to front. Then, all too soon, Cappy's voice bellowed, 'Is it clear?' And scurrying into our bedroom we replied, 'Yes, all clear,' and he limped along in his pyjamas and we waited for the roar of rage which would thunder through the house if we had mistakenly left any of our clothes in the bathroom – once he threw an offending garment out of the window. But we didn't care because, it was only Cappy in a temper again, *making a mountain out of a mole hill*, something we were frequently urged not to do.

Anyway, now that we knew for certain that he loved Josephine best, we twins had subconsciously started to distance ourselves emotionally from him. Sometimes after the clearing of the passage we would see, as we wandered in the garden, Cappy's hot bath water gushing down the wall from the overflow pipe, for he loved deep baths. If, on the other hand, Winnie, or her successor, had failed in their job and the water was cold, breakfast became a very disagreeable meal. Mamma offered as usual to *speak* to the culprit again. The heap of bills in brown envelopes seemed higher, the aggrieved silences longer. Then after Cappy had finished his shredded wheat, whose colour matched his moustache, the next crucial moment came as he picked up a spoon and chopped the top off the first of his two boiled eggs. At seven I, who had once longed for a hard-boiled one, held my breath. Would the egg be right with its white beautifully set and its yolk runny? Or wrong with a soft white or hard yolk? If it was right, silence followed while the important matter of eating continued. If wrong Cappy flung down his table napkin and shouted 'She's done it *again*,' and Mamma reiterated a long-worn promise to *speak* to the cook. Cappy then made do with toast and at eight-fifteen donned a bowler hat and left for the London train on the first lap of his journey to a job he hated. I think in the end I came to despise Cappy for his rages, and he knew it, and sometimes they diminished his always fragile self-esteem. Once, at the height of a family quarrel, he shouted to Mamma, with a male's natural inclination to blame the nearest woman in any argument, 'Why don't you *manage* me?'

I am sorry now that Mamma never talked to us about Cappy's arthritic pain and the after-effects of one of the cruellest wars the world has known. I believe that, since we were not hard-hearted, such an explanation could have entirely changed our attitude to Cappy and made his life happier. But I may be wrong because we might have sounded patronising and Cappy scorned pity and needed to feel the strongest of us all. Indeed, one of his frequent declarations in times of family discord was, 'I will be master in my own house,' an irony since The Grove could not have been bought without Cannan money.

If *clearing the air* is, as some counsellors suggest, a sensible way of keeping human relationships happy, I was handicapped from the first. Disdaining rages and often incapable of *saying* what was wrong, I sulked when offended. I sulked so badly once that Mamma, shouting 'I'm tired of your beastly, gloomy face!', threw all the table mats at me one by one and, she said laughingly afterwards, I just stood there without making any attempt to protect myself. Sometimes, filled with remorse, I left a note on Mamma's writing table – never Cappy's – saying *Dear Mummy, I'm sorry I was cross today*, and, although she never mentioned them, I felt an apology had wiped the slate clean.

The dogs were a great emotional stand-by. When overtaken by the *nobody loves me* syndrome, you turned to Barney. You stroked his lovely, dark fur and he licked your hands and offered his paws until you felt better.

In 1935 or thereabouts Mamma began writing *A Pony for Jean*, which was to start a new genre in children's books. Up to now pony stories had been written with the pony as the central figure. But this story is told by Jean, who cares for horses more than anything else in the world, and turns the thin, discarded pony Cavalier into a winner.

Every Sunday evening Cappy read to us the latest chapter in the book in typescript and, although the character of Jean is mainly based on Mamma herself, we claimed it also contained the nicest part of each one of us. Many of our animals are there with different names: Barney and Dinah as Shadow and Sally, Freddy, our second gander, now called Harold and our dear goose, who hatched her eggs every year amongst the violets, as Edith. And there was Bluey, too, Christine's alarm clock, not working very well after being dropped over the banisters. And Jean, like us, had come to the country after her father lost money in business. Mamma dedicated the book partly to us as follows:

> For all children who ride; all children who would ride if they could; but especially for those intrepid though unorthodox horsewomen, Josephine, Diana and Christine.

A Pony for Jean is beautifully written – 'A little piece of literature', commented one reviewer – and its style and story captivated us, for now, as we contributed to *The Grove Magazine*, we were beginning to see ourselves as budding authors. Words had become important. And Cappy read well, passing round butterballs when his throat got dry, so that we looked forward to the evening and the next instalment. Soon after *A Pony for Jean* was finished he started on the next one, *We Met Our Cousins*, which is set at Roshven in the Scottish Highlands and was more about Mamma's childhood – she had unsympathetic cousins – than ours. 'Cannan can write the heads off almost all her rivals,' enthused a critic. 'Here is a book that neither child nor adult can set down, bubbling with humour, packed with adventure, marked by the keenest observation.'

Another Pony for Jean followed the next year. In this story Milky appears as a bucking grey mare called Charity, and Jean tries to make a hen house, which collapses – a minor disaster which happened to Mamma herself in Wimbledon when, like her eponymous heroine, she burst into tears. Only Mamma was grown up and watched by her small son, Denis.

We loved Sundays, because of the readings and in summer the ice cream man, Eldorado or Walls, who pedalled to our gate ringing his bell. Usually we had the cheapest, a penny water ice in paper, no wafers, and occasionally a twopenny, creamy vanilla ice cream.

We were never taken to church, except on Armistice Day, when Cappy wore his medals and prayed, I suppose, for his comrades who had died in the First World War. Once, I remember, Mamma and I were next to a refined lady who sang 'O God Our Help in Ages Past' in such a high trilling voice, laced with gentility, that we got the giggles. It was awful. The vicar, a handsome man in early middle age, was known in the village as Gentle Ernest, because of his quiet and tranquil nature. When he bought himself a small car, the villagers took advantage of his kindliness, and, although he had lost an arm in the war, constantly asked him to drive them here, there and everywhere. No doubt they thought their requests were reasonable, but in the end they became too much for Gentle Ernest, who, unable to say *No*, sold his car in self-defence.

Sometimes when the sound of the church bells travelled across the fields and Spring Wood into our garden, I wondered whether we *ought* to be there, but Mamma advised us to be 'Blue Domers' – a term which I thought was widely accepted, but I believe now was invented by her. 'It means,' she said, 'that you worship under the blue dome of the sky rather than in church.' This suited me well, since I had chosen 'There is a Green Hill Far Away' as my favourite hymn, because of the hill rather than the crucifixion.

Nevertheless our conversation was littered with proverbs and biblical quotes and there still lurked in the back of my mind the thought that God sees all and would punish me for my misdeeds.

But high spirits and giggles were endemic at The Grove. 'Beware of the female nude,' Mamma cried, stealing across the grass on the nights we slept outdoors. And then we hid our faces, but she wasn't naked, only flimsily clad. Her words were a joke, which became a ritual. The villagers claimed that summer had only truly arrived when the Pullein-Thompsons moved their beds out on to the lawn. Mamma and Cappy had camp beds, but we children shoved our horsehair mattresses out of the windows and made them up with sheets and blankets as though we were indoors. The dogs and their baskets came out, too. We chattered for a bit. Then, snug and warm, we lay counting the stars until sleep came and sometimes we heard the hooting of the owls and the birds' first songs and felt the dew on our cheeks. One of my most abiding memories is the smell and texture of damp Witney blankets under my chin. They were very thin, because we had picked off most of the wool for those little fluffy balls Christine has described, and they had tapes on them saying *First Housemaid* or *Parlour Maid* or *Cook*, because they had been bought originally for the Magdalen Gate House servants some thirty-five years earlier. Later Rupert Brooke's 'and the rough male kiss of blankets', in his poem 'The Great Lover' struck a chord, for although I in no way shared his sensuality, he was right; the feel of the blankets was male rather than female.

Sometimes the weather broke in the middle of the night: someone shouted 'It's raining,' and we pulled ourselves out of bed and dragged our mattresses – now damp, for there were no groundsheets underneath – up the stairs, remade our beds indoors and fell asleep almost at once. Other times we woke when the dogs barked at the postman, who politely averted his eyes, and then the puritan work ethic which had somehow taken root in our beings would make me feel guilty. Why were we not up, too? How awful to be caught sleeping so late.

When it was very hot Mamma packed a picnic and Cappy drove

us to Shiplake church and parked where it said NO PARKING and opened a gate which said PRIVATE and we walked down to the towpath to swim in the Thames, along with the spaniels.

We always picnicked in the same spot in a thistle-ridden field, close to where the cows stood, keeping cool, in a shallow inlet. By now we could swim breast-stroke and on our backs and we could tread water. The river was narrow enough here for us to swim to the far bank, rest awhile and swim back. When Denis came he sometimes chased and caught us among the thistles, and then dropped us into the river, and he taught us all the honeypot jump-ins Josephine has mentioned.

It was lovely to be cool, but sadly, stuffed in the car with three dogs, we always grew hot again during the four-mile drive home and then I longed for a river at the bottom of our garden and saw myself paddling barefoot into the house still cool in my deliciously wet swimsuit.

When Christine and I were eleven, we came, with Josephine, to an arrangement with Mr Sworder out of mutual need. We needed ponies to ride: he needed riders to show off and school the ponies he bought to sell. If we could get more than the asking price for them we kept the change.

Mr Sworder was a greengrocer by trade irredeemably drawn to horses, although we never saw him on one. He especially loved carriages of all sorts and sizes, which he bought in large numbers in the 'thirties – probably Milky's phaeton was among them. He kept these beautiful relics in his yard at Crowthorne, Berkshire, because, I believe, he could not bear to see them broken up; an admirable sentiment which made him rich when war came and people turned back to horse-drawn vehicles.

His appearance did not suggest such good taste. A short, rotund figure, usually in a checked suit complete with watch chain, brown-moustached and pallid, Mr Sworder, who was nobody's idea of a horse dealer and indeed knew little about horses, came to play an increasingly important part in our lives.

'Going to gay Paree?' he would ask Mamma before 'gay' became a euphemism for homosexuality, when we met him by chance at Reading's monthly horse sale, which we visited sometimes with horror and fascination. Knowing that Mamma stayed sometimes with Granny in France, he would buy her a revolting 'cup of *real* French coffee', and we children ice creams.

This monthly sale of horses was presided over by a terrible red-faced, beer-bellied man called Wilkins, who held a stockman's whip in his coarse right hand and lashed any hesitant, frightened or stubborn horses with it as they were trotted up and down to show their paces to prospective buyers. Wilkins took no account of the animals' age or condition, indeed the lash fell hardest on the starved, old or lame, and each blow seemed to lacerate my own heart. I hated him, but did nothing. It was a grown-up world, which did not in those days listen to children. Outside the great shed in which the horses waited to change hands were the cattle pens, where farmers moved calves from place to place by hitting them on their noses with sticks.

Mr Sworder, however, was of a different ilk. He sometimes made growling or shooing noises to persuade a horse to sharpen-up his paces or walk up a trailer's ramp, but I never saw him carry a whip or stick.

The first pony he brought us was Rainbow, a sweet, unbroken mare under twelve hands, whose colour was hard to specify, for she was a mixture of chestnut, bay, brown and dun. We consulted what books we had on breaking-in ponies, backed her carefully without mishap and, because she was small, we schooled her meticulously as a beginner's pony, teaching her not to jump or run away when we dropped sheets of corrugated iron behind her or let newspapers blow around her feet.

One cold morning we were surprised to find the hair on Rainbow's legs and fetlocks lightly singed and realised that she had ingeniously and endearingly slept on the ashes of a bonfire to keep warm. After two months we sold her reluctantly for five pounds more than Mr Sworder's asking price, and opened our first bank account. Mamma, who now described us as 'horse copers', put some of the people who came to see Rainbow into her book *They Bought Her A Pony*, and the remark by one that riding was a 'social asset', became another quote to be giggled over. Other ponies in need of schooling followed one at a time.

Of course, sadly, all the Sworder ponies had eventually to be sold. Parting with Rainbow was fairly easy, because she was too small for us, but it was harder with the others. Later when we started the Grove Riding School we were able to buy those we liked by instalments, but in the meantime we had to cope with the heartache of frequent partings. Worst of all, Mr Sworder sometimes sold his ponies to unsuitable people and afterwards we lay in bed at night worrying about their future.

In 1937 Josephine moved into Winnie's room and a new influence entered our lives when Joan Harris, who was seventeen, came to work in the house. Joan was the plump brown-eyed daughter of a handsome gamekeeper and a loving mother. She lived in Shiplake Bottom, and her aunt, pretty, aristocratic-looking Phoebe Harris whose face was like porcelain, lived in a cream-painted cottage opposite the Kews and took in our washing. Joan's only sister had died when eleven in 1934 from diphtheria. Her elder brother, Jim, a plumber, had developed lead poisoning, which turned to TB and killed him in January 1937 at the age of twenty-three, leaving just one brother, Pete (who became a gamekeeper). But, despite these tragedies, Joan had an unquenchable, earthy and often ironic sense of humour. She was calm, with a slow unconsciously seductive smile. Mamma liked her immediately and, after a happy and pleasant job interview, Joan left gaily, only – she laughingly relates now – to be bitten on the back of her leg by Pippin as she went through the gate. She didn't complain. She had fallen in love with The Grove. Dogs were dogs. And she had taken to Mamma, whom she was to hold in deep affection for the rest of Mamma's life.

Cheerfully, Joan arrived on foot every morning at seven-thirty and left at six. She cooked breakfast and lunch, put tea on the dining-room table and prepared dinner before she headed homewards. An avid reader, who particularly liked Mamma's novels, she quickly became a friend who joined in our joys and sorrows.

Soon the kitchen became a place where we could all meet together for elevenses, consuming slices of the Kews' delicious warm lardy or dough cakes, the like of which I have never found elsewhere. Here Joan later opened our eyes to another world, as we listened to stories of doctors who dallied drinking sherry with rich patients while those who paid fourpence a week into a panel to secure health care anxiously waited for a visit; we learned of men who beat their wives after having 'one over the eight' on a Saturday night, and of frightened women who went to a chemist in Reading to buy a bottle of purgative to abort their unwanted babies, and much else. And when home from school Denis would sometimes sit in the kitchen talking to her as she cooked.

Joan had a way with men, too, which, combined with her habit of politely answering criticism back, ensured she managed Cappy – a bonus for us all.

Since the age of six we three had covered pages of lined paper in our sixpenny Woolworth's exercise books, with everything which caught our imagination or infuriated us. When in 1933 Mamma decided that the best of our work should be included in a *Grove Magazine*, she was following a family tradition; for in 1911 and 1912 two of the Cannan girls, with Carola and Dulcie Oman and several school friends, had produced a magazine, called *Inter Multos*. This lively handwritten enterprise ran to ten numbers and was eventually bound in two volumes by the Oxford University Press. Mamma, who contributed many drawings, was at first Sporting and Literary Editor, and later Editor in Chief, and Carola Oman, who clearly had a penchant for painting in watercolours, was Artistic Editor. Along with May, a future poet, they also wrote prose and poetry for the magazine and Dorothea, Mamma's eldest sister, contributed a play, but appears to have dropped out in 1912, probably because she had by then become a boarder at Downe House School. All the contributors were dons' daughters, so it is perhaps not surprising that the writing in *Inter Multos* is of a high standard for girls in their teens. Nor is it surprising that the three most enthusiastic contributors, Carola Oman and May and Joanna Cannan, were all to become authors.

Gilbert Cannan had cut his authorial teeth several years earlier with stories in his own family's magazine, *The Star*, which his indolent father Henry (our Cannan grandfather's first cousin) had started, so carrying on a family tradition. I suspect that, although the prime reason for encouraging these magazines was probably educational, the grown-ups also enjoyed having a forum for their own work.

* * * *

Christine writes:-

It was not difficult for us to find material for *The Grove Magazine*. Since we were six years old we had been attempting to write books. This is borne out by a letter written describing Mamma's life to someone called APC – I do not know the purpose of the letter or who signed it. I quote the relevant lines: 'Incidentally her smaller children spend their time in writing novels, which seem to deal mostly with "the cat is on the mat" and "the cat has caught a rat." When they have filled an exercise book they insist the manuscript must be typed just like mother's. And there is always a scene of tearful disappointment when they find how small their book is.' The letter is dated February 1932, and could have been to Doubleday in the USA.

As Diana writes, *The Grove Magazine* was Mamma's idea. Now, more than fifty years on, reading the three volumes published between 1933 and 1940, I am impressed by our grasp of words at such an early age, how opinionated we were, and how little our views changed between those years. Mamma typed all the magazines but didn't correct our grammar. Denis supplied illustrations for the first two.

Josephine edited the first *Grove Magazine*. She contributed more to this than to the two later ones. In her article 'What Children should be fed on' she begins, 'I am sure no children like rice pudding,' and later adds, 'pancakes are very good for children,' and more in the same vein. She also writes on 'Poultry Management', which is full of sensible advice. Diana contributed 'The Brave Old Days of Old' which begins:

> *In the brave old days of old,*
> *Everyone was bold.*
> *Now everybody runs away even this day.*

My piece called 'Modern Houses' states, 'Modern houses are very nasty inside, don't you think so?'

Then there is Josephine's philosophical 'Today's Great Thought'. 'If machinery had not been invented, it would be the brave days of old, so in the future there will be a curse on engineers.'

Diana's 'In Olden Days' was probably her first complete story. Because of this I include its first lines:

IN OLDEN DAYS
By Diana Aged 7 or 8.

I was born in a country called Scotland. I was named Joanna and I was a dog and my master was James and his son was called Christopher and had a pony.

> *We lived in a thatched cottage, and in that time people smuggled. One night some smugglers came and stole me and took me on a ship. I had never been on a ship before, but James had told me what it was like so I knew*

that I was on a ship, and that they were smugglers.

After a bit I was taken to the Captain. He was a very stern man. He had a good look at me and smiled and then said, "That's a good dog." I was a puppy and not used to this.

Diana also wrote an article called 'Animals' which appears mainly concerned with which ones are useful – it seems we were very keen on practicalities at that time. I contributed a short piece on school: 'School is beastly especially Miss Coopers. You learn nothing. They are very sloppy indeed. Children ought to be taught well, else not at all. Schools would be better if they were kept warm in winter.' Miss Coopers was of course Highlands School and it was not surprising that we learnt 'nothing' since Diana and I spent most of our time in disgrace reading in the cloakroom. The best of our poems in this volume is I think Josephine's 'Captain Ren', which I include in full:

CAPTAIN REN

Josephine Pullein-Thompson
(Aged eight or nine).

O, bold Captain Ren,
Who roamed the ancient seas,
He strove to find the Spanish Main
But all he found was bees.

THE END OF CAPTAIN REN

O, bold Captain Ren
Who roamed the Lively seas
He loved to hear the distant sigh
But he, like all, must die.

We left him far behind us
Far below the sea,
Far, far behind us
With the starfish on his knee.

There were other contributors. Our cousin Jim, Aunt May's son, contributed 'Tune for after Tea', a musical score and a piece entitled 'On Ranches' which begins: 'When going shooting a gun should be used not a rifle', and more such advice. (Later Jim went into the army.) He also wrote 'Adventures of Trapper Tom, Trapper Bob and Arkansas Jones'. Tom is an inventor who manages to turn two cars into flying machines.

Aunt May's poem 'The Ballad of the Sword' appears in this one. It is not up to her usual standard and maybe had been rejected for one of her collections. It is set in the First World War.

Mamma wrote 'Answers to Correspondence', which were entirely fictional. Here is her reply to 'Eater, Oxon':

> *'Your fears are well founded. Bursting is painful and an un-becoming process and should be avoided. Thirty apples a day is enough for anybody.'*

But surely the best contribution is Mamma's 'A Grove Alphabet'. It describes perfectly how life at The Grove was at that time. In it Josephine Mary is of course Josephine, who was christened Josephine Mary Wedderburn. Judas was Denis's ferret.

A GROVE ALPHABET
by
Joanna Cannan

A   *is for Authors. At The Grove they abound,*
     Like leaves in the autumn they cover the ground.

B   *is for Bertha. She leaps and she hops,*
     She bounces and flounces and sometimes she stops.

C   *is for Cappy, so sturdy and strong,*
     No one else at The Grove is so broad or so long.

D   *is for Dinah, who bristles with rage,*
     If she bites me again, I shall buy her a cage.

E   *is for Eggs, which we look for in vain,*
     We'll be all dead and gone 'ere the hens lay again.

F   *is for Farmers, both poultry and dairy,*
     Christine and Diana and Josephine Mary.

G   *is for Gander. He's fierce in the spring,*
     But the rest of the year he's the dearest old thing.

H   *is for Heavy Hen. Though she's not slim,*

When she fell in the tank, she proceeded to swim.

I   is for Ice Cream, Eldorado or Walls,
     I hope I have tuppence next time the man calls.

J   is for Judas. His size is no merit,
     He's as big as a bear but he's really a ferret.

K   is for Kitchen. I know of a sinner
     Who opens the door and asks what's for dinner.

L   is for Larder. Without saying please
     Some people go in there and finish the cheese.

M   is for Mummy. We call it all day,
     What we want we don't know, but it's something to say.

N   is for Nursery. There's sharks on the floor,
     And booby traps fall as you open the door.

O   is for Orange, so pleasant to eat,
     And six lumps of sugar and you'll have a treat.

P   is for Pony, white, brown, bay or sable,
     We'll have nothing to wish for when he's in the stable.

Q   is for Quicklime. It gets in our eyes
     When we whiten the hen house, but nobody cries.

R   is for Rabbits. They scratch up the lawn,
     We rise from our beds and pursue them at dawn.

S   is for Summer, that glorious time,
     When to stay for a moment indoors is a crime.

T   is for Teatime. We wash with a fuss,
     There are lard cakes and dough cakes for Barney and us.

U   is for Useful. That's what we must be,
     And shut up the hens when we've finished our tea.

V   is for Vauxhall, so cold she won't start.
     Let's save and buy Cappy a donkey and cart.

W   is for Water. To wash we are made,
     But we like it to drink when there's no lemonade.

X   We don't mention. But sometimes it's clear

That everyone's horrid and nothing is fair.

Y   *is for Yawning, a horrible sight,*
     But don't think we are tired, we could sit up all night.

Z's *for Zip Fasteners. Some people wear 'em,*
     When we take off our clothes, it's much quicker to tear
     'em.

Diana edited *Grove Magazine* No 2 which was published in January 1935. In it is possibly Diana's first horse story called 'The Life of a Carthorse'. Called Crown, the horse begins by pulling a coal cart, has many adventures and eventually returns to his old home having been bought for the then princely sum of one hundred guineas. There are echoes of *Black Beauty* in this one and a mare called Ginger.

My first horse story is included too. About New Forest ponies, which predictably are rounded up and sold, it also has a happy ending. 'A Dreadful Day', by me, is a rambling story in which children sell all the eggs there are in the house to a strange lady who knocks on the door, resulting in no eggs for father's breakfast and much fury both from him and an upset maid. It has a tailpiece by Denis.

I also contributed to a piece entitled: 'Why Should England Take Money from Scotland for Repairing England' – it seems I was by then a Scottish Nationalist – and 'Pirates', a story running to two chapters entitled: 'Captured' and 'Escaping'. Included too is Diana's 'In Danger of Death' which is another one which begins in Scotland and is full of danger and smuggling. It ends happily. Her 'Olden Days are Best' is included as well. It seems we have not changed much!

Diana's 'In Danger of Death' takes up a great deal of space in Volume No 2 which may be why there is less of Josephine in this one, or possibly it was because she was already away at school. Her best contribution is 'The Wilds' which begins:

The Red Deer browses on the hill,
Against the skyline bright
You can see the cattle graze
Black, brown and white.

Mamma contributed a poem about a fish shop in Reading called 'Colbrook's' (the name of the shop). The last verse is as follows:

I hope there is a heaven for us all,
but mostly for the beasts, green woods, deep seas,
that some day I may hear a bird's voice call,
Send Mrs Partridge two knight's widows, please.

She also wrote 'Woodcote' reviling the line of pylons which had suddenly appeared there. Denis wrote a poem on the same subject entitled simply 'Pylons'. There is no 'correspondence' in this volume.

Grove Magazine No. 3 was a long time in the making. It finally appeared in January 1940, but I think many of the contributions were written long before then. I believe I had to be persuaded to edit this one by Mamma. With Denis now a soldier we had lost our illustrator, and the front is covered with Christmas paper. Included is a piece by Granny called 'A Visit to a Snake Farm', which took place in South Africa in 1929. (Maybe because she was born at sea Granny was an inveterate traveller who went round the world three times.)

In it too was Diana's 'The Fate of the Georgian Manor'. Below are three of its nine verses:

But their days are over now
The Manor is not there,
The stately trees have gone now,
And sordid villas stare
Out onto a slippy highway
Where there used to be a track.

In the coach house cars are kept
In the stables tools abide,
Where the happy horses slept
In their stalls side by side.
In the kennels where gun dogs used to dream
In the paddocks sordid dustbins gleam
In the paddocks where horses used to roam.

For in the happy days of sunshine
The Georgian Manor was pulled down.
Gone now has the oak and pine
Where they stood there stands a town.

I contributed a piece on the dangers of barbed wire which is equally relevant today, particularly to horse owners. Our visit to

Scotland in 1938 had not diminished our love for it and Josephine's 'A Wish' begins:

> I wish I were in the West Highlands
> Out in the mist and the rain,
> Standing on Morar's silver sands
> And watching the gulls again.

On the same subject my effort, 'A Longing', begins:

> Oh to smell the sea, the soft green Highland sea,
> And see the waves lapping the sandy shore
> And to know that it is scones and jam for tea.
> Oh for all this and nothing more.

On the same theme was Mamma's 'Highland Lament' which I have included at the end of this chapter. Diana also wrote a piece deriding battery hen houses, a view much in advance of our time, and a long poem called 'A Londoner living in the Country'.

Perhaps influenced by Keats, Josephine's poem 'To An Oak' ends thus:

> And now you lie a huddle of glory in the dust
> A broken tree to satisfy some thoughtless mortal's lust
> A headless Hector on a Grecian plain
> Your friendly branches writhéd round with pain.

There is also Mamma's wonderful poem about 'Milkmaid' whom she sometimes exercised when we were away at school:

> All round about our white farmhouse
> The tall green beechwoods stand;
> they bar the hill and secret keep
> this ancient secret land.
> The tracks the timber waggons make
> wind north, south, east and west;
> Milkmaid and I don't fear to try
> the one we like the best.
>
> The leaves of half a hundred years
> lie soft upon the ground,
> and Milkmaid's little iron-shod hoof
> pass there without a sound.
> And north and south and east and west
> the wheeling tracks divide,

111

and I don't know which way they go,
but on and on we ride.

There are no signposts in the woods;
no people walk so far;
and when night falls the branches hide
the friendly evening star.
I'm not afraid of getting lost
however far we roam;
I just sit back, the reins lie slack
And Milkmaid takes me home.

I also wrote a poem about the death of three cats, and a piece anti flower-preservers, and another on the stupidity of wearing gloves in summer, in the style of Frances Cornford.

Surprisingly there are two poems written by both Diana and myself. Why were we suddenly together again? It seems distinctly odd. Personally I recall Mamma saying that there was too much of me already in this edition, particularly as I was editor; so any more poems must be in collaboration with Diana. I remember inwardly squirming because once again we were to be the twins. I can think of no other reason. Diana disagrees. However, I remain convinced that at least the first verse of 'Reading' is solely mine. (We also combined on a poem about hunting.) Here is 'Reading', a town with which I suspect we had a love-hate relationship:

Reading, you are sordid, dusty, dreary,
Full of women cold and weary,
Always tired and never cheery,
Tramping back to Nottingham lace.
What a poor, dejected race.

Full of dentists smug and clean
Always earnest, always keen
Never dirty, never mean.
Full of surgeons, squat and stout,
Sometimes in and sometimes out.

Reading, you are ugly, grim,
Sunless, smokey, squalid, dim,
And yet in some parts strangely trim.
Your factories shine against the sky
And in your streets the babies cry.

112

You have bloody butchers' shops
Filled with fat gruesome chops,
Confectioners with no acid drops,
Fishmongers, greengrocers, bakers,
Shoe shops, clothes shops, undertakers.

Oh you daily-growing town,
You spoil the spinney and the down,
Every hillock you hideously crown.
With your vile suburbs stretching wide
You spoil the neighbouring countryside.

Mamma also wrote 'Letters To The Editor' for this one, plus the answers. I give you one example:

> *Sir*
> *I live in a small villa on the outskirts of Birmingham.*
> *I want to own a dog. But I can't give it much exercise,*
> *and cannot afford meat for it. What breed do you advise?*
> *Enquirer*
> *Wy/wurrie*
> *Black Road*
> *Birmingham.*
>
> *In view of the fact that you can neither exercise nor feed*
> *a dog, our advice to you is to give up thoughts of*
> *becoming a dog owner and to purchase a cat or a white*
> *mouse. (Reliable cats can be obtained at a moderate*
> *price from The Misses Pullein-Thompson, The Grove,*
> *Peppard, Oxon. Ed.)*

One cannot but wonder why we wrote what we did. I think Diana's and my early work was influenced by the books we were reading at the time: *Smugglers All*, *The Ghostly Galleon*, *Who Rides in the Dark?* are full of pirates and kidnappers. *Treasure Island* and *Kidnapped* also fuelled our imagination, as did *Black Beauty*. Josephine, who had rather different literary tastes, nevertheless shared our obsession with Scotland. Later horse stories eclipsed our more violent offerings. But even in these, violence and dishonesty are rampant. Fox hunting appears in Numbers 2 and 3 of *The Grove Magazine*, including articles justifying and in defence of it – once again we appear ahead of our time.

In our youth we pored over a book of tartans. We mourned

the defeat of the Scots at Culloden as though it were yesterday. Sometimes we even raised our glasses at meals calling out to 'The King', then passed them over the water jug before drinking, so signalling to each other that we were actually toasting Prince Charles Edward across the water in France, not King George – a Jacobite habit. But then, as Josephine has written earlier, one of our ancestors was hung, drawn and quartered after the battle of Culloden, so maybe we had good reason.

The Scottish obsession has not left me; four of my books are set in the Highlands as were Mamma's *We Met our Cousins* and *Hamish*, which was one of the first Penguin books for children to be published, about a pony from the Shetland Isles loose in London.

And finally Mamma's 'Highland Lament' from *Grove Magazine* No 3:

> *Over the loch the gulls are wheeling,*
> > *Achnatallasaig!*
> *There is no fire in the lone sheiling,*
> > *Achnatallasaig!*
> *Down from the hills the wet mist wanders,*
> > *Achnatallasaig!*
> *The cow stands in the byre with glanders,*
> > *Achnatallasaig!*
> *From the dim grey sea the night comes creeping,*
> > *Achnatallasaig!*
> *The roar of the waves prevents us sleeping,*
> > *Achnatallasaig!*
> *Over the Sound the wind blows harder,*
> > *Achnatallasaig!*
> *There's nothing to eat in the wee sma' larder,*
> > *Achnatallasaig!*
> *The wet rain falls on the hills of heather,*
> > *Achnatallasaig!*
> *The scones we have made taste just like leather,*
> > *Achnatallasaig!*
> *Up on the moor the storm clouds gather,*
> > *Achnatallasaig!*
> *Why did we come to the land of our fathers?*
> > *Achnatallasaig!*

Traditional.

Beside writing and riding, we canoed. We had shared the cost of the Folbot canoe (or was it really called Foldboat?) taking much of the money Granny had given us each Christmas from our Post Office accounts to buy it. Denis paid the most. We called it Foy after Foy Quiller Couch. It took us about fifteen minutes to remove it from its bags and put it together. We did not have the usual single paddle, but two shorter ones. Denis, already an oarsman, took us out in Foy, and I remember him taking us in turn up or down the Thames before depositing us on a small island covered with nettles before returning for the next one. Left usually in shorts, aertex shirts, sandals and without socks, one was horribly stung if one moved in any direction, but I don't remember ever complaining, and we soon became experts with a paddle.

Diana has described our caravanning holidays in Cornwall. On our way we stayed in the grounds of public schools, where Cappy lectured in term time and discussed job prospects with the boys there. I remember swimming in Canford's swimming pool and finding it shady and cold, and stopping at Monkton Coombe which I preferred. We already knew these schools by name and many others, having cheered them on at Henley Regatta.

The unpleasant side to these holidays was the jobs which we – Diana and I, in particular – were given. Peeling potatoes was boring enough, but infinitely worse was emptying the latrine buckets which Mamma, being cook, was excused. The rest of us took it in turn dragging the bucket across a field, trying to hold our noses as we went – then pulling it up a bank, before with a final desperate heave we tipped its unsavoury contents over a stone wall on to the clump of nettles below; then we lugged it back, thankful that the task was done.

Diana and I shared the double bed in the caravan. For some reason we hated this. Mamma said that we should be like knights of old and sleep with a sword between us, but we had no sword and could think of nothing to put in its place. Mamma and Josephine had the single beds and Cappy and Denis slept in the lean-to tent with Barney in his basket. Dinah, being car sick, had been left at home. As far as I can remember there was no one else staying on the farm, and by today's standards the site left much to be desired. To reach it one drove through an incredibly old-fashioned farmyard, where sometimes, when an animal had recently been slaughtered, the drains ran red with blood. During our last stay there was a great deal of rain, and on leaving we became bogged down. We were rescued by two enormous Shire horses who easily pulled our car and caravan out of the mire, proving what we had been saying all along – horses are better than cars.

Much of our time was spent with our horses. Our ponies were hogged. Sometimes Mamma cut their manes with red-handled clippers, but more often we rode to the Maxwells' stables near Kingwood Common, where the groom clipped them for a tip. Otherwise clipping was done with a machine driven by a man turning a handle, while another held the horse and the third, the expert, did the actual clipping. Milkmaid and Rum were clipped once a year and, when turned out, wore New Zealand rugs which were quite an innovation then. Our nearest forge had three farriers and was only a hundred yards away. A set of shoes cost around six shillings, depending on the size of your horse. When a pony staying with us developed colic, it was put down to eating the husks of acorns by the vet who called. The pony recovered, but it was an expensive visit and for years afterwards we kept two bottles of drench collecting dust in the stable. One bottle was given at the onset of colic, the next if the symptoms persisted after forty-five minutes. And what a struggle ensued when this was done! I remember much of a drench smelling of linseed and, I believe, turpentine running down my arm. Some vets insist now that such drenches only made matters worse and these days such concoctions are mostly give by a stomach tube; but I do remember them working on the few occasions when we used them.

Our ponies were fed meadow hay in the winter, delivered in trusses and cut from a stack. Their feed consisted of oats, bran and chaff. On wet days when the ponies stayed in we amused them by playing records on Nana's old wind-up gramophone. We would write down their preferences, decided by pricked ears, calm expressions and shining eyes. The hymns always won. The dogs also seemed to prefer hymns. Sometimes we gave them lessons in the nursery. Religion was a popular subject with us, if not with them, and to this day my Bible has pages daubed with Dinah's paw marks.

Mamma believed in labour-saving devices and when Milky had stable stains on her, rather than washing her these were rubbed out with a chalk block called CLEANFUR, which was actually intended for dogs.

We loved riding with Mamma, who always dismounted in what

she said was the Russian way, flinging one leg over the pommel of her saddle before sliding down. Personally I think it had more to do with riding side-saddle in her youth than Russia.

Our saddles were flat-seated with almost no cantle and the knee flaps were so small that, as one grew, one's knees were off them most of the time. Eggbutt snaffles were yet to be invented and sore mouths were quite common-place. At first our girths were made of webbing, and, since there were two of them, it was easy for flesh to be caught between. Worse than this, sweaty webbing dries stiff and hard so girth galls were quite prevalent. We wore crash caps, as they were called then, and were not allowed to ride without them. Mamma wore a bowler hat and we all wore lace up shoes; our previous breeches and socks had now been replaced by jodhpurs which in those days were flared at the sides.

My legs flapped wildly as I rode, like windmills it was said. Sometimes Mamma would say, 'See how long you can keep a leaf between your knees and the saddle.' Sadly even quite a large leaf vanished in minutes, while my legs continued working overtime.

We were not short of rides. Mamma gave them names: The Ipsden Gallop, The Plough, Binfield Heath, The Kidmore End Gallop and The Nutwalk were a few of them. And we did gallop. The Ipsden Gallop was one of our longer rides. We rode past the Devil's Churchyard to reach it, an eerie place with dark yew trees and a smell of thyme; then on down the long hill to Ipsden. Here, because the road was slippery, we always dismounted and led our ponies. Remounting we would see the Goring Gap ahead, so open and wide and quite different to the beech woods nearer home. We would ride along a long straight road and then turn right up the gallop itself, which was wide and straight too, downhill at first and then uphill for the final furlong. The ponies were keyed up and jogging long before they reached the gallop which must have been a mile in length; afterwards we rode on loose reins through Hailey and on to Checkendon where the beech woods began again.

Sometimes, riding through Splashers Bottom past where Dinah went when she was in season, where the middle-aged woman living with her mother was still called Baby (which caused much merriment among us), we would turn right, and see the inhabitants of Boro' Court – a huge mausoleum-type lunatic asylum built by Lord Wyfold for his mistress, it was said – pulling carts through the dark garden there. Years later a gardener told me that when he worked there he had been given permission to hit the inmates, but had never in fact touched them.

The Wyfold Gallop passed nearby as well, and here one stopped to open small hunting gates, something at which we soon became experts, which stood us in good stead later. There was a ride through the park near Cane End House, and another further down the road where one passed huge rusting machines belonging to the owner of the house. Steam engines predominated, for he was apparently certain that one day they would be needed again, and in a way they probably were, melted down in the war, I believe, for guns or ammunition. To me they added mystery to an old man living alone in the ancient slowly decaying house, so beautiful but so neglected. The Kidmore End Gallop ended near his brother's house, which was smaller, and it seemed that he too was a recluse.

The ride called Binfield Heath really began near the Bottle and Glass pub and skirted Crowsley Park which contained another beautiful house. Huge, with an impressive ha-ha, it was inhabited by two brothers, both bachelor clergymen, it was said. In the days when Colonel and Mrs Baskerville had lived there, Crowsley Park had boasted a garden good enough to be open to the public, but little of it still remained. A herd of deer roamed free in the park and there were notices warning walkers to keep away during the rutting season. Thinking of *The Hound of the Baskervilles* added more mystery to this house, which one could only glimpse beyond the big fences which surrounded it. On the way to the Bottle and Glass one passed the old stable yard, and what tales I wove around it. There was a ride through Bottom Wood to Satwell where the artist Cecil Aldin had lived next to the hunt kennels which were there then and where in later years the Woodland Foxhounds were kept.

There was The Plough, from which one could ride on to Bolts Cross and through Lambridge Woods, then down a steep hill and on past the cemetery to the Traveller's Rest, a large townlike pub, long gone. Here we could never resist cantering to Henley along the Fair Mile which was mostly wide and empty except for a few goats tethered, and a drive to a large house also called The Grove. Having completed our mile we would ride back and then home through the Fleming estate, always quickly for fear of being stopped, as it wasn't quite a bridlepath. Many of our rides ended at Kingwood Common where Polish troops were stationed in the war and which later became a prisoner-of-war camp. Sometimes we rode through Witheridge Hill and then past the cottage belonging to Alistair Sim, and then on to Nettlebed. Other days we rode past the Maharajah's Well at Stoke Row or down a lane where we stopped to eat bread and cheese and drink cider at a remote pub called the Crooked Billet. Here in the beech wood nearby were groups of dark-complexioned men making chairs beneath the tall trees, and riding by we would shout, 'Good morning' as one did in the country in those days. Loud engines were switched off at our approach for people knew then that horses are easily upset, and most had or were still working with them; so a nervous horse would be led past a frightening object with many a pat and kind word.

As a child Mamma was allowed only one day a season with the Bicester Hunt. This left her with a great yearning for hunting. She had ridden side-saddle then and jumped all the fences which came her way, though she had never had a jumping lesson in her life. Her favourite hunter was Sweet Briar who came from Mr Rhodes' stable at the Lamb and Flag in St Giles, Oxford.

Before we hunted properly Mamma sent us beagling, which she said would help us to understand how horses felt in the hunting field. Effie Barker was the Master of the Beagles (later she became a highly respected Master of the Garth Hunt). Mamma greatly admired Effie, I think because she was dashing, strong and independent. Personally, I never understood much of what was going on. I ran wildly in my plimsolls, which grew wetter and wetter and more and more slimy inside, enjoying the opportunity to tear around places where I had never been before. I never thought about the unfortunate hares which were being hunted until one day there was a kill. My sisters and I had been helping Effie Barker all day. Due to a broken collarbone she had one arm in a sling and we had opened gates for her and held up strands of wire. So after the kill she presented us with the dead hare's pad. I cannot remember which one of us accepted it, but looking at the small paw I was overcome by a feeling of melancholy. But to everyone else it was a well-earned trophy, which Mamma took to the taxidermist in Reading to be preserved and mounted on wood with our names inscribed underneath.

Real hunting was much more fun than beagling. Having too few ponies meant that two of us usually stayed behind to muck out and make the bran mashes. Being left behind and having lunch alone with Cappy was always an ordeal for me. Those hunting always hacked to the meet, usually a distance of four or five miles but occasionally as long as twelve. At first we hunted with the Woodland Harriers, started by a young army officer who greatly impressed Mamma by calling in a suit to request her help in persuading the farmers to let hounds cross their land. His name was Captain Fane and the hounds were called Harriers because, as a serving officer, he was not allowed to be a Master of Foxhounds. The name was of course a mere formality; we actually hunted foxes. I don't think any one of us was interested in killing anything, but we loved the sound of the horn, the cry of hounds, the thundering of hoofs, a distant holler. We were brought up to treat a Master of Hounds as God. At the meet one greeted him or her by saying, 'Good morning, Master.' At the end of the day before setting off for home, one said, 'Goodnight, Master.' During the day a Master could do no wrong. Heading a fox – turning him back towards hounds – was the worst crime one could commit in the hunting field, for it spoilt the day for everyone else. We did not hang back, galloping ahead to open gates, holding the Master's horse if needed; we were always around calling out, 'I'll do it.'

I must have been nine or ten when, after we had been hunting all day, a fox was killed at dusk in the osiers near Playhatch, and there were only Mamma and I left of the field to witness it. I dismounted and loosened Milky's girth and was then surprised to be blooded and given the brush of the dead fox while Mamma was given the pad. They must have been hung on our saddle Ds for the long ride home. Mamma was delighted for me, as it was a great honour to be given the brush, but I was a trifle bewildered. It seemed unearned, for all I had done was to enjoy myself. But to Mamma who longed for us to be 'Fair girls . . . who never went wide of a fence or a kiss', it was another step in the right direction. So, as darkness fell that day, we remounted and hacked home, stopping to loosen our tired hunters' girths and walking part of the way, bearing our trophies with us.

There were many other wonderful hunts. And although sometimes we would ride twelve miles home after a particularly good run, by the light of a winter moon, the ponies loved hunting as much as we did. The joy of crossing the countryside on a good horse was such fun that even when I was in my twenties sitting on a train I would still in my imagination be on a horse, choosing the best way across the landscape outside the window. Without hunting, life would have held few excitements during the long winter months and before long I was addicted to it. My first trilogy was about children who start their own pack of hounds; though it sold thousands over several years, it is of course unacceptable today.

After Captain Fane went to war and was subsequently killed, the Woodland Harriers became the Woodland Foxhounds and that great horseman Henry Wynmalen became joint master with a Colonel Hill. They employed a professional huntsman but it remained a small and friendly pack.

Sometimes we had lunch in Aunt Dot and Uncle John's charming house at Headington. They had it built themselves and called it Bareacres. Great-uncle Teddy, hating any exaggeration and deciding that the whole property was little more than an acre in size, always addressed it as 'Barely an Acre'. On one occasion when we lunched there, I remember Mamma and Aunt Dot sitting in the sunny drawing room which overlooked the garden, while we children sat squashed together at the kitchen table with our young cousin Paulla, in a high chair flanked by Maud, her nanny, and Mrs Hicks, the enormously fat cook. The kitchen smelt of gas, and Mrs Hicks, hot from standing over the hot stove, smelt too. We ate boiled suet pudding while I longed to be sitting in the drawing room with Mamma and Aunt Dot. I think we all did. Paulla says now that when she stayed with us in the war, Cappy did not address a single word to her. As a child, I cannot recall Uncle John speaking a single word to me either. I remember him as a slightly eccentric and very erudite figure, Printer to the Oxford University Press, who spent his free time in his study working on a collection of memorabilia made up of the sort of things no one had ever collected before – the paper used to wrap oranges, posters, cigarette cartons, prospectuses and much else. We considered it a crazy occupation, but we could not have been more wrong, for it is now the highly respected Doctor John Johnson Collection of Printed Ephemera at the New Bodleian Library in Oxford. Our first, and I think only, prospectus for the Grove Riding School is in the collection, having been printed and designed by Uncle John.

Uncle John and Aunt Dot showed me great kindness in later years, and when Denis while up at Oxford appeared at Bareacres in winter shivering and without an overcoat, an outfitter was despatched to Christ Church to fit him out with an overcoat. Denis was equally surprised to receive a small allowance from Uncle John with a letter stating that he was not to write a thank you letter or mention it. Later in the war when Denis was in Italy he received an equally cryptic letter saying something like: 'I understand that you have been promoted to the rank of Captain so are no longer in need of money, so I am stopping your allowance forthwith.' In other ways Uncle John was tight with money. He and Aunt Dot did not have a car and it was said that they bought a machine which turned butter into cream because butter was actually cheaper. But this may have been family folklore.

Uncle Percival, known as Uncle P, was tall with a moustache and had been gassed in the First World War, when he had been a balloonist. He became a solicitor and later an ADC to the Queen, whose signed photograph he kept on his desk. It was said that his mother, a German, was the only person killed when a bomb was dropped on Walsall during the First World War. But again this may be just folklore. I remember Uncle P taking us to the Royal Show and to our great surprise, when the time came to go home, being unable to find his car. Fortunately, after much frantic searching I found it to much acclaim. Uncle P was very kind to Denis when he was at prep school in Warwickshire and our parents were too busy or too hard up to fetch him home for half-term. He and Aunt May would collect him and take him camping, which he much enjoyed. Looking back I think we were lucky with our uncles. We were lucky too with our aunts, May and Dorothea. Aunt May was invariably kind. Aunt Dot, as we called Dorothea, was colour blind, so rare a phenomenon in women that learned doctors came to examine her when she was young. Aunt Dot could not tell green and brown apart. She liked mending and sometimes our brown jodhpurs were patched in green and our green socks darned with brown wool. I am glad to say we were too polite to remark on such a minor misfortune.

We continued playing with our farm animals on the nursery floor for a long time. But the game became more involved. Josephine's main character, Captain Alec Horseshoe, was made from pipe cleaners with black boots and white breeches and became an expert on equitation, while Diana's and my characters, Squadron Leader Charlie Hoof and Commander Duncan Snaffles, remained in permanent sitting positions because they had been bought sitting on tractors. They wore large hats and bright shirts.

All three had small farms and, more important, horses. Captain Alec Horseshoe had a favourite black with a white blaze called Dauntless. Charlie Hoof's favourite was a lightweight spotted horse called Trooper, while Duncan Snaffles's unbeatable jumper was called Spider and was soon so worn with use that he became the colour of metal. Fortunately, after a time we acquired pots of enamel paint and then Spider became a strange chestnut-cum-dark bay with a blaze. Loose-boxes were made out of shoe boxes and I remember nailing kindling wood together to make fences and then creosoting them. Commander Duncan Snaffles had a charming white farm house. Josephine made one using Denis's fretsaw for Captain Alec Horseshoe, but it had no interior. She painted its walls to look like grey stone and glued on appropriate curtains to each window; brocade for the drawing room, crimson velvet for the dining room and a learned dark brown for the library. I have the feeling that Captain Alec Horseshoe was in a different class to his two companions!

There were other characters too – labourers in smocks, milkmaids with stools, milkmen with milk churns and carts always pulled by thin-legged prancy horses. We gave many of the humans strange mannerisms, and on one amazing day one came to life. He was Ronald, a red-faced middle-aged farmer who wore a bowler hat and had the most annoying habit of saying 'Hm ha' between his sentences. His arrival was always dreaded by the farmyard people, and when one day a man appeared to see Cappy and, though not so red-faced as Ronald, also said 'Hm ha' between his sentences, we were flabbergasted. Cappy, soon bored by his company, told us to show him our bantams, but whenever he said the fatal 'Hm ha', whoever was nearest collapsed into un-controllable giggles and had to be relieved by one of the others. He must have thought us three very silly girls.

In later years Diana's chickens and donkeys became a less important part of her farmyard, and my dairy herd diminished. Captain Alec Horseshoe and the other two started a riding school and ran horse shows. But strangely in all the years that we played with our farms, none of the three main characters ever married or had a girl friend.

I don't think I read much until I was twelve or thirteen. Children's books of the time were not very exciting. Besides I found it difficult to sit still for long, unlike Josephine who always seemed to have her head in a book and refused to play anything but farm animals, and whom Diana and I were soon calling 'Bookworm', for we enjoyed playing on the lawn, jumping on imaginary horses over a course we set up, for hours on end. One day we followed this by running into Henley and back, a distance of eight miles, just to prove that we could do it. We were incredibly healthy at this time; but I don't remember thinking of anything beyond Scotland and horses. I don't even remember education being discussed, but I do recall Mamma saying, 'If anyone asks you what you are going to do when you are grown up, say, marry a rich husband.' We all knew a lot of poetry, and when we had less help in the house and sometimes washed up in the evenings, we would talk in rhyme all the time.

When we were younger we had run round and round the nursery table singing hymns at the top of our voices. Now we recited poetry instead, (something I still do for comfort in moments of stress). Diana learnt the whole of 'The Ballad of Reading Gaol', and Scottish ballads were a great favourite with Diana and me. Mamma believed fervently that 'One crowded hour of glorious life is worth an age without a name' and also that 'They are not long the days of wine and roses'.

As Diana has written earlier, Mamma had been reading poetry to us since infancy: 'Drake's Drum', 'He Fell Among Thieves' and 'The Fighting Téméraire' by Henry Newbolt were great favourites. Personally I was much inspired by the lines in 'Horatius' by Lord Macaulay which run:

And how can man die better
Than facing fearful odds,
For the ashes of his fathers,
and the temples of his Gods.

But Mamma did not only read warlike poems; there was 'Fidele's Grassy Tomb' and 'The Lady of Shallot' which seemed to last for ever. And G.K. Chesterton's marvellous poem about a donkey, which ends with the evocative lines:

Fools! For I also had my hour,
One far fierce hour and sweet:
There was a shout about my ears
And palms before my feet.

One called 'The Canadian Boat Song' by an unknown poet, which begins: 'From the lone sheiling on the misty island,

124

mountains divide us and a waste of sea . . .' And so many more.

She would tell us the parable of Martha and Mary when she thought we were working too hard, or recite 'Consider the lilies of the field, how they grow; they toil not, neither do they spin: And yet I say unto you, That even Solomon in all his glory was not arrayed like one of these.' Mamma was witty too and I remember when someone said to her, 'I never have time to read because of the mending,' she replied, 'I never have time to mend because of the reading.'

As we grew older we had poetry readings when we chose what we would read. I remember Diana reading poems by Emily Brontë and Josephine reading those haunting lines from 'Oleanders' by Humbert Wolfe: 'Rosebay, rosebay where are your roses now?' (In later years her eventer, whom we bred ourselves, was to be called Rosebay.)

Often I chose to read Yeats. 'When you are Old', and 'The Lake Isle of Innisfree' were two of my favourites. I remember Mamma saying that Cappy had read poetry when they were engaged but stopped once they were married. Certainly he preferred playing cards with us to reading poetry. But like Mamma, and perhaps because he was a vicar's son, he could quote long passages from the Bible. Sadly, as the years passed I saw Cappy more as an ogre than a friend, which was unjust for he was the first to leap to our defence in any dispute. I remember when I must have been in my early teens Cappy saying, 'I want "He was a bloody fool, but he did his best" inscribed on my tombstone.' I'm sure he longed for someone to say then, 'Darling, you are not a bloody fool,' but no one did.

Once he related that after lunching with a business acquaintance at the Metropole Hotel at Brighton, he called for a taxi and the taxi door was opened for him by his estranged brother Edgar dressed in the uniform of a commissionaire. In a fleeting second he decided that Edgar would not wish to be recognised in such a lowly situation and so he ignored him and passed by without a word, but forever after he wondered whether he had done the right thing. I do not think any of us offered an opinion for, though Edgar was Diana's godfather, we hardly knew him, though we were aware that he had lost all his money in the crash in the 'twenties.

Although we had a small but charming spare bedroom which looked out on the stables, we did not have many people to stay.

Aunt Dot's son Charles came. Older than us by a few years, he impressed me by learning to ride Countess in a few days. When Cappy paid us to collect round pebbles for the steps he was building into the ha-ha, Charles always made the most money – it was the same with blackberries. Josephine says that Denis and Charles once carried her around the garden in a sack and that she was infuriated and deeply humiliated by the experience. I can only recall her red face when they tipped her out at Mamma's feet as she sat on the lawn.

John Gardner, the well known musician and composer, another cousin, this time on the Pullein-Thompson side – sometimes stayed when Denis was at home. The house seemed full of laughter then. Once John and Denis walked through the streets of Reading pretending that one of them was blind. I don't think anyone was taken in; maybe they laughed too much.

Paulla, Charles's younger sister, often stayed with us in the war; but as her visits grew longer she lodged with Joan, because Cappy could not tolerate a guest in the house for more than a few days. Paulla soon became a talented rider and later jumped Tarragona at local shows with great success.

When bombs were falling on London, Georgette Heyer sent her son Richard, now an eminent judge, to us for the summer.

Richard had wonderful manners but I think was always hungry. He did not like riding and must have found us the most terrible bores. I recall that once he ate the best sandwiches at a Horse Show before we had a chance even to look at them, but having been brought up with the laws of hospitality ringing in our ears, we said nothing. Granny stayed sometimes, too. Mamma, nervous that she would tell Cappy that he was not keeping his wife in the way in which she had been accustomed – something she had said to Uncle Percival – would rise early on these occasions and make exotic dishes which she would then claim had been made by our daily help of the moment. Granny adored Mamma; all the same I found her visits fraught. She seemed distant and I don't think she had any inclination to get to know us. She was not a cuddly granny and I cannot remember ever talking to her or her to me.

By this time Granny had ceased to rent Highclere, and Nana had retired as her housekeeper which she had been more or less ever since we left Wimbledon, though with Granny in the South of France much of the year, she had sometimes spent more time at The Grove than at Highclere.

Granny had provided a pension, as was the custom then, but it must have been a dreadful moment for Nana. We and the Cannan girls had been 'her babies' ever since she was twenty-four. She was now seventy and destined to live for more than twenty years. Until now she had never needed nor wanted friends; her charges had been her life. She was given the choice of living in Oxford or near to us in Peppard. She chose Oxford which was closer to her relations and a place where she had spent so many happy years with the Cannans at Magdalen Gate House. Highclere was cleared. But first Nana had her pick of the things there, or maybe certain items had been allotted to her. Either way, she took Granny's cane-headed bed which had originally come from Heal's in London and been one of a pair. She took chairs, one with the arms of Trinity College underneath its cover, and a chest of drawers and a fine wardrobe, and a pretty sofa and much else besides. They were a little big for the two small rooms she rented in Summertown, Oxford, but no doubt they made them feel more like home.

We all hoped that Nana would make friends at Oxford, but she soon fell out with her relations. Jim's old Nanny, probably encouraged by Aunt May, tried to make friends with her, but Nana did not wish to be befriended, least of all by a Nanny whom she had always despised for holding opposite views to hers on the upbringing of children.

As well as the two rooms Nana rented, she had use of a kitchen and a bathroom, never an ideal arrangement and one which soon caused difficulties, resulting in her doing little cooking for herself.

Aunt Dot had Nana to lunch on most Sundays and also visited her in Summertown. Whenever we were in Oxford we visited her too. Later during the war years when at last we had money in our pockets from giving riding lessons, we took it in turns to spend several hours with her each week, often accompanying her to the cinema and theatre. Sometimes we had to queue endlessly for buses to return home, when I would read the tiny pocket dictionary I took everywhere with me. And at least once a year Nana spent time at The Grove with us. All the same she did complain that she was lonely and that sometimes she did not see a soul for days. In later years she confessed to going to Christ Church cathedral – 'Not for the service,' she would add hastily, 'but for the singing.' Sometimes we would walk round the colleges with her and while she told us how it had been in our grandfather's day, and about the famous people who had lived there, a crowd would collect around us, delighted to have a free guide.

One summer at The Grove when one of us was hosing a swollen hock which belonged to a temperamental thorough-bred mare called Bittersweet, she came out of the house in her slippers and said, "Ere, let me do that, you've got better things to do.' Reluctantly the rope and hose were handed over to her; but there was no need to worry, horses saw Nana as firm and trustworthy, and Bittersweet was not at all perturbed by the sudden change of handler.

Sometimes I hear Nana's voice echoing down the years, shouting, 'I might as well speak to that there wall as speak to you.' But as a mother does, she forgave us all our misdemeanours and left everything she had to us in the end. Her bed went to Josephine because, in Nana's words, 'She had never had a decent bed to sleep on.' (For years Josephine had been obliged to sleep on the last cook-general's bed, which had a dip in the middle.) We all had some of her jewellery and a share in the few Government securities which remained from those bought with the thousand pounds Granny had left to Nana in her Will. Her funeral seemed like the end of a chapter in our lives, a very long one going back as far as I could remember.

I like to think that we all owe something to Nana. It's true that she was cruel to insects, unlike Mamma who called earwigs her brothers and gave a name to a beetle which crawled across the drawing room carpet at the same time each evening – Emily. Nana taught us not to whine, to eat what we were given, to read and write, to sew, to climb stiles and walk for miles without complaining. She was always the same, her views on life unalterable. Of course she over-dressed us in our early years and over-fed us too, except for Josephine who resisted. With Nana around I, for one, always felt secure, and unlike modern nannies she demanded little, neither car nor television set nor their equivalent then. Legend has it that when our parents were particularly hard-up, Nana worked without wages for weeks without complaining, a thing impossible to imagine happening today.

* * * *

Josephine writes:-

Mamma's next two novels, *North Wall* and *Underproof* – published in 1933 and 1934 – both expressed disillusion with the modern world. The death of the old order, the war and depression had produced a less principled generation and perhaps this, she suggested, was to be expected, for peaches do not grow on north walls. Though the South of France and a less romanticised view of English country life had added to her backgrounds, I don't think either of these rather gloomy books did well.

The parents' rows about money grew in intensity. When Denis was at home I always assumed that he was in charge, but when he was at school I felt that it was my duty to listen. As soon as the row began downstairs in the parlour I would creep out of my room and station myself on the top stair. Denis tells me that he sat there too, and once, hearing divorce mentioned, he rushed down shouting 'No, no, no.' Another time, when older, he intervened. My role was always passive. I found it hard to grasp exactly what the rows were about, but the voices, unfamiliar in their anger, proved that the parents were not to be trusted and I felt that my presence on the stairs might avert some unimaginable catastrophe.

As well as the family rescues that Diana has written about, Mamma's diamond necklace, which, she told us, was to pay for any operations we might need, vanished without comment and her letter from Rudyard Kipling was sold shortly after his death.

I suspect that it was this constant need for money which caused her to embark on her first thriller. The hero, James Raeburn, educated at Eton and Oxford, was a mountaineer of some repute. Mamma had climbed with her father, his friends and her sisters on holidays in the Lake District and in Switzerland. She loved mountains and used her experience in a number of books, giving exciting and very detailed accounts of climbs. The romance of mountaineering was passed on to us. In the hall, among the umbrellas and walking sticks, were two ice-axes and she had also kept a climbing rope. I would gaze reverently at the magical red thread which ran through it, giving, she explained, the strength that held the roped party together when a climber lost his or her footing.

The Hills Sleep On, set in the Himalayas, was the first of her books in which I took an interest. Every day at lunch-time I would dash into the parlour and read the latest instalment right up to the piece on the typewriter. 'James' did make money, the agent sold an option on the film rights for a thousand pounds, and the publishers produced three impressions in a year. Mamma reduced the overdraft, paid the bills, bought a motor mower for my father, a large refrigerator for the family, and spent twenty-five pounds on Rum, a sixteen-year-old mare, for herself and Denis to ride.

The second 'James', set in Brittany and published in 1936, was dedicated *To Josephine Pullein-Thompson. A Candid Critic.* So I suspect that my interest must have become tiresomely carping. *A Hand To Burn* did not have the success of *The Hills Sleep On*, but from the research trip to Brittany which Mamma and Denis had made with Granny, they bought the red trousers worn by the fishermen of Concarneau, and a length of the same cloth to make shorts for the twins and me. So for the next year or two we were all dressed in the romantically fading red of Brittany sailcloth.

Although I made no protest, I felt that Mamma's 'Jean' books, which Cappy read aloud to us, were too young for me; after all we had had Jean's adventures and moved on – I preferred to read about James. And there was a feeling of discomfort when Mamma, protesting that hearing her work read aloud set her teeth on edge, fled the parlour.

According to Mamma, the ownership of a refrigerator ended our childhood bilious attacks, but it was Rum who changed my life. She was fourteen hands, two inches in height, a red roan with black points and on her forehead a small, white crescent moon instead of the usual star. Nothing to look at – she had an imposing front but was hollow-backed and her body trailed away to weak quarters, topped with a 'jumper's bump' – but she was possessed of great character. She could give kisses, by stiffening her rather bristly upper lip, but when we became too demanding and she tired of a row of upturned faces all calling 'Kiss *me*, Rummy,' the kisses would become increasingly rough and perfunctory. She also used her 'twitch lip', as we called it, for opening doors and gates and for investigating likely-looking sacks. She was a thief and, if the granary door was open, would seize bags and sacks in her teeth. Once she cantered across the orchard spilling nails from a purloined paper bag. She loved jumping, adored hunting, but was bored by hacking. When slipping and stumbling along the road in a geriatric manner, the appearance of a horseman in a scarlet coat would transform her, instantly, into a prancing steed with shining eyes.

All the spaniel puppies but Pippin had found homes. I don't know why he was rejected, perhaps it was his lack of a white waistcoat, but the parents decided to keep him. This turned out to be a mistake, because the inevitable jealousy between father and son soon developed from growls and snarls into dogfights. We became expert at separating them, but once they fought in the back of the car and Diana's hand was badly bitten. Barney had always been the most genial of characters – it was assumed that he would greet burglars with a wagging tail – but Dinah, belying her meek appearance, would slink up on the postman and deliver a sharp nip, and Pippin seemed to have inherited her aggression.

Mamma acquired an Irish wolfhound. Darkie had been a champion show dog who, on retiring from the ring, had failed to breed and the owner of the kennels wanted a good home for her. She was a very inconvenient dog but Mamma became deeply devoted to her and, writing a short story about a wolfhound for one of the women's magazines, announced that she was endowed for life.

Darkie was not house-trained, so the bean hole was converted to a kennel in which she was to sleep at night. She hated it and, having kept everyone in the neighbourhood awake by howling at the moon, finally gnawed her way out. A large dog bed was then provided in the dining room and the first person down in the morning was frequently confronted by a lake of pee. Luckily the ancient brick flags of the floor stood up to it and the maids, being country girls, didn't object.

Darkie's other disadvantage was that she took up the whole of the back seat in Bouncing Bertha, leaving only a tiny ledge among her paws, on which the twins and I had to perch.

I suppose we were all growing tired of sharing everything, for after the arrival of Darkie, who plainly belonged to Mamma, the twins suggested to me that we shared out the spaniels and had one each. I remember the knotted feeling in my stomach as I suddenly became aware that I had given my heart to Pippin. Apprehensively, I asked which of the dogs they wanted and remember an enormous flood of relief when Diana answered 'Barney' and Christine 'Dinah.'

Almost every day, if we succeeded in borrowing enough ponies, we rode through the beechwood cathedrals, pillared by pewter-grey trunks and carpeted with centuries of leaves, soft and muffling to the thud of hoofs. The woods changed dramatically with the

131

seasons: the white anemones of spring, the drifts of bluebells, the green canopy of high summer, the seductive melancholy of autumn with rosebay willow herb and the orange brown of falling leaves, all brought their own heady pleasure. Winter could be beautiful too and it was possible to canter on the carpet of beech leaves when the fields were frozen iron-hard, but I always hated the cold.

Though we were encouraged to love and admire and write poetry about the countryside, sentimental gushing was not permitted. Mamma mocked flower-arranging ladies enthusing over autumnal tints, disdainfully alluding to them as 'autimnal tunts'.

The countryside of the 'thirties offered little room for sentimentality, for though the farms boasted meadows bright with wild flowers, fields fenced with hedges and ancient orchards that had never known a pesticide, they were also gloomy reminders of world recession. Ruinous cottages, unrepaired barns and sagging barbed wire fences abounded. The ubiquitous corrugated iron rusted as it filled gaps in hedges, patched up roofs and walled the shanty town sheds that passed for farm buildings in many smallholdings.

It was a time when old horrors lingered and new ones appeared. Dogs could still spend their lives chained to damp kennels, but the first battery hen houses were being erected. Rheumaticky farm labourers lived without electricity, baths or indoor lavatories; in the winter their bent figures moved across the sodden landscape cloaked against the weather with sacks. But we watched swathes being cut through the woods for the erection of the first pylons. Stephen Spender wrote a poem of admiration, Mamma and Denis penned hate poems, which appeared in *The Grove Magazine.*

We would ride through the hamlet of Nuney Green, deep in the beechwoods and reached only by lanes, where the thatched cottages were collapsing one by one, through Stoke Row, a dull straggle of a village except in cherry blossom time, where the men who worked for the Star Brush Company, fashioning the wooden parts of brushes and brooms, were said to be of a different race. They were small, dark, round-headed men, whose forebears had been charcoal burners, and it was considered rather a disgrace for a girl from another village to marry one of them. We would visit the well, presented by the Maharajah of Benares in 1864, as an expression of gratitude to an engineer from Stoke Row. The oriental dome, bedecked with elephants, the cypress walk and the small round house provided for the custodian, looked incongruous among the dripping beechwoods, and the concept that the best way to honour a man was to bore a well for his village conjured up visions of a different, dryer world.

Nearer home, the Crowsley Park road branched beyond the Kews' and the downhill road, heading for Sonning Common, passed between the Butchers' Arms (in those days a small whitewashed pub) and the bottomless pond. Dark, shaded by trees except where it was walled against the road, it lost its mystery for Christine, she says, but not for me. The pond's bottomless reputation rested on the seventeenth-century attempt to drain it. According to local accounts, they had drained and drained for days and finally, coming to the topmost branches of a standing oak, they gave up. It was also said that a coach and four had gone in one winter night and never been seen again. I viewed it with respect and wondered what other horrors were concealed in the black waters, but all that emerged in our day was the annual migration of frogs – presumably to mate – and hundreds of them filled the road and died a grisly death under the wheels of passing cars.

Years later, I discovered in the British Library a seventeenth-century account of the draining. The local stories were true as far as they went, but no one had told us of Dr Plot's conclusion, that the pond was a Roman silver mine and when our colonial masters withdrew they had attempted to fill it, even dropping in whole trees.

The summer I was eleven, Mamma suddenly announced that she and I were going to a gathering of the Wychwood School old girls. All three Cannan girls had attended Miss Batty's classes for the daughters of Oxford dons – then affectionally known as the Battyhole, which had grown into Wychwood School, with Miss Lee (who had taught English in Mamma's day) now the headmistress.

I remember only a buffet lunch in the garden of Miss Lee's house at Dorchester-on-Thames and being warned not to approach a horse in the field alongside, as the previous year it had badly bitten the nose of a senior girl. Afterwards I learned that I was being considered for Miss Lee's personal scholarship, which would have covered tuition fees throughout my schooldays.

When the offer of the scholarship came – it obviously owed more to Mamma's record, she and Carola Oman were the school's most distinguished old girls, than to any sign of academic brilliance on my part – the parents turned it down. Peppard was twenty miles from Oxford so I couldn't go daily, and they decided that I was too young to be a weekly boarder. They told the school that I would go as a paying pupil the following year.

It may have been pride, but I suspect they feared that I could become Miss Lee's child, and they wanted to fashion their daughters in their own mould. Eton was a different matter; Grandfather Cannan had judged it the best and they seemed prepared to let it mould Denis as far as he was mouldable. I don't think it occurred to them that I needed older companionship or that the longer we spent at Miss Fryer's, the harder it would be to adjust to the curriculum of a conventional school.

At Miss Fryer's I was moved in with the older girls, who worked largely unsupervised at the round table in the sitting room of the cottage. I much preferred worldly conversation with Jean and Bernice to essay writing and they had great difficulty in persuading me to work. One of my many inquiries, wisely put to Bernice – the blacksmith's daughter – was, 'Are there any worse swear words than bloody?'

She reeled them off without hesitation and I was deeply disappointed. They seemed so short and meaningless, so much less satisfactory than 'bloody': I began to wonder if she was fooling me.

That evening, alone with the parents, I chose one at random and asked, 'Is bugger really a swear word?' Cappy exploded; shouting, he demanded to know who had told me? Where I had heard it?

I instantly became obstinate and Mamma, trying to calm him, pointed out that if he insisted on knowing, I would never confide in him again. He repeated that it was a terrible word, only used by men in prison, and that I must never, never let it pass my lips.

As Bernice's father was a perfectly respectable blacksmith, Cappy was obviously wrong. This, with his absurd shouting and his demand that I told tales, angered me. However, I now knew that Bernice was trustworthy, and, though I confined myself to 'bloody' until I was adult and never divulged my secret store to the twins, I hugged them to me; knowledge was power.

Cappy admired a sexual knowingness in Denis, but he seemed to expect innocence in his daughters. Hearing him warn Mamma that a certain novel had better be kept away from me, I naturally searched for it and, balanced precariously on the back of an armchair, reached it down from the top shelf of the bookcase. He need not have worried, the sex act demanded in a regimental initiation ceremony was baffling to me and while a pair of lovers coupled in a wood I worried about the horses they left tied to trees.

Apart from sex, Cappy's cry was always 'It's not the things you've *done* that you'll regret in later life, it's the things you *haven't* done.' He took a fitful interest in our education, which usually ended in him saying that we were learning nothing. Once he laboriously typed three copies of the dates of Kings and Queens of England, and offered half a crown to whichever of us learned them first.

He was having no success with his writing, despite evenings and weekends spent at the typewriter, but these rejections did nothing to diminish his passion for the theatre. When we were first at The Grove I was taken to see Harry Lauder at the New Theatre, Oxford, Cappy saying that I would remember the great man all my life as he had remembered seeing Sarah Bernhardt when she had only one leg, but could still hold an audience spellbound. He took an interest in the repertory company which played in the little eighteenth-century theatre in New Street, Henley and later threw himself into organizing the Friends of the Theatre. We enjoyed being taken to *Maria Marten or Murder in the Red Barn*, and the villain's soliloquy on the scaffold, 'See where my education has brought me,' provided an invaluable quote.

Denis, who had also been passionate about the theatre since Carola Oman had given him a model one at the age of eight, began to help at the Kenton in the holidays. We saw him act for the first time as Richard Hare in *East Lynne*, and 'Dead, dead, and never called me mother!' became a quotation that could be used in moments of stress. At Christmas there was usually an amateur production, and once Mamma took the three of us and Nana to a production of *Iolanthe*. The vet's youthful assistant played the part of a lord with great vigour and we all fell in love with him. As we grew older we became regular theatregoers and saw the Barries, the A.A. Milnes, and the Priestleys which made up the repertoire of the company.

We put on our own plays too. The end of the dining room with its four doors was fine for entrances and exits and the audience could be seated at the table. Our plots were very rough, the actors improvised the dialogue and the finale invariably disintegrated into mayhem and murder, my antique blunderbuss, a birthday present from the twins, being used to shoot most of the cast.

When I discovered Cappy's collection of plays, I thought *On Approval* by Frederick Lonsdale the most racy work I had read. I tried to put it on, but it was too old for us and when the twins, who didn't believe in learning parts, would giggle, the performance had to be abandoned. After that the plays ceased.

The twins' vocabulary had grown enormously, but their early diet of pirate books, rousing poetry and Nana's euphemisms had made it decidedly idiosyncratic. They talked of swabbing floors and used *might* as a term of reproach – 'You *might* get up, play farms, come and ride etc.' One of my most heinous faults was 'sipping'. The twins *drank* milk or water, I *sipped* tea.

We had been brought up never to fight two against one but once, when there had been a twin rift, Christine and I began to gang up on Diana. Mamma spoke to us seriously and confessed that she and Aunt Dot had treated Aunt May in the same way when they were young, but it was wrong and their parents should have stopped it. However, though ganging up was wrong, democracy was right and, as the twins discovered their voting power, I learned the frustration of being in a minority.

When they took the clippers to Milky's mane and hogged her so that she matched Rum, I pointed out that as part-owner I ought to have been consulted, but my protest was shrugged off with, 'Oh well, it would have been two against one, anyway.'

Being smaller than my younger sisters was also humbling. They had taken to handing me their outgrown garments with an airy, 'Here, you'd better have this.' I made a joke of it, saying that I now had two of everything, but I began to call myself 'Dustbin'. I think this was a protest, for I don't remember any feeling of worthlessness; but my teenage letters to Mamma are all signed 'Dustbin', so I suppose it assumed the status of a pet name.

Mamma always said that I held my own and used a lot of low cunning in dealing with the twins. I remember playing on their fear of death. I had only to say 'When you die, you go out like a candle,' to make them block their ears and scream. And when one of them beat me at high jump and the other at long jump, I would challenge them to jump the garden seat back to front, or the extremely prickly paddock hedge. To preserve my seniority, I could force myself over, but without this spur they couldn't and, like overfaced horses, refused.

I began to ride Rum. She was a safe, experienced and passionate jumper but, unlike many good horses, she needed a jockey; she never jumped in and out of fields on her own. Denis had leaped five-barred gates and ridden her in Handy Hunter classes, Mamma had led the field over trappy timber fences out hunting, but Rum and I began to showjump. I was the pupil, Rum the teacher and we communicated in some mysterious way. Flying over far greater heights than I could jump on my feet gave me great pleasure and boosted my self-confidence enormously.

The Silkies were very dear to me, but it became apparent that some of their progeny had to be sold. Owing to their blue skin the cockerels couldn't be eaten, and I needed a second blood line to provide breeding pairs; the Kew family's congenital deafness had alerted us to the dangers of inbreeding. I bought new stock, Young Lochinvar and the Pentland Daisy – named after a Scottish ancestor from Penicuik – and Mamma got in touch with the pet department at Harrods. Later we took a pair up to London in a hamper. I suspect Mamma paid both our fares, giving me an exalted idea of my profit.

Fred Kew had bought me some Mallard duck eggs with instructions to set them under one of my bantams. They hatched and horrified their bantam mother by plunging into the duckpond. When adult they didn't join the geese and other ducks – Mamma's Aylesburys and the twins' Khaki Campbells; they lived a semi-wild life, taking off on daily flights, but always returning to and nesting at The Grove.

Cappy had lost interest in the White Wyandottes and Rhode Island Reds, who had sensibly escaped from their exclusive runs and joined the other hens. He suggested rearing turkeys; we would have a free one for ourselves and sell the rest for large sums. Local wisdom told us that the mortality rate was high and you must set twice as many eggs as you wanted turkeys at Christmas, so we filled the incubator and I found myself tending the turkey chicks in the brooder and later in the abandoned chicken runs. All went well until the adolescent turkey cocks began to grow their wattles, then depression seemed to overtake them. They died willy nilly of a dozen unrelated diseases and, as a last resort, hanged themselves by putting their heads through the wire netting. I believe that modern turkey farmers feed anti-depressants, but with us the local prediction proved correct and we lost half our hatching. The survivors didn't grow enormously large, perhaps because we let them out to roam in a flock. Then, at the approach of Christmas, Bowley and an assistant killed them. When the gentle sound of turkey gobble ceased, a terrible silence reigned over the orchard and we resolved never to rear turkeys for eating again. For some unremembered reason one female was spared, we called her Lady Precious-stream, and later Mamma bought her a magnificent white husband and named him Fujiyama.

I decided not to be a poultry farmer, I now knew too much about the hard work and hazards, the awful harvesting, and the modest profit. I announced that I would be a vet. Bowley took my ambition seriously. We discussed the health of the 'Sooners' – his name for those animals who would 'sooner' be upstairs in the bathroom than outside in the yard. When one of the silkies injured a toe, which gradually withered and died, we took her to the bathroom for an amputation. Cappy's precious nail scissors were borrowed and my tears fell with the toe. 'You'll never be a vet if you cry over that,' said Bowley briskly.

So far we had relied on the *Complete Book of the Dog* and *First Aid Hints for Horseowners* – which dealt with cuts and colic, splints and spavins – for our veterinary advice, but then Bowley presented me with a Victorian manual, retrieved from another employer's bonfire. Illustrated with engravings of embryos in cross-section, with foaling mares and aborting cows, all attended by a veterinary gentleman wearing a frock coat and top hat, it became one of my most cherished possessions.

Though we were still unorthodox riders – we shocked the conventional by mounting indiscriminately from either side – we had grown in confidence and were proud that we had the reputation of being able to ride any pony that came our way. We began to long for an unbroken pony. We loved Milky and Rum, but they were our mentors. Milky looked both ways before she crossed the road and took you home if you were lost. Now we wanted to reverse the process and train a young pony.

When Mr Sworder agreed to try us, we took our new profession seriously. I spent the evening before Rainbow arrived making notes on schooling from Golden Gorse's *The Young Rider* and we worked out a plan for training the child's perfect pony. I am not sure if Rocket was the second Sworder pony, but he was one to whom I lost my heart. However much you love horses in general, you cannot offer equal affection to them all. There are stupid and ungenerous horses, horses who bore or irritate you and those with whom you just don't dovetail. Rocket was a narrow four-year-old, dark brown 12.2 and of Dartmoor type, and we fell for each other at once. We seemed to be young together, we loved to gallop like the wind and we did it as partners; there was no worry about starting or stopping.

Out hunting with the South Berks, this reckless galloping brought us to grief. Rocket put a forefoot in a rabbit hole and we both had a crashing fall. I lay on the cropped turf and a ring of middle-aged farmers gazed down on me, their concerned faces topped with bowler hats. To everyone's surprise, we were only shaken and, reunited, we galloped on, but I had learned to watch out for rabbit warrens.

My next great love among the Sworder ponies was a red roan mare of 13.2, named Lassie. She was very gentle and rather nervous, but I found I could supply the self-confidence she lacked and inspire her to race and jump. Mamma, observing my love, told me sadly we couldn't afford the twenty-five guineas that Mr Sworder was asking. Later Christine, who disliked nervousness, bonded with Pennywise, an uncomplicated brown pony, and they made a wonderful gymkhana pair, while Diana developed a special relationship with Northwind, a blue roan, who needed great patience and persuasion.

I disagree with Diana about our profits from the sale of the ponies. My memory is that Mr Sworder brought his customers to The Grove, we put the ponies through their paces, and if he got a good price he rewarded us with five pounds, which we paid into our joint bank account. It was only as teenagers that we did the actual buying and selling ourselves.

Some of the ponies Mr Sworder brought us were not suitable for children and, as we grew more experienced, he would readily accept our verdict. There was Brecon, a little grey who reared, and Black Tulip, a mare of uncertain temper. He would then enter them in sales, without a warranty that they were safe for children; in those days, with no market for horse meat for human consumption, such ponies were worth very little.

A publisher once asked me how we had produced so many pony books when most of the other writers in the genre only wrote two or three, and I've always believed that this was due to the huge cast of equine characters we met and rode as children.

We had begun to win rosettes. I was never very good at dressing-up races or anything demanding haste, as Christine had written in her poetic description of the family:

Josephine is low
and very slow.

I preferred to stay on the pony. The exception was the 'Handy Hunter' competition in which you had to dismount to lead your pony over a slip rail, but the rest of the course, including a trappy 'in and out', made it worthwhile. Rum enjoyed 'Handy Hunters' too, and always used her twitch lip to assist in the opening and shutting of the gate.

Show-jumping was becoming more and more important to me, and I remember my indignation at the Kidmore End Show when the judges – all male and very red-faced after an alcoholic lunch – muddled the results and called in one of the twins on Milky to receive Rum's and my rosette. I wanted the parents to object but they wouldn't. They said that life wasn't fair. Everyone else seemed to think that as it was 'all in the family' it didn't matter. I sulked.

In those days middle-class parents had not become competitive, and unless you were a professional you simply hacked to the nearer shows and gymkhanas. We entered for only two or three each summer and the Woodcote Show on Bank Holiday Monday was the highlight of the year. It was the largest horticultural show in the district. Diana has described how one year a man died from drinking a wasp in his beer, and another year a member of the Royal Berkshire Regiment's gymnastic team fell in a vaulting display and died because his comrades, not realizing that his neck was broken, carried him off without a stretcher. Both disasters were added to Mamma's list of awful warnings.

Then there was Captain Angier whose name always appeared on the programme as an entry for the adult jumping. But when, year after year, he scratched at the last minute, we didn't believe his explanation that his horse was sick or lame; meanly, we suspected him of cowardice.

The first year that I rode Rum in the children's jumping we did well, but the parents wouldn't let me take her in the adult class; instead they invited Christina Edward-Jones from the riding school to be her jockey. Rum had taught me exactly how she liked to be ridden round the boringly uniform courses of those days. Brush, stile and gate were all straightforward, but the wall unnerved her. Denis had made a wooden wall and painted grey stone on one side and red brick on the other, but she was still apprehensive and it was my duty to put the reins in one hand and give her a tap with the whip on take-off, which supplied the courage she needed. Then, turning up the centre of the ring for the solitary triple – her favourite fence – you rode fast and saying 'Come on Rummy,' gradually gave her her head. The audience always exclaimed 'too fast,' but that was how Rum liked it and she would soar over with a whisk of her tail.

Christina's round was clear until she took control and approached the triple at a measured pace. Deprived of her speed, and appalled at this interference, Rum made a spectacular last-minute refusal, shooting her rider head first among the poles. Christina got up shaken and with a rapidly blackening eye, and Cappy, who admired tall slim women, hurried her away for an unwise brandy. The next year I was allowed to jump Rum in the adult class. We won a prize, beating the local horse dealer, who was heard to say, 'Damn that child!' as he rode out of the ring.

Chapter Five

Josephine writes on:-

Perhaps because of my Dustbin campaign, I was kitted out quite stylishly for Wychwood school. Mamma balked at the clothes list, providing, as she had with Denis, about half of the school's demands. But when it came to linen I took new yellow sheets and towels and my eiderdown was re-covered to match. She refused to provide two pairs of slippers and walking shoes or Clark's expensive sandals, but bought me an elegant pair of dancing shoes. Then at the last moment she presented me with a charming little writing case, the writing paper deckle-edged and yellow, with envelopes to match.

Observing gloomily that 'Shades of the prison-house begin to close,' Mamma seemed far more affected by our parting than I was. I minded leaving her and Pip and the ponies, but it was only until Friday and then I would be home for the weekend; she saw a gulf opening between us.

I think the family finances must have improved at that moment, for Bouncing Bertha, incapable of twice-weekly drives to Oxford, vanished to the scrap-yard and a small, brand new Ford took her place.

On the way to Oxford (the twins having stayed at home), Mamma told me about menstruation. Apparently a recent new girl at the school had suffered untold misery, for, believing she had a terrible illness, she had tried to conceal her bleeding. The brisk Scottish matron had now decreed that all mothers were to give their daughters full explanations, and instructions to go straight to her if a period began. As Mamma linked her explanation to Dinah being in season, which I knew to be a very messy business, I fervently hoped that my 'curse' would not start for years.

The next revelation was the medical inspection. The doctor was unprepossessing; to me he seemed old and fat, and suitably named Higgins. He listened to my heart and chest and then announced with a series of irritable tuts that I had an inverted sternum. I knew I had a hollow, Mamma had it too, and Nana dismissed it as 'the Cannan chest'. Then I was weighed and with even more tuts I was pronounced 'severely underweight' – at twelve and a half I still couldn't make five stone. Then he found fault with my feet; they tended towards flatness.

I don't think I was cast down for long. I had to meet my 'Housemother', a remote and very senior girl called Diana. She was distantly kind, but won my respect by painting a stylish watercolour of two riders in my autograph book.

We slept in mixed-aged groups, three or four to a room, with cubicle curtains around our beds, which were only to be drawn for dressing and undressing. I warned my room mates about my sleep-walking and explained that my sisters had found that, if ordered back to bed in a commanding voice, I obeyed.

I think I found an enemy before I made a friend. Rosemary, who had darting eyes behind pale spectacles, was one of those unpopular people who batten on to new girls. The reason she was shunned was an obsession with Harrison Ainsworth, a long dead but still popular writer of historical romances. She could talk of nothing else and she spent all her spare time poring over telephone directories in search of people whose names were either Harrison or Ainsworth. Then she pestered them, writing or telephoning to ask if they were related to the writer.

An early letter home states 'I have just had a fight.' I can't remember this quarrel, but the saga of the dancing shoes which vanished, still in their packaging, the moment they were put in my locker, remains clear in my mind. The dancing mistress, displeased at my clumping through her class in leather slippers, demanded a new pair. Mamma, consulted at the weekend, resolutely refused. Various mistresses and I searched in vain. The lockers were in the basement passage, opposite the kitchens. It was a very public pathway, along which supplies were delivered; they had obviously been stolen. The following week I wrote to tell Mamma that it has been resolved: 'No need to write an angry letter, they are getting me some more dancing shoes and *paying* for them . . . I hope my new hen house has arrived.'

I had been assigned to a form called the Lower Remove, but after a day or two I was told quite tactfully that as I hadn't done

Algebra or Geometry and didn't speak French I was to be moved down. I didn't mind. The Lower Remove people seemed too tall and sophisticated for me. I felt much more at home in M.1, where, though one of the oldest, I was still one of the smallest in the form. Lack of height meant I was hopeless at netball – I never shot a goal, even in practice – but it had one advantage, for in the endless games of horses I was in great demand as a jockey and never had to play the part of a horse.

Wychwood had a policy of taking one or two mildly mentally handicapped or 'backward' girls, as they were called at that time. The intention was, apparently, that their company would teach the rest of us understanding, compassion and benevolence, but I'm not sure that it succeeded. We were told we must be kind to them and the staff set a good example, but it was hard to overcome physical repulsion, especially of Joy who breathed heavily and had clammy hands. Always picked last for teams, at dancing they were forced to partner each other and, if one was missing, our desperate rush to avoid partnering the lone one must have been both obvious and hurtful.

The surplus women left without hope of marriage by the First World War had provided a multiplicity of schoolmistresses. They had grown middle-aged in a badly paid and not always chosen profession, but that first year at Wychwood they didn't seem too bad. There was Miss Ruddock, the senior housemistress, severe, rather masculine, but admirably decisive, who taught us maths; Mademoiselle, mild and kindly, but over-tall with a long neck and prominent eyes, who had trouble in keeping order. Mamma, who regarded xenophobia as a sin, had forbidden me to torment the French mistress, so I sat passively while the bloods of the class used their rulers to catapult their rubber erasers in her direction. Miss Lyons, who had taught scripture in Mamma's day, was also under her protection on the grounds of age. But she made the mistake of trusting us to do our homework and usually let us recite en masse what we were supposed to have learned. This meant that only a few of the virtuous actually recited; the rest of us mouthed in unison. Once I was highly embarrassed by being singled out for a solo performance, but Scripture prep remained something that one skipped.

Miss Vaughan, who taught English, was fair game. Though younger, she had been at the Battyhole with Mamma, who confessed to tormenting her endlessly, mostly by tying her long plaits to the back of her chair. I had a strong feeling that I reminded her of Mamma and that she disliked me. This was sad, as English was my favourite subject. I still learned poetry for pleasure and had discovered that if I said a half-learned poem to myself just before falling asleep, I was word perfect next morning – a great time-saver. I even liked grammar when it was a question of parsing sentences and underlining the component parts with crayons in different colours.

Miss Chandler, with her wide frog mouth, was neutral towards me. She taught Latin from a cheerful modern picture book, the antithesis of the grim tomes we had used at Miss Fryer's. I can't remember who taught history and geography, but history, which I wanted to like, was incredibly dreary. We were 'doing' Charlemagne and the Holy Roman Empire, which seemed a remote period for twelve-year-olds, few of whom had ever been abroad. As for geography, I was incapable of tracing neat maps – mine were always dishevelled and dirty – and I had no visual memory for the shapes of countries and continents.

Carpentry I liked but not Miss Pinhorn who, fair and fringed with her hair in a bang, also taught nature. The workshop, with its smell of sawdust and gleaming tools, was in a loft above the wooden building known as the Hut, where we had prayers every morning. I enjoyed prayers; providing an undemanding interlude between breakfast and lessons, they gave one time to wake up. Gym was also taught in the Hut. My first lesson passed in a daze after someone had let the bar down on my head and, later, I found not knowing my right hand from my left a distinct disadvantage. Having no rhythm made it impossible to do exercises in time with the rest of the class, and being so small meant that the vaulting horse and the bar were always too high for me. My only gymnastic prowess was on the ropes; I shinned up them with ease and was accomplished at something called flying angels.

As winter came on, the three houses – two facing the Banbury Road and the one in the Bardwell Road – all built in the red brick of Victorian North Oxford, became freezing cold. Most of us had chilblains; I had them on my hands and feet. We licked the ones on our hands and held them to the anthracite stove in our classroom. They oozed disgustingly, but Matron didn't treat them, they were considered a normal hazard of childhood.

The only civilized room open to me was the library. I had been directed there early on my arrival. Someone, eager to inform, had suggested that I hurry to a book which described the facts of life. I was given the title, shelf and even the page number.

The book was a disappointment; sticking to birds and bees and flowers, it offered no real enlightenment on sex and was much less explicit about birth than my veterinary book. But I liked the library. There were several comfortable chairs, an open fire in winter, and window seats for the summer. As a sitting room it was under-used, the seniors had their own common room and the chatty were discouraged by the rule of silence. With one foot of my chair in the grate, I began to read my way through the books.

My new friends were indignant. Angry faces would appear round the door and mouth demands that I played horses, Truth, or just *came*. I never understood why I belonged to the élite of my year, for all the others were good at either games or work and my only accomplishment was learning poetry. They wanted to call me Jo – unisex names were popular, we had a Tony and a Charlie – but my old hatred of Jo hadn't abated. When I threatened them with disgusting names in retaliation, they tried Cheshire Cat, on the grounds that I was always smiling, but finally settled for J P-T.

The younger half of the school was regularly swept by fashions. Crazes, we called them. The first one was for yo-yos. When I returned home and announced my desperate need for a yo-yo, Mamma was unmoved, but Cappy, whose wardrobe was full of discarded fashions, from spats to plus-fours, was more sympathetic. He posted me a yo-yo at school and bought them for the twins as well. The next craze, a term later, was for pot plants; it was essential to have some flowering object on the chest of drawers beside your bed. The third one was for wretched little white mice in tiny cages and Mamma refused to allow mine in the house. After the mouse's lonely and miserable end, I think I became less susceptible to fashion and acquired a grim trophy from biology, a partially dissected toad preserved in a jar of formaldehyde. It too was banned from the house, so I kept my disembowelled corpse in the laurel bushes by the coalhole and when in a mean mood would brandish it at the twins, who fled shrieking.

I rather enjoyed horrors at that time, but I liked them inanimate. On a nature lesson with Miss Pinhorn, fishing in a stagnant backwater near the Trout Inn at Wolvercote, I had the misfortune with Anne, my pair for the afternoon, to net a rare and utterly repulsive water beetle. It was the catch of the day and Miss Pinhorn was delighted. She pronounced it carnivorous and ordered a diet of raw meat. Anne, known as Bully, was a day girl, so she swiftly opted out and I had to make daily visits to the kitchen to beg raw meat and feed the unlovely creature, now in an aquarium in a junior classroom. Either I overfed it or the meat was not to its taste, for the glass tank and the classroom soon began to smell of rotting flesh. We were told to clean the aquarium, but I don't think we did and eventually, after a weekend at home, I returned to find the tank empty; someone had thrown our monster out with the stinking water.

The summer games field, where we played tennis and rounders, was some distance from the school on the way to the Rear, the dark tree-shaded stretch of the Cherwell where we swam. The timetable was tight and you had to run most of the way back if you were to be in time for Art. I began to lobby for a bicycle, my friends all had them. Mamma withdrew from the discussion, but Cappy said that if I had the money he would help me; we went to Reading and bought a second-hand one for 27/6d.

Winnie was being courted by Georgie Parker who worked at the brewery in Henley and now spent his evenings at The Grove. As they were both poor conversationalists, teaching me to bicycle provided an occupation. They arranged testing courses in the paddock and, steering round jumps and bending poles, I gradually became efficient. Miss Lee made a habit of using her pupils with bicycles to deliver notes to her friends in North Oxford. When Mamma heard I had been used in this way she was furious and wrote one of her scathingly erudite letters of complaint. I suppose I suffered from a comeback, because in a letter home I told her, 'I am very annoyed with you for writing to the Lee.'

Schools didn't like our reading matter. Denis's housemaster, shocked at finding Philip Lindsay's *Here Comes The King* in his room, and then learning that it had been provided by his mother, had only instructed, 'Keep it to yourself, old man.' But Wychwood wrote asking that my beloved veterinary book, 'be kept for holiday consumption as it upset the other children'.

My attempts at singing were also banned. Miss Cholmondley, who took choir practice at which the whole school tried out the assembly hymns for the week, took me aside and asked if I would mind not singing, as my efforts put the other children off. A little indignant, I decided to capitalize and later took her aside to point out that if I was not to sing there was no point in my being there. She agreed to excuse me and I then spent a few happy choir practices in sole possession of the communal swing. It was sited beside the Hut windows, so I was able to make triumphant faces at my friends as I swung. Eventually observed, I was told to go to my classroom and get on with my prep; this was acceptable as it meant less to take home at the weekend. My banishment from choir practice gave me more ammunition for my campaign to give up Musical Appreciation. Mamma was totally unmusical and always admitted that at the end of ten years of piano lessons she could only play 'The Bluebells of Scotland', but the Pullein-Thompsons were musical and she felt that there was no reason we should all have inherited the Cannan lack of ear. So as Musical Appreciation wasn't an extra, I was forced to go on taking part for a whole year. As it was apparent that I couldn't tell one note from another, I was given simple tasks – one clash of the cymbals, one tinkle of the triangle – but even then I would go into a dream and miss my cue.

One of Wychwood's more interesting and original ideas was their House of Commons. It met in the Hut once a week; the senior girls provided the officers and the front benches, while we junior back-benchers were supposed to scour the newspapers for topical matters to bring up at Question Time. I think we mainly concentrated on Question Time, but speeches were delivered and when you reached the Lower Remove you were required to make your maiden speech. I panicked, but Mamma was happy to write me a speech on the urbanization of rural England; I seem to remember poetic sentences about the pastoral heart of England being engulfed in a tide of creeping red brick. I read the speech nervously – I could only perform publicly on the back of a horse – and it was galling afterwards when everyone congratulated me on 'your mother's speech'. Later I became interested in Civics, which was suddenly introduced as a subject, and I think if I had stayed at school longer I might well have played a part in the House.

At that time we were all more concerned with our own small world. Tony Craker, who had an older sister in the school and had been there longer than the rest of us, was usually our leader; but Ann Mullins, who joined us, was interestingly wicked and had been expelled, rumour suggested, from all her previous schools. Joan Aiken, who came a term later, was quiet with red hair and wore her tunic unfashionably long. We didn't object to this for we had been taught at least to pay lip service to plain living and high thinking. Prepared to accept a degree of eccentricity, we scorned acquisitiveness. Two sisters from the Midlands who wore dresses with bows (instead of the skirts and sweaters most of us changed into for supper) and had their own radios, and were sent lavish, be-ribboned boxes of chocolates by their parents – they were the ones who were given a hard time.

Joan Aiken was the only one among us to have divorced parents. Her father, the American poet Conrad Aiken, had left her mother who had married again. We were fascinated, and I remember her sitting on a table and the rest of us gathered round asking about the surnames and relationship of her various half – and step – siblings. My other memory of Joan is that when we drew horses I laboured long over the hideous angularities of hocks, fetlocks and pasterns, but she drew them with wings and lost the legs among the clouds.

Encouraged to read newspapers, we came upon a guarded advertisement for disposable sanitary towels which offered a booklet, entitled *Marjorie-May's Twelfth Birthday*, to help mothers explain menstruation to their daughters. Feeling wickedly subversive and hoping for revelations, we sent for it, but there was the usual disappointment. At the birthday party Marjorie-May's slightly older cousin is much quieter than usual and later Mother explains that she has her first period and is now a woman. In saccharine language Marjorie-May looks forward to becoming a woman too. I took the booklet home for the delectation of Mamma and the twins. Mamma giggled over its awfulness and 'Marjorie' became an alternative euphemism to 'the curse'.

Despite the fecundity of The Grove, my racy reading and strong interest in veterinary matters, I seemed almost wilfully slow to grasp that sex was a human activity. I didn't worry when, at a mutual examination of legs, mine – thin, and long in proportion to my body – were pronounced 'not sexy'. A captive audience in the dormitory, I laughed heartily at Ann and Jean's dirty stories – pretending to understand punch lines about husbands not being bicycle pumps. In fact I had left Wychwood by the time the long-known facts of life suddenly manifested themselves to me. It was by the pond at The Grove, where the ducks were engaged in their usual copulation, that I realized, and choosing the most dignified couple I knew, I told myself 'Aunt May and Uncle Percival do that.'

At Wychwood 'Dares' became fashionable for a time, and Ann

was our most persistent and imaginative darer. At first I felt bound to accept these challenges, which ranged from standing on second-floor window ledges to telling some unfortunate mistress that she looked like a turkey cock; but it seemed that the more you took, the more were made. Gradually I realized that this was a form of tyranny and announced I would accept no more. Then I was tempted by dozens of easy ones, but I stood firm and eventually the craze died.

Ruth Napier, who was in the form above me, was the daughter of Elizabeth Sprigge, and Ruth's younger sister had written to tell Mamma that she much preferred the Jean books to her own mother's *Pony Tracks*. We agreed with the critical judgement, but to admit it seemed an act of treachery which, as we were reared in the Scottish belief that blood is thicker than water, shook us to the core.

In my third term Eleanor Dawson was a room-mate. She was a year older, but as her father trained racehorses, all the family rode and her brothers went to Eton, we had a lot in common. After sharing a room for a week or two, she was amazed to find that I hadn't noticed she had only one eye. She took out her glass one at night and flopped a lock of hair over her face to hide the cavity. The accident had happened on her fourth birthday, as she opened a parcel with a pair of scissors. To me it became a Mamma-style awful warning; I still think of Eleanor as I take up scissors to attack a parcel, and remind myself to point them downwards.

The summer I was ten I had been considered civilized enough to attend the Fourth of June celebrations at Eton and had much enjoyed an elegant lunch given by Denis's housemaster, C.R.N. Routh. I remember the salmon – far more of a luxury then – and the huge homemade meringues, buff-coloured and far more delicious than the white objects one usually ate. After seeing round the school and eating a picnic dinner in the car park, we sat on the river bank to watch the Procession of Boats and then the lavish firework display. The dramatic set-pieces of Catherine wheels and waterfalls on the far bank were interspersed with rockets; I was thrilled with the ones that made multiple bursts, and joined in the audience participation when the whole crowd counted. The other memorable moment was Mamma fainting in the crush on the way to the car park and having to be supported to the car by Cappy and Denis.

That summer at Wychwood, Eleanor was horrified to hear that

I wasn't going to the Fourth, particularly as it was Denis's last half. She arranged with both sets of parents that her eldest brother Dickie, who was up at Oxford, should drive us to Eton after lunch and deliver us to our families.

Clothes weren't a problem because ever since the family dressmaker had retired, Mamma had decided that we must each have one good frock a year, and she bought them mail order from Harrods. We would help to choose the dress and then the twins would decide on one colour and I on another. Mamma did offer them different colours – they never wore matching sweaters or pyjamas – but for some reason their dresses were always identical. In linen hats that matched and tidy socks and shoes, we were considered equipped. We never had summer coats and Cappy loathed cardigans, so if the day turned cold we had to freeze in silence. Any appeal to Mamma would be answered with one of her favourite quotes: 'It is necessary to suffer to be beautiful.'

Dickie Dawson appeared to be satisfied with our appearances but halfway to Windsor, after a further inspection in the driving mirror, he suggested that I removed the brace from my teeth. Obediently, for I was used to elder-brotherly advice, I wrapped it in a handkerchief and put it in my pocket.

Denis was rowing in the traditional Procession of Boats, which then took place before the fireworks, as the light faded. The audience watched from the river bank and as the boats passed each member of every crew, dressed in white duck trousers, a striped shirt and a straw boater decorated with flowers, had to get to his feet and stand, holding his oar vertically in front of him. When Denis's *Arethusa* drew level we were all in terror that one of the crew would lose his balance and capsize the boat, but they rose in turn until the whole crew stood erect and brilliantly illuminated by spotlights.

On the whole Eton seemed to have very little influence on the twins and me. It had taught us to call sponge cakes sandwiched with jam and cream French Cream Jesuses. But I think the various strictures Denis tried to impose had as much to do with his growing sophistication as with his school. 'You *can't* go to the pony club, Miss Ferrand wears a *hairnet*,' he would tell us; or 'You *can't* like china animals.' But I think numbers gave us the strength to ignore him, for we accepted the hairnetted lady and continued to collect china animals, and Denis, always a generous brother, relented enough to give me a magnificent pair of china horse's-head book-ends for my birthday. I think he must have been about seventeen when he announced that parents could not be called Mummy and Cappy, they had to be Mamma and Papa. While we were at Wychwood all our letters were written to Mummy, but as we became teenagers she changed to Mamma, quite happily. Cappy hated Papa – perhaps it was his unloved father's name – but he finally accepted it when we were adult.

In the autumn of 1937, when the twins joined me at Wychwood, I found many changes. Most of the old staff had disappeared. I heard that on learning the whole of the Shell form had failed school certificate, a furious Miss Lee had sacked the deputy principal, and many of the staff had resigned in sympathy. Even Matron had gone; in fact I think only Mademoiselle, Miss Baker and Miss Pinhorn remained. Miss Snodgrass the new deputy headmistress was an improvement, but some of the other staff were not. I remember one who wore cotton wool in her ears, answered no questions and obviously disliked us intensely.

The twins were warmly welcomed and allotted the most popular seniors for their housemothers. I showed them round and introduced them to everyone, displaying them as an interesting rarity, for there were no other twins in the school. I also made use of them. When my over-energetic friends demanded that I joined them in jumping garden seats, I would say, 'Take the twins,' and make a swift retreat to the library.

Though I was conscious that I had less energy than other children, it never occurred to me that there might be anything wrong. I used to feel very odd when I played tennis – I would play quite well in the first set and then lose my coordination completely in the second. In swimming races I would win the first heat and then disappoint my cheering friends by being quite unable to produce the same form in the finals. I would arrive at art lessons, which followed games, in a state of collapse, but I knew from experience that I always felt better after tea, with its liberal helpings of golden syrup. As I grew older and became more motivated, energetic exercise was an increasing problem. At least when riding the horse did most of the strenuous work; but mucking out stables before breakfast or a day's hunting with only a sandwich at lunch-time would leave me feeling half dead. It didn't occur to me to complain, or to consult a doctor, until I was adult and then I learned that I was suffering from hypoglycaemia.

During the 'thirties Cappy had realized that the changes wrought by the First World War and the Depression meant that many more public school boys had to earn their livings. Younger sons had traditionally entered the law, the church or the services, family banks and businesses took on their own, and the administration of the Empire had provided a living for those who could take exile. Cappy felt the new generation of young men needed career guidance and to be brought together with the new national and multinational firms that were coming into being. He persuaded the Headmasters' Conference schools and Trueman and Knightley, one of the well-known education consultancies, to back him, and set up The Public Schools Employment Bureau with an office and an assistant in London. He then spent the term-time travelling round the schools interviewing and advising. We accused him of hurrying the poor unsuspecting boys into miserable careers in chartered accountancy, but he was convinced that this was the area of future growth. He admitted that he always advised against careers in the arts because he felt that writing, painting and music all offered such hard and uncertain lives that only those who went into them despite discouragement were likely to survive.

With Cappy visiting schools, Denis at Christ Church and the three of us at Wychwood, Mamma was alone at home. She hated it, and if anyone sneezed on Monday morning she would persuade herself that we were all about to have colds and keep us at home for the rest of the week. Our parents' disregard for the authority of school obviously had an effect on us and we were always in trouble for minor infringements, for which you were awarded an 'N.D.' or 'not done'. The lack of name tapes on our clothes clocked up N.D.s by the dozen. The punishments were fines deducted from your pocket money, but as we had no pocket money they went unpaid. At the end of each term the unpaid fines were doubled, and a list on the notice-board named the offenders. As the P-T debt grew and grew, more law-abiding girls would gasp in horror at the huge sums we owed, but we knew that the school was helpless; our bank and post office accounts were out of their reach.

In the summer of 1938 poliomyelitis, or infantile paralysis as it was then called, struck Oxford. It was a terrifying illness which left children and young adults crippled or suffering a living death in an iron lung. There was no immunization and no cure and I

153

think people had only just become aware that swimming in polluted water contributed to the spread of the virus.

Mamma removed us from school instantly and we spent a glorious summer at home. But when the outbreak was over we were returned in time for exams and it was deeply humiliating to find that one could no longer compete with one's peers. Our parents, inconsequently, used our appallingly low marks as proof that we were learning nothing and that Wychwood was a waste of money. They decided we were to leave, they would find a governess and educate us at home; but meanwhile they had to give a term's notice.

* * * *

Diana writes:-

Looking back now to Wychwood I see myself an untidy girl struggling to be liked, in gaunt, red-brick houses with windows open to the damp cold of the Oxford air; I remember hockey on barren fields, chilblains and despair; I see a place where my half-understood dreams of being a normal schoolchild slowly fell apart like a bright jersey eaten by moths, until each day brought further confirmation of my failure both in lessons and relationships, and paranoia started to take root.

When I arrived, with no special sheets or writing paper and the minimum items of uniform, my confidence had already been undermined by the entrance exam. Many questions in it had foxed me, although I now remember only one, which was about the significance of King Alfred. Of course I should have mentioned education and the navy, but we had never *done* King Alfred at Miss Fryer's and all I could recall was a picture of him with a tray of burnt cakes in our illustrated nursery history book. So I answered, 'King Alfred burnt the cakes,' and, not realising the school was at a low ebb, I was surprised to be accepted.

Tackling a new, unfamiliar curriculum, we struggled to understand lessons like people trying to find their way through deep country without the signposts and maps available to others. Worse still, we were, once again, 'the twins' rather than individuals; and potential friends had to take both of us or neither, for, homesick and lost, we stayed together like abandoned puppies. Outwardly cheerful, ill-written postcards sent by me from

Wychwood showed how quickly I regressed. Yet the staff tried to make us feel at home and our form mistress, Miss Woodward, who I suspect admired Mamma's books, tried to encourage us.

The first term we shared a dormitory with our 'house mother', Joy, an amiable sixth-former appointed to show us the ropes and be available for questions. But, although there was no bullying and little cattiness, the place became for us the prison Mamma had anticipated. How could it be otherwise with almost every minute of the day organised and life punctuated by rules, which we rarely remembered? At home we hogged the nursery fire, here in the Banbury Road there seemed no permanent escape from the raw penetrating cold of an Oxford winter. While other girls wore tunics and white blouses Christine and I shivered even with games sweaters and blazers on top of that uniform, our faces marred by dental braces, mine on both top and bottom teeth. And while Josephine found warmth in the Library, Christine and I eventually sat in front of a coal stove in our class room which was adjacent to the Hut. Here, where no one else came in the evenings, we, too, could read in peace.

Seeing Christine hunched and miserable was to see myself, except for those braces – she only had one at the top – which made me loth to smile. Inept but optimistic, we tried to make friends with two day girls in our class, tall Jean Chalk and the shorter Sally Foley. They had paired off and, conscious that people without friends were 'wet blankets', we tagged along after them. When spring came Mamma, anxious to encourage us, asked Jean and Sally over to tea. They rode Lassie and seemed to enjoy themselves. But the fact that they never asked us back fed my own suspicion that they came for the ride and to talk with the writer of *A Pony for Jean*, rather than because they wanted to be with us – a sad realisation, because I needed so much to be *liked*. With no friends, Christine and I feared we might one day be linked to the mentally disadvantaged Joy and Mary, whom Josephine has described. If you came in last for a meal the only vacant place would be next to one of these poor girls and secretly we thought this might one day be our scenario, too.

The 'picking teams' ritual confirmed that dreadful possibility. My cherished hope that the leaders' fingers might one day point at me first was never realised. Their keen eyes passed Christine and me over like dust among the diamonds until there was nobody else left. Although I liked netball and tennis, I loathed hockey, because we were always on the boundary, shivering while we waited for the ball to come our way and conscious of Nana, a dumpy little old lady in a hat, standing face pressed against the wire mesh, or sitting on a bench, a mother hen watching her chicks.

Occasionally I have wondered since whether our feeling of rejection was merely a symptom of mild paranoia, but when I meet women who were at Wychwood with us they put me right. 'You were,' they say, 'very peculiar.' And one asked me recently how I had learned to speak properly? *Did I see somebody?* – meaning, I suppose, a psychiatrist, although perhaps a speech therapist would have been enough. She said, also, how sorry she had felt for me as I stood humiliated in an elocution lesson. 'They asked you to try a tongue twister, which they must have known you couldn't possibly manage. It was so cruel.' Another experience edited out by my brain's censor.

I suspect, however, that kind dark-haired Miss Woodward considered us to be a challenge. She raised our spirits by giving us the best parts when we read from Shakespeare in class and later, when we became less manageable, bribed us with chocolate to be quiet. Accustomed to women with outdoor complexions, I remember her as a fine-featured woman with dark shadows under dark eyes in a pale face, and elegant fingers slightly yellowed by nicotine. I see her now in a long dark skirt, sitting in a small, smoke-filled room, as she checked that we had cleaned our teeth and been to the loo. And we were first each night for this chore, because, having soon discovered that there was no hot bath water after half past eight, we opted to be the first to bed.

The other teachers are less clear in my memory, although Snodgrass and Pinhorn are names not easily forgotten. Formidable Miss Snodgrass, who later became headmistress, was a fine history teacher, although I felt a childish prejudice against the kirby grips that kept her hair so firmly behind her ears. Fair Miss Pinhorn, whose glasses seemed to match her skin, I resented because she insisted, in carpentry lessons, that we made easels for the use of fifth- and sixth-formers. Wanting to take home some elegant box I had made, I suspected our efforts were being exploited to save the school money.

For me the least successful and most unforgettable teacher was Mademoiselle – a Russian, I believe – whose great brown eyes sometimes brimmed with tears, as children played her up. Poor Mademoiselle, young and lost in the claustrophobic atmosphere of an English boarding school, found Christine and me impossible. And who could blame her, for, since we could hardly pronounce English, how could she be expected to teach us French? Years later when I was signing books at a Russian bazaar, Mademoiselle, now a tall, distinguished old lady with a stick, hobbled up. 'You *can't* be one of the twins,' she exclaimed. 'You *must* be Josephine.' Her difficulty in accepting me as an author confirmed a childhood suspicion that she had considered Christine and me beyond recall (a view which first surfaced when she refused to give us extra French lessons after we had opted out of eurhythmics).

Perhaps the unrealistic dreams we brought to Wychwood, a liberal and enlightened school, contributed eventually to Christine's and my bad behaviour. Imagining hunt balls, we wanted to learn ball-room dancing, but found ourselves instead attempting to sway gracefully in eurhythmics, or skipping, which we told Miss Lee we did not consider *beneficial*. We longed to learn more Scottish history, but found ourselves once again in the Stone Age, which had so fascinated Miss Fryer, while in geography we concentrated on the Colonies instead of Western Europe.

In the spring term Christine and I were put in different dormitories, but because we were still untidy and disorganised we were again, against normal practice, provided with housemothers. Mine was tall, flaxen-haired Noël Clifton, who lived on Dartmoor and rode. Feeling she was a kindred spirit I confided in her my hopes for success in a spring gymkhana. I won a first prize there – was it for best rider? I can't remember – and eagerly sat beside her the next term, expecting her to ask how I had got on. But she didn't, and family rules against *swanking* prevented me from telling her; so to my great disappointment, the girl I admired never knew that I was good at *something*.

Josephine, who always looked on the bright side, is certain Christine and I were not as miserable as we say, but Ann Mullins, whom Josephine sent to play horses with 'the twins', remembers us as unhappy. Ann, who became Ann Dally, a distinguished psychiatrist and medical historian, had already the knack of noticing behaviour and mood in others. 'You were gloomy,' she told me, 'because of your speech problem, but Josephine was always smiling.'

During our first summer at Wychwood the teachers took a day

off, leaving the senior girls in charge of lessons. Noël gave Christine a starred 1 for a picture of Jesus in the desert, a mark withdrawn by Miss Lyons the next day, because, she said, none of us was fit to draw Our Lord.

Each Sunday or Monday we three returned to school loaded with apples, a passport for Christine and me to a temporary popularity. We kept the apples hidden amongst our clothes to offer around when no teachers were about. But the dress box full of chocolate and grapes which Denis sent us in a typically spontaneous gesture, when he left Oxford after a year for the theatre, was a different matter.

Denis had won a Kitchener Scholarship to read History at Christ Church, an expensive college for a young man trying to live on a pound a week provided by Granny and a small parental allowance, which Cappy often only sent when dunned for it. Aunt Dorothea paid for a tailor to make Denis an overcoat, but he could hardly keep up with his polo-playing, sherry-drinking fellow undergraduates. Besides, his first love was for the theatre and, when he should have been reading history, he spent much of his time at the Playhouse. When he sent us the parcel he already had a job waiting for him as Stage Manager at the Bexhill Repertory Theatre, which was run by Matthew Forsythe, the producer of Cappy's play *It's Folly to be Wise* at the Kew Theatre in the 'twenties. Matthew Forsythe joined the Air Force in the war, but afterwards ran The Citizens' Theatre in Glasgow, where he immediately offered Denis another job. Later Forsythe became Director of the London Academy of Dramatic Art.

We ate the grapes straightaway and some of the chocolate. Then, before going home for the weekend, Josephine put the box under clothes in the bottom drawer of her chest of drawers, but someone discovered its hiding place and we returned to find it gone.

The only frightening experience at Wychwood was, for me, fire practice, when all the girls in my house assembled in an attic. A webbing band was put round our bodies under our arms, and in turn we were gradually let down the side of the house on a pulley with a teacher turning a small wheel. With little faith in our elders' competence, I clutched at the wall's creepers, scraping my knees and ashamed of my cowardice.

But if imitation is the sincerest form of flattery, Christine and I did at one time gain respect from our peers when, on Denis's suggestion, we chose to recite in turn A.E. Housman's poem, 'Farewell to barn and stack and tree', our voices rising as we reached those memorable lines:

> And here's a bloody hand to shake,
> And oh, man, here's goodbye;
> We'll sweat no more with scythe and rake,
> My bloody hands and I.

'I don't think that's a very nice poem,' the teacher said, not liking the bloodys. But afterwards other children begged us to lend them our copy of *The Shropshire Lad*, and the next week recited the same poem, accompanied by their classmates' giggles. Thereafter free choice ended and we were back to Walter de la Mare's 'Is there anybody there?' said the Traveller, Knocking at the moonlit door', which we hated, and to Christina Rossetti.

In the summer term Josephine was put in the main house, Christine in St John's and me in the Flat, where we slept only occasionally because of the polio epidemic, which Josephine has mentioned. When we did return to school we were, as usual, late for Assembly – a source of complaint from the teachers, to whom Cappy replied in a sharp, short letter saying that his wife's health was more important than his children's prayers.

Earlier in the year Mr Sworder had left with us Northwind, a blue roan gelding of 14 hands with a large dark head and black points, who became one of my special, most challenging favourites. After much schooling I rode him in a jumping class, judged by the notable Reading vet, G.P. Male. At the approach to each obstacle he half-reared and ran backwards, but in those days there were no time limits and somehow I got him round with only one or two refusals. I came out of the ring despondent, obeying the cardinal rule never to blame one's mount for failure. Then, at the end of a long, hot day, I was astonished to be called back to receive the cup for the Best Rider in the Show – a quirky decision by Mr Male based entirely on my battle with Northwind, which suggested that the struggles with Jenny and Daisy had paid off and, for me, that some disasters turn into triumphs. When Mr Sworder eventually sold Northwind, he handed us ten shillings or a pound as usual for our work, which, of course, could in no way compensate for losing a pony whom I had felt was my own; but I think we had all learned by then that life is punctuated with goodbyes.

Meanwhile, with so many lessons missed, Wychwood became for me almost unbearable, and secretly I decided to run away. Josephine's initial attempts to make Christine and me feel at ease made my lack of friends all the more painful. Jean Chalk and Sally Foley had become distant. The apple season had not yet begun. And there was no one else remotely interested in us. During lessons I struggled in a fog of incomprehension.

'If you don't like something, don't whine, change it,' Mamma had advised on innumerable occasions. All right, then. I hated being a failure, so next term I would run away – with Christine if she wanted to come. I would disappear for a whole day and then, as evening fell, turn up at the house where Nana lived. She would contact Mamma and then perhaps everyone would understand how totally inadequate and fed-up I felt.

Then our parents told us that we were to leave school, because they could no longer afford the fees and we didn't seem to be learning anything. I hugged this information to myself, thinking how amazed our unfriendly schoolmates would be when our names were read out at the end of term. But first there were plans for an end-of-term midnight feast. Mamma gave us fruit and ever-popular Lyons Individual Fruit Pies, and, tribal still, we agreed that all three of us would meet at the main house for the feast. The Flat had a balcony on the first floor, from which daring girls sometimes jumped down to the grass below when no teachers were around. Were doors locked at night or was it bravado which made me decide to jump from it too on the night of the feast? I don't know what Christine's plans were for leaving St John's, but they, like mine, were pre-empted when we were both ordered to spend our last night in the main house sick beds, and we realised sadly that the teachers knew exactly what was going on and had decided to turn a partially blind eye. With deceit ruled out, the feast became a staid affair.

None of this mattered, of course, once we were back for good at The Grove, where half-disturbing, half-exciting talk of war was in the air, and we had our first very own pony, whom I have not mentioned, though we bought him on an autumn Saturday during our last term at Wychwood.

We came across Shandy (full name, Shandy Gaff) at Reading Market, where Mamma had left us on her way to shop in the town centre. He was one of scores of wild, recently-weaned foals from the New Forest, huddled miserably together in pens. Golden-coloured, yet more dun than chestnut, with a cream underbelly and a star which turned into a trickle running down to a pale muzzle, he seemed to me the most loveable foal in the world. Then, as we looked at him, he became the boldest, too, as he jumped over the bars of the pen and fell on his nose the other side. When a strong man picked him up and threw him back inside, our longing to buy him grew into an agony of hope, but we had no money on us and, very soon, we sadly watched him auctioned and sold to someone else. Then, too late, Mamma returned and drove us home.

Over lunch the vision of Shandy jumping the railings haunted us. Bought with several other suckers in one lot by a dealer, his fate seemed horribly uncertain. Was it possible he might be sold for dog meat? 'It may not be too late,' Mamma said. 'If he's still there his new owner might sell him on to us.' And so, in a wild rush of hope, we decided to take the last of our money out of our post office accounts.

There was a dash to find our passbooks, an agonizing wait for the post office to reopen after the lunch break, and then at last Mamma drove us, with money in our pockets, swiftly down Gravel Hill, through Sonning Common, Emmer Green and Caversham, over the wide Thames to Reading. Would we be too late? We each had our own imaginary scenario.

With fast beating hearts we ran into the Market and – miraculously, we thought – the foals were still there, Shandy among them, his nose still bloody from his fall.

I don't remember which of us asked the dealer whether he would resell Shandy, who was the smallest of the lot – only that after a tantalising pause, in which no doubt he worked out his profit, the dealer said, 'All right, seventy-five shillings.'

Thrilled, we dug deep in our pockets, gave over the money. The sale was clinched and we probably shook hands, as was the custom in those days. Pleased with his sale, the dealer promised to drop Shandy off at The Grove soon after four.

So we achieved in one afternoon something other girls only dream of. And, in the dislocated weeks ahead, Wychwood could not compete with such an event. How indeed could we attend to Miss Lee's often sensible homilies at Assembly or to dull lessons or much else when our minds were on home and the pony book lives we led there?

***

Christine writes:-

For years I could not hear the sound of a piano being played without recalling Highlands and the Miss Coopers. So it is with Wychwood, for the cry of owls on a winter night still reminds me of the owls in North Oxford which hooted so mournfully while I lay homesick trying to sleep. Beside my bed I kept a picture of Mama. And photographs of Dinah and Milkmaid in blue Woolworth frames.

Carola Oman had given Diana and me small cases in which to carry our toothbrushes and pyjamas backwards and forwards between home and school. They had our initials on them. Arriving on Monday mornings we would already be looking forward to returning home on Friday. Everyone tried very hard to make us happy; our housemothers were kind – we had them far longer than anyone else – our teachers were tolerant. There was no bullying of any kind and the school was known to prize individuality. It was not Wychwood's fault that we were naughty, unhappy and quite incapable of fitting in. We did complain, particularly about tea which consisted of bread, butter, and jam one day, and bread, butter and slab cake the next, as we thought that we should have all of them every day. We also objected to one of the teachers insisting that we should say 'pardon' when we failed to hear something, instead of our usual 'what?' Mama wrote to Wychwood about both with words which were both scathing and elegant. Unfortunately she misunderstood our complaint about tea and objected to our being given Danish butter rather than English.

Josephine made lasting friends at Wychwood. Diana and I did not. People were kind to us because we were different and we knew why they were being kind. I constantly feared that I would be put on the same level as poor Winkle and Mary who were definitely odder than us.

Used to piles of blankets on our beds, the two plus eiderdown which we were allowed was not enough for us on cold winter nights. So we went to bed earlier and earlier so that we could have baths while the water was still hot and our hot water bottles to comfort us through the freezing owl-hooting nights. In the mornings there were two bells, and one had to be up by the second. Before going to breakfast we were expected to strip our beds and open the windows. When we returned later the sheets often felt like ice.

Wiggy, my second housemother, wore a bra. It was the first time I had ever seen one. I would lie in bed watching her dress, marvelling how long she took and then, when she had gone, I would drag my clothes on willy nilly, pull back my sheets, fling open the window and hurtle downstairs to breakfast.

In the winter we played hockey on a ground adjoining Oliver and Gurdens' cake factory. Standing around, as a back without much to do I would grow cold, and with the smell of cakes cooking, got hungrier and hungrier. Fortunately Nana would be waiting by the way out to push chocolate into our eager hands as we passed by. Nobody said anything about this. Did they turn a blind eye? for all food and sweets were supposed to be handed in to one's house-mistress or to matron. Perhaps because of this I always ate Nana's gift immediately without offering so much as a crumb to anyone else.

But for me, like Diana, the worst part of being at Wychwood was feeling a misfit – which we were. In spite of Cappy having once played rugger with the Harlequins and in the doubles at Wimbledon, we were bad at games. We used long out-dated words, had no social graces whatsoever, and we were farouche too; but, what I dreaded most of all, we were 'peculiar'. As Diana has said, we were often absent, which hardly helped us to fit in. And it was not long before Mamma arranged for us to leave early every Friday to see our dentist Mr Robert Bruce in Reading who she said needed to check our braces. (Afraid that we might swallow them, she insisted we took them out while riding, and often we hung them on a damson tree in the paddock.) Our braces had to be made a little tighter every day. I always forgot this and much frantic tightening was done in the car on the way to Reading. Once, on a Saturday, we appeared in Mr Bruce's surgery wearing MacGregor ties and he immediately asked how we were entitled to wear the tartan. Fortunately we were able to explain that the Wedderburns were related to the MacGregors and so we could wear their tartan ties, but not the kilt.

There were several things about Wychwood which remain indelible on my mind: getting up early to play tennis with Diana, sitting on the swings taunting our classmates who were attending a singing lesson in the Hut. (We were excluded from such lessons for previous bad behaviour.) Being called before the senior girls for the way we left the bathrooms after we had used them; looking down before muttering that we should have used a swab, sensing the hidden laughter in their eyes. I can never forget the hollow feeling inside when I looked at a geometry exam paper and realised that I couldn't answer a single question. Nor the joy I felt when I gained an A for an essay entitled 'Rain'. The longing for Friday, which never left me, and eating cress I had grown for tea. And the thick green knickers we wore with white linings inside. I remember making a green snood to wear in my hair and waiting for admiration in vain. I recall asking Josephine's friend Tony Craker what she thought of me, and her reply, 'You're bumptious', which left me flummoxed. I cannot forget devotedly making Mamma a pyjama case in sewing class, laboriously blanket-stitching the edges, then embroidering JMP-T on the front. I gave it to her and waited for a rapturous response. It was not forthcoming. Did she hate it? Or was she already worried by such unswerving devotion, or thinking of what the materials had cost her, or simply tired at that moment? I shall never know.

When we were not visiting Mr Bruce on the way home, we had tea with Nana who now lived in rooms in Summertown. Granny had given her furniture and I remember a large Victorian wardrobe too big for her small bedroom and a Heal's bed with a caned head-piece. But before we had tea we would visit the little antique shop on the corner. We hunted for bargains there and Diana bought a little hunting crop, as they were called before they became hunting whips. We bought a picture there too which now hangs in Josephine's house.

In winter Nana toasted bread for us on a long fork in front of her fire, and boiled a kettle on it. There were always cakes from Oliver and Gurdens' for tea and with a roaring coal fire one was never cold.

Sadly I feel my short stay at Wychwood only increased my feelings of inadequacy as an individual, though not as part of the Pullein-Thompson clan. Perhaps if Diana and I had not stayed at home so often, we might have done better, but I doubt it. I think a one-to-one approach and a great deal of encouragement might have helped me, but it was not available and besides Mamma did not think education really mattered. As it was, when I left Wychwood for good I can recall nothing but joy in my heart.

Chapter Six

Christine writes:-

One of the happiest moments of my youth was when Mamma called us to her bedroom and said, 'I have something to tell you which will please Christine most of all – we're going to Scotland for a whole month.'

Though Scotland had been part of me for so long, I had never been there and I still cannot recall my feelings at that moment. I had pretended to be Cluny and Macduff and fought their battles against my sister's heroes. I had loathed the dirty Campbells and admired the Macdonalds so cruelly massacred by them at Glencoe. I had learned Scottish poetry and sung Scottish songs, and now at last I was going to Scotland. The news was overwhelming. Even so, I do not remember saying much. We were brought up not to be effusive, which Cappy considered behaving like a foreigner. (It took me a long time to discover how wrong he was and that a simple thank-you is hardly ever enough.) So probably I just looked happy and cried, 'Hurray'. But whatever I said my heart must have been pounding with excitement, while my mind was already reciting Scottish poetry. We were going for the whole of September 1938.

Once again Bowley and his family were to look after the house and animals, and this time the dogs were staying behind. There were four of them by now, and Darkie the wolfhound would take up the whole back seat of the car. We were not hiring a caravan; a cottage had been rented near Arisaig. The fact that we were all to miss nearly three weeks of school didn't deter any of us, least of all our parents. War was brewing, but I did not know it then, nor did I know that six long years would pass before I had another holiday.

It had been decided that while we were in Scotland Mamma would finish her novel and Cappy would do the cooking. Mrs

Macdonald, a lady of great charm whom we later persuaded to teach us a smattering of Gaelic, would do the housework. So without Denis, who was holidaying elsewhere, we set off in high spirits. We spent our first night at the Lockerbie House Hotel. Cappy, forever worried about money, had booked us rooms in the basement which were cheaper. It was the first time I had ever stayed in a hotel – on previous holidays we had always stayed in boarding houses or a caravan – and it seemed very grand to me. The next morning we had a large breakfast in an impressive dining room before setting off for the Highlands. I cannot remember where we stopped for lunch but I recall being tremendously impressed by the desolation and grandeur of Glencoe. I had read so much about Scotland and gazed so often at the watercolour painting of Eigg and Rhum by Granny, which hung in the nursery, that I felt as though I were returning home. By evening we had reached Achnatallasaig, the grey, clean, spartan cottage which was to be our home for the next four weeks. It looked out on a grey, green Highland sea. A black and white cow was wandering slowly across white sand, while birds wheeled calling in an empty sky. The only other house was the farmhouse nearby.

It was to be an unforgettable holiday. As agreed, Mamma worked on her novel in the mornings, while Cappy did the cooking and the shopping. Loving rice puddings, he made one every day, and there were trips to Mallaig to buy the kippers there which he insisted were the best in the world. We shopped in Arisaig as well where Diana and I were shocked at the price of apples, to which we were addicted, and which now took all our pocket money.

After a week, our parents sent a premeditated telegram to Wychwood which read: 'CANNOT RETURN HOME. CAR'S BIG END GONE'. (The big end was an important part of a car in those days.) On returning to school we were asked why there were no garages in Scotland – a difficult question to answer!

We had brought our folbot canoe with us and spent many happy hours paddling between rocky islands in a quiet sea. Of course it rained, but it was warm Highland rain and we swam with it falling on our backs. Sometimes Josephine and I caught cuddy fish for breakfast which Josephine, intending to be a vet and not being squeamish, gutted. One morning Mamma and I left the canoe beached on the grass above the sea. Next morning it had disappeared and though we searched and searched we never found it.

When questioned, the locals laughed at us, saying that a hater of foreigners had thrown it into the sea or that it had blown away and was now 'awa' to the Isle of Skye.' Either way it was gone for ever.

In the afternoons we went on expeditions. We stared into the deep, dark waters of Loch Morar and ran across the white sands of Arisaig. We climbed the hills hoping for a glimpse of Roshven, the place where Mamma had spent perhaps the happiest days of her childhood. Situated in Moidart, one of the wildest parts of the Highlands, Roshven had belonged to Mamma's great-uncle, Hugh Blackburn, a retired professor of mathematics, and to his wife Jemima Blackburn, a well-known painter. But it was their daughter, Lady, whom the Cannan girls loved. She let them run wild amidst the heather and taught them to row and all the other things town children never learn, like how to tie a reef knot and use a penknife. They rode the Highland ponies, and the donkey Rosie, whom they soon considered theirs. The post came by pony. There were thatched cottages with earth floors, and picnics on Goat Island. And they must have climbed the mountain after which the house was named.

In Aunt May's autobiography *Grey Ghosts and Voices*, published posthumously, she wrote: 'The Roshven boat with four men in red shirts, blue coats and tam o'shanters with red bobbles came up to the head of the loch to meet us. The Railway stopped at Fort William then, and we drove in a wagonette from there to Inverlott.' She was four years old at the time. Later she wrote: 'If it was too stormy for the boat, the ponies came over the hill and, clutching a bag with your night things, you rode.' She called life at Roshven 'heaven'.

Mamma had talked often of Roshven, telling us how the piper there had played to them on their arrival and again on the night before their departure, 'Lochaber no more,' and, 'Will ye no' come back again', beneath their bedroom window. To us, addicted to the old days, a house which you could only reach on foot or by horse or boat, without electricity or telephone, sounded like the house of our dreams. So soon we were climbing higher and higher into the hills hoping for a glimpse of Roshven, while Cappy, unable to keep up with us because of his hip wound, stayed by the car smoking his pipe.

But to no avail. Every hill seemed to lead only to a higher one. While I climbed I looked also for Cluny's Caves, in particular for the one called, 'the cage' where he was reputed to have hidden Prince Charlie and which is so vividly described in Robert Louis Stevenson's book *Kidnapped*.

Soon Mamma's novel was almost finished and we were growing weary of Cappy's daily rice pudding. We had almost given up hope of ever seeing Roshven when we had an unexpected stroke of luck. One evening as the shadows lengthened and September was about to give way to October, a caravan arrived and was parked in a nearby field. At first it seemed like an intrusion, for its owners were obviously English, while we throughout our stay had become steadily more Scottish.

'Tourists, interfering foreigners,' we muttered scornfully. But Cappy had better ideas. The owner of the caravan was a Mr Carr. 'Carr's biscuits,' suggested Cappy hopefully, and hastily made friends. Then, ingenious as ever, he persuaded Mr and Mrs Carr to share the cost of a motorboat to take us all to Roshven. I don't know what he said, maybe he simply suggested that they might enjoy a trip around the loch. Anyway, a few days later we set off in a hired motorboat with its owner to see the house of our dreams.

The sea was choppy, the boat's engine stuttered and spluttered and gave out a terrible smell. I was beginning to feel distinctly sick when at last we saw Roshven, the mountain, the house and behind it the wild hills. The boat stopped. We jumped out and ran up a shingly beach. It was a moment I will never forget. It was so wild and beautiful, without road or electricity – the olden days suddenly in front of my very eyes. Mamma had not been back to Roshven since the death of Hugh and Jemima Blackburn, when the house was bequeathed to a cousin who had grown up in Canada. Their daughter Margaret (Lady) went to live in her house in Edinburgh. Peter Blackburn and his wife had been left the estate but no means for maintaining it, so Peter, who I believe had farmed when in Canada, needed to make Roshven pay. He bought tractors and tried modern methods – which meant that there was no work for many of the people who had laboured there all their lives, and they had to go. Hating changes, Mamma and her sisters had never been back to Roshven. Not until now.

We found the house empty, blind behind its shutters. The square, a yard with stables and a cow byre which Mamma had remembered with such affection because the Highland ponies and Rosie had lived there, was now overgrown and empty. The peaches and the arum lilies, which Mamma said had flourished because there was no frost, had gone too.

'It's all so much smaller than I remembered it,' cried Mamma in anguish.

The Carrs picnicked. Wandering around, we met a few elderly inhabitants, who remembered Mamma and embraced her. At some time we ate our lunch. We could see Goat Island and, in the distance, Eigg and Rhum, and Loch Ailort where it reached the sea. It was Prince Charles Edward country, and it was there in 1883, while being rowed on Loch Ailort by Roshven boatmen and listening to their sea shanties, that Harold Boulton conceived the words for the 'Skye Boat Song'.

Was Mamma disappointed by the visit? I think she must have been. Over the years it has strengthened my feeling that one should never return to a place beloved in childhood. The time came to go back. I don't think the Carrs made any comment as we climbed back into the boat and set off across the water for Achnatallasaig. Someone must have talked to the owner of the boat, but I can no longer recall what was said. Mamma was pensive. Roshven must have been full of ghosts for her; but at least the quest was over.

Soon after our visit to Roshven, it was time to return to England. I do not remember much of the journey home. I think by this time we were ready to pick up the strands of our ordinary lives again.

Nothing had changed when we reached The Grove – no animals had died, no disaster had struck. The Bowles's friendly faces were there to greet us. Our beds were made up. I do not think I was perturbed at being nearly three weeks late for school. Whatever our parents decided I still considered right, however inconvenient; besides I hated school, so any time away was to be celebrated. And if nothing else, our Scottish holiday must have proved to our parents that we could exist for a whole month without a single ride, so might never become the horsey bores they so feared.

We were soon back in the saddle and by the next summer we were riding further and further to horse shows. On one memorable occasion we rode many miles to a training stable near Chaddleworth in Berkshire, which belonged to the parents of

Josephine's schoolfriend Eleanor Dawson. To us the stables there appeared immensely smart, with rows of superior loose boxes, grooms and thoroughbreds. Our ponies Penny Wise, Milky and Rum were soon turned out and they did look like poor relations compared to the many well-bred horses looking at them so keenly over their loosebox doors.

Mamma arrived in her car, bringing food and a tent as well as blankets. We erected the tent in a field in the shadow of the grand house and the stables. Watched by amused grooms, we cleaned our tack. I cannot remember what we ate that evening, but as darkness fell we discovered that Mamma had taken back home the blankets meant for us. So, wearing pullovers to keep warm, we lay down covered with our one blanket, a horse-rug which smelt deliciously of horse. Later we were woken by a raging thunder-storm. Josephine says that at some point a fraught governess appeared and persuaded us to sleep on a verandah. I can only remember the thunder and lightning and the rain lashing our tent.

Next morning we groomed our ponies, and in the early light they still looked very plain, with their hogged manes and pony features, compared to Eleanor's and her brothers' well-bred mounts. I suspect that our clothes were not up to scratch either. But I pushed all this to the back of my mind. I believe the grooms helped us groom our ponies, still with amused faces. I think the sun shone. I tried to feel hopeful, but the fences in the ring looked enormous and our rivals appeared unbeatable in their shiny boots and well-cut jackets.

But, as in the best pony books, we triumphed. Watched by Mamma, Josephine jumped off repeatedly against Eleanor's brothers and won. Milky was given a medal for the Best Trained Pony. Penny Wise excelled in the gymkhana events. The expressions on the grooms' faces changed; it was obvious that never in their wildest dreams had they expected long-backed Rum ridden by Josephine to beat the home horses. Loaded with congratulations and bedecked with rosettes, we rode home through an evening which became night before we saw the welcoming lights of home ahead of us. I suspect we walked on foot some of the way leading our mounts. I remember riding through Gate Hampton and Goring Heath and that the ponies were tireless. And although we had probably ridden more than forty miles in two days and competed in a show, they were none the worse for it. But perhaps most importantly we had proved something to ourselves, which was of lasting importance – that you don't need expensive horses and grooms to win, that you can do it on a shoestring.

There were other triumphs. We became smarter. Milky and Rum wore rugs now with P-T on them. We wore riding coats which fitted. People started calling us the P-Ts and groaning when they saw us arriving at shows. Rum jumped better and better and we gradually became experts at the Handy Hunter class. Winning does not endear you to people, but at last we had found something at which we could succeed, and Diana and I needed success – me most of all, if I was ever to emerge from my personal feeling of inferiority. We did not know then that in future years we would be actually holding our own horse shows at which a very small Alan Oliver would compete, looking tiny on huge much-martingaled horses, and Henry Wynmalen and R. S. Summerhays, the editor of *Riding* would judge.

But, long before this we held dog gymkhanas in the Top Meadow. The first one was rather disorganised. I believe either Miss Lawrence or Christina Edwards-Jones judged it. There was a jumping class for dogs under eighteen inches and one for those over, a flat race, and best-trained dog classes. Josephine says Cappy organised an owners' race at one of them, which she won, to everyone's surprise; but sadly, because she was family, the prize had to go to Claudia, an acquaintance, who always seemed so much tidier and self contained than us. I remember there was much growling and snarling, and dogs who ran away and wouldn't come back, but thankfully no dog fights. Mrs Mooring, who for some time had mended our socks for fourpence a time and who lived in a tiny cottage with a dour husband and a daughter who was our first pupil, sewed the rosettes. Any profit we made was intended for the RSPCA, but I'm not sure that we made any.

* * * *

Diana writes:-

Reading my sisters' recollections, I recognise again how selective my own memory is. I cannot, for instance, recall the blood in the foul-smelling farm drains on our caravanning holiday, nor emptying the latrine bucket, although I would have certainly taken my turn, nor the ganging-up against me mentioned by Josephine. What did I do when I was the odd one out? Often I must have wandered around playing my beloved mouth organ (no doubt to everyone's irritation): 'Loch Lomond', 'The Isle of Capri', 'Daisy' and 'Goodbye My Bluebell'.

In Scotland, when my sisters went fishing in the canoe I tried to teach a friendly cow to shake hands – for me a scientific experiment: I had taught a pony and a dog, so why not a cow? Every morning Christine and I swam together in that grey cove, peeling off layers of clothes before plunging into the cold Highland water. Afterwards we prepared breakfast for everyone, but our attempts at cooking failed; my hot bread rolls were again hard as stones. Later in the mornings we paddled close to shore in the folbot or played on the knoll which looked out across the sheltered sea to the blue outlines of Rhum and Eigg and Skye, which were already familiar from the watercolours Granny had painted of them.

My sisters have forgotten the rowing boat our parents hired in Arisaig from a drunken fisherman. Cappy arranged to pay for it weekly, but, as the fisherman kept running out of money, the weeks got shorter and shorter, and he became a frequent, slightly dreaded figure on the cottage doorstep. In the evenings we rowed our parents out towards the glory of the setting Highland sun and trawled in vain for mackerel. One day our drunken fisherman brought us a live lobster to buy and, as luck would have it, there had been an article in *The Times* that morning on how to kill lobsters humanely. The usual method of plunging them into boiling water was apparently cruel. Far better, the author said, to put them in a large saucepan of cold, salted water and bring them slowly to the boil, a method guaranteed to send the lobster to sleep. Cappy followed these instructions and, unable to escape – it was raining and the cottage was small – we listened miserably for ages while our victim crawled round and round, his claws clinking against the saucepan's sides, until at last there was no sound except the boiling water and we knew he had expired. Inevitably, his white flesh, extracted laboriously from inside his pinkish shell, gave us no pleasure when it eventually it arrived on our plates and I, for one, ate it only to please our parents.

Cappy's temper seemed to improve in Scotland – partly, I suspect, because his job running the Public Schools' Employment Bureau now suited his temperament. Known as 'pull-through

Thompson' by boys at Repton, he enjoyed driving across the country staying with careers teachers or headmasters, and lecturing pupils, and to this day we meet from time to time men whom he advised in their youth.

But that year there was cause for sadness, too, because in May his brother Edgar – handsome, womanising Edgar, who had had his father's charm, polished by Marlborough College – died of TB, so adding remorse, perhaps, to conflicting emotions mentioned by Christine. Cappy dealt with the funeral arrangements and afterwards handed me Edgar's watch, because I was his godchild. It was too big and, since I never knew Edgar, of no sentimental value – and how could I bear to wear something taken from a corpse? Sickened, I put it on to please our parents and later lost it. But I still treasure Edgar's christening present to me, a delightful silver porringer and spoon, each engraved simply *Diana* – I like to think he knew that when I grew up and used them for sugar, I would not wish my birth date there for all to see.

*   *   *   *

Josephine writes:-

I don't think I was quite so Scottish-minded as the twins, but I found the journey there very exciting. Glencoe, magnificently sombre under storm clouds, was an indelible memory; another at the very end of the arduous drive, was a nerve-wracking confrontation with the Lochaber Laundry's van on a single-track road with a precipice on one side and the wreck of at least one lorry lying in the valley below.

The cottage, Achnatallasaig, stern and grey with neat gables, stood quite alone on unfenced land; only a stretch of grass divided it from the sea. The twins and the parents had the large front bedrooms with views across the Sound; mine was a horrid little room with only a skylight. I swam on the first morning, but the sea water was freezing cold, and, emerging blue with orange splodges all over, I refused to go in again for the rest of the month. The twins, either better-covered or of higher moral fibre, swam every day. Mamma spent the mornings working on her crime novel for Gollancz and Cappy made his endless shopping trips to Arisaig, or to Mallaig if kippers were needed. We explored, searched for caves and canoed when it was fine, read and played Happy Families when it was wet. I remember Christine sobbing endlessly over *Jane Eyre*.

We fetched the milk daily from the farm. I made friends with the farmer's wife, another Mrs Macdonald, and I was soon invited into the kitchen and found myself learning to make soda scones. I don't remember what we talked about, but cold wet mornings passed in the warmth of her kitchen with its blazing range, kneading the large round scones before we cooked them on the griddle, seemed infinitely preferable to swimming. At eleven we would cut sections from a scone, slice them open, spread them with butter and golden syrup and, sitting sociably at the kitchen table, down them with cups of tea. A scone, taken back for the family to sample, was so approved of that the parents later bought a griddle and, whenever there was sour milk at The Grove, I was called upon to make some.

I feel certain that the main reason for Cappy's constant shopping trips was to acquire the latest possible copy of *The Times*. The news was appalling and we had no wireless. In March Hitler had incorporated Austria into Germany and now it was Czechoslovakia's turn. I don't remember the parents talking to us about the situation – perhaps they didn't want to spoil our last holiday – but all through that month they must have been reading about the air raid precautions; thirty-eight million gas masks distributed to regional centres, trenches dug and Britain's pathetic stock of anti-aircraft guns deployed in London parks. When an evacuation scheme was announced eighty-three per cent of London parents had applied for their children to go. As the crisis mounted the House of Commons was recalled from holiday and on September 23rd the French began the mobilization of their forces. I was delegated to ask if we might listen on the farm radio to a speech Hitler was making; this must have been the ultimatum he delivered to the Czechs from the Sports Palace in Berlin on September 25th. We trooped over to the farm and sat stiffly in the Macdonalds' formal front room. At the end of an untranslated extract Mrs Macdonald asked in her soft Highland voice, 'And would that be Cherman?'

To me Hitler's raving and ranting was still something of a joke and was he not rumoured to bite carpets when in a rage? But the parents were filled with gloom and they took no comfort at all from his famous assurance: 'This is the last territorial claim I have to make in Europe.'

Hitler's ultimatum was to expire on September 28th and orders were given for the mobilization of the British fleet. Then, as we seemed on the brink of war, the four powers agreed to meet in Munich, and Prime Minister Chamberlain returned with his agreement, saying that he had '. . . peace with honour. I believe it is peace for our time.' Our parents felt only dishonour at the abandonment of Czechoslovakia, and this was communicated to us.

After our wet holiday and the twins' birthday celebrations, we finally arrived at Wychwood on October 2nd. I don't think anyone had believed Cappy's telegram about the Big End of the car failing, and my friends also refused to accept that we were leaving. When on the last day of term our names were not included in the list of departing seniors, they turned to me in triumph and said, 'There you see, you're *not* leaving.' I don't think the school staff really believed it either and the final report on us threatened, 'Gaiety and high spirits will not find them jobs in life.' This description of us makes me wonder whether the twins were quite as unhappy there as Diana remembers?

It was at Easter 1939, with Denis now working in the theatre, that I was considered old enough to accompany Mamma on her visit to Granny in St Jean Cap Ferrat. On the journey out we saved money by not having couchettes. I found sitting up all night rather arduous, especially as I had developed a boil on my bottom, and on arrival I was deeply disappointed for instead of the incredible blue of the postcards, both sea and sky were grey.

Granny, who had a suite of rooms in the Dardes' private hotel, had booked an extra bedroom for Mamma and me. It was all very comfortable and, as there was Dubonnet at eleven, on an empty stomach, and wine at lunch and dinner, I was deliciously drunk most of the time. I didn't like Madame Darde – sycophantic, short and rounded into a ball by her own good cooking. I would avert my eyes from the two bushes of grey underarm hair which emerged from her sleeveless dresses. The Darde dogs were also a disappointment: small, dingy white, yappy animals, with curly coats and tails, they answered to names like Bou-Bou and Frou-Frou.

We went out with Granny's friends. Mrs Singer took us to lunch at a very grand hotel in Nice – the Réserve, I think – where you could choose your fish, live, from an ornamental pond outside. I decided against fish. The meal was endless and I was persuaded to eat and eat, delicious chocolate ice cream being forced on me when I was already bursting.

When we didn't have enormous lunches, my need to eat at teatime was recognised and I was sent into a patisserie to choose a delicious fruit tartlet. I enjoyed shopping except for the cries of excitement French women gave at the sight of my blue eyes and blonde hair and the constant necessity of explaining that I was not Swedish.

I was rather hurt when on Easter Sunday I presented Mamma and Granny each with a chocolate Easter egg and didn't receive one in return; but later in the day we visited the headmistress of Mamma's old finishing school and she gave me a tiny Russian Fabergé-style egg to wear on a chain, which restored my faith in human nature. Granny loved Mamma but really had no interest in children, and I was good at being seen and not heard. I remember only one real conversation with her, when she advocated the learning of poetry by heart. She told me that now she was old and didn't sleep well, she spent the long nights reciting the poems she had learned in childhood.

Every day there was an expedition. In Monte Carlo, Granny bought Mamma an evening dress. A creation of lace, black taffeta and cherry-red velvet ribbons, it was lovely, but I knew that Mamma would have preferred the money to pay the coal bill. Hanging about in the dress shop was boring, but walking along the terrace outside the Casino, where so many ruined gamblers had cursed their luck for the last time before shooting themselves, was much more to my taste. Another time we drove to Grasse and lunched there with some more of Granny's dignified friends.

The parents had decided that we would all holiday in France for the whole of September that year, so Mamma and I viewed and booked a large apartment in Villefranche. The idea was that Cappy would sunbathe and live a café life, the twins and I would acquire impeccable French accents by doing the household shopping, and Mamma would spend a good deal of her time with Granny. I have always wondered if this was a fantasy born of desperation, for all around us were the signs of war, including the grim, grey battleships gathering in the harbour outside. In Menton Granny wanted to cross the frontier so that I could say I had been in Italy, but we had to leave Silvio, as his papers were mysteriously 'not in order', and walk. It was then, seeing the threatening stance of Mussolini's Fascist troops, that I felt for the first time what

Churchill called the 'hush of suspense, the hush of fear'.

Chapter Seven

Diana writes:-

When the parents told us we were going to have a governess, visions of that often down-trodden breed in Victorian novels leapt to mind. But Hope, a communist and, I suspect, a feminist too, was very different: a graduate, brisk, intelligent, and, at times, amusing. I remember her as brown-haired with, I think, green or hazel eyes, and a fresh complexion. She was of medium height with a bust made prominent by the uplift bra of those days. Her husband Owen, an architect, was finding it hard to get work and, although war seemed inevitable, a medical condition made him unfit for the armed forces; I expect the money our parents paid Hope came in useful.

Hope, who lived locally, arrived every morning at nine o'clock and stayed until twelve-thirty. We all sat round the nursery's gate-legged table, in winter close to a roaring fire, each fortified during our eleven o'clock break by a glass of Australian burgundy, which Mamma said would give us iron and ward off colds and 'flu. Sometimes we slipped away into the kitchen, saying we needed the loo, and returned with a plate of cakes from a batch Joan had cooked; other times we pretended to be drunk and giggled a great deal, and then Hope told us not to be so *bloody silly*. When it rained we were late because, we claimed, the ponies needed drying. But Hope, who called a spade a spade and not a bloody shovel, never got rattled, except when we wound her up by expressing outrageous right-wing views, for we soon learned that we had only to gabble on about grinding the faces of the poor and the laziness of the British worker to interrupt whatever lesson she was taking.

Mamma decided we should study *Julius Caesar* for School Certificate, and continue with *Macbeth*, which we had 'done' at Wychwood. We were each bought for English a copy of *Modern Poetry 1922–1924*, an anthology selected by M. Wollman. I still have my copy and suspect now that some of the poets in this book have been almost forgotten; but there is a poem by one of Josephine's favourites, Humbert Wolfe, and I remember liking 'The Zebras' by Roy Campbell, and 'Cambridgeshire' by Frances Cornford, some of whose work was already known to us. The notes I made in this anthology show how thorough Hope was; no unusual word was left unexplained, and although she accused me of reciting poetry like a vicar preaching in sepulchral tones from a pulpit, I enjoyed our English lessons. We all loved learning 'Friends, Romans, countrymen lend me your ears'. We already knew much of Macbeth by heart and frequently pretended to be the three witches; for who of our age could not revel in 'Double, double toil and trouble; Fire burn, and cauldron bubble' and 'By the pricking of my thumbs, Something wicked this way comes'? Soon 'Open, locks, Whoever knocks' became a frequent cry before closed doors.

We rode most afternoons and every evening we spent at least an hour and a half on homework. Before Hope came I had been living in a sort of intellectual fog, but now, with individual tuition, I started to understand even geometry and algebra for the first time, while in private I tried to write sonnets, which were morbid and naïve but technically sound.

Hope had a knack of criticising without wounding, perhaps because she often balanced her criticism with praise and encouragement. Of course there were boring moments – Civics I hated, although later I was to become very interested in politics. Surprisingly, I can't remember which period of history Christine and I covered – the Tudors?

Mamma, who was happier with us at home, sometimes asked Hope for a glass of sherry along with Mrs Grattan, a don's erudite daughter, who worked as Cappy's secretary for the Public Schools Employment Bureau, typing busily in what was once Denis's bedroom. Other times Hope joined us for lunch and came riding with us afterwards.

Josephine rode nearly a mile on Milky to Hope's house on two evenings a week for extra tuition, because she hoped to study veterinary science at Edinburgh University. But over the years, when Mamma was asked about careers for Christine and me, there had always been a short pause before she said, jokingly, 'The twins will marry rich husbands' – words which seemed to confirm my suspicion that she could not see us fitting into *any* jobs. Yet I did not feel equipped to find a rich husband, for I was ill at ease with men and sexually and emotionally backward. Although I fantasised about hunt balls and love, as expressed in some Victorian poetry, I did not consider myself attractive and when it came to touching other human beings I was hopelessly inhibited.

Then one spring day Hope said to Mamma, 'I shall have no trouble getting Diana through School Certificate,' and I felt as if a window had opened. I was going to get there after all. Netting a man was not the only option. Work became easier. I began to look in the mirror and consider my appearance without being cast-down, and I probably became a little arrogant, because Cappy, who had in the past been irritated by Christine, was now aggravated by me. But I didn't care. Long ago my remark after some slight – 'I walked away with my head held high' – had entered our list of oft-repeated sayings. So no doubt when Cappy seemed to pick on me unfairly, I appeared haughty instead of mortified, and I don't think he ever quite forgave me for that response. I don't blame him, for what father can bear a daughter, for whom he feels he has made financial sacrifices, treating him with disdain? But we were not allowed to argue or answer back; and, with hindsight, I know a wiser man would have had it out with me and cleared the air.

These days Shandy, the pony we had bought as a foal at Reading Market, came with us when we walked with the dogs, happily jumping the stiles we met on our way. And about this time Lady Precious Stream, our turkey hen, temporarily solved a major problem in her life. Her mate Fujiyama had died of bronchitis in a basket by the hot-water pipes in the scullery – our intensive care unit – and Lady Precious Stream had twice sat on her eggs in vain. So, realising she was infertile, she took over a guinea-fowl's nest, with two or three eggs, into which she rolled with her beak a few oval stones and potatoes. Then, puffed out and broody, she settled down to hatch her collection.

Miraculously the fox didn't find Lady Precious Stream and, to her intense joy, two tiny guinea-fowl chicks were born. Fearing perhaps that they might be stolen by their natural parents, she immediately took them away into Spring Wood, to live on blackberries. She returned a few days later, a proud and slightly ridiculous figure towering above her chicks, which she looked after with obsessive care. We called them White Waistcoat and Bow Tie, because of their markings, and watched them grow and turn away from their adoptive mother until eventually they joined their own species, who slept at night in the tall Blenheim apple tree. Then poor Lady Precious Stream keened terribly, as she had after Fujiyama's death, and, too heavy to fly, crouched below the tree. Fearing the fox, we carried her each night as dusk fell to the henhouse. At last she gave up; her mournful turkey cries ended and she never again tried motherhood. Disheartened, Mamma decided not to buy her another mate.

Meanwhile Christine and I had read and were reading more grown-up books. The favourites *Kidnapped* and *Jane Eyre* were followed with whatever interesting books we could find on our parents' shelves, particularly detective novels by Agatha Christie and her contemporaries. Mamma had read *Oliver Twist* and *David Copperfield* aloud to us. And, like Josephine, I had enjoyed three novels by E Nesbit. With the money Granny gave us for Christmas and birthdays, I had also bought books illustrated by Cecil Aldin – I still treasure his *Dogs of Character* and *An Artist's Model. The Studio*, which Denis sometimes left lying around, introduced me to a wider field of art.

Although he visited, Denis no longer lived at home. But the mural of a French café scene, which he had painted on the garage wall, remained to remind us of him. When he *did* come, he usually made some comment about Christine or me, because, after we left Wimbledon, he more than almost anyone else had seen us as individuals rather than as 'the twins'. On one occasion he announced that Christine was suffering from an inferiority complex – he was probably right – and on another he asked why Diana always jumped up first when there was something to be done.

With Hope I became at last a person in my own right, perhaps able, I thought, to catch up with Josephine. Suddenly ambitious, I tried unsuccessfully to write stories about Barney for *The Tailwaggers' Magazine* and a year or so later I won first prize for the best review of an article in *Riding*. With all the arrogance of youth, I had chosen a piece by a well-established expert – was it Faudel-Phillips? – on jumping with the Weedon seat, which I tore slowly apart, unfavourably comparing the style he recommended with the Italian forward seat. For once *Riding* broke with tradition and did not publish the winning entry, for fear, I suppose, of offending the expert.

But before this, Hope's husband Owen found a job in London

and she gave in her notice. War broke out, as Christine will describe, and our parents interviewed another governess. She arrived on a hot summer's day in hat and gloves. While our parents talked to her on the lawn, we hid behind shrubs with a gander and a ferret, wanting to test her courage. When we emerged the poor woman shrank at the sight of the animals and failed on every count.

A few days later our parents asked whether we would like to abandon our formal education, and we said, 'Yes'. 'Promise you will never reproach us,' they said, and we promised. Afterwards Josephine lit a fire and we burned our books on geometry, algebra and mathematics. Deciding to become writers, we appropriated a huge and ancient typewriter Cappy had thrown out. The letter 'R' was missing, but we would write it in ink. We had no pocket money, so Josephine suggested we should start a proper riding school. Christine and I wondered whether we were good enough riders to teach others, but Josephine was adamant. Denis would paint us a sign of a grey horse's head on a black background, to advertise our business to all those who passed down the road. Then we decided to educate ourselves by reading up the subjects which interested us. Suddenly life seemed full of new possibilities. We would write a pony book, too. Perhaps one day we might even be famous.

I suspect that by now I had developed that fine balance of arrogance and insecurity described by Terence Blacker in the 1995 Summer edition of *The Author* as the driving force behind most authors, whatever their calibre.

* * * *

Christine writes:-

As Diana has explained, lessons were never boring with Hope. But we were still naughty, and her enthusiastic lectures on communism had absolutely no influence on me. (Indeed, in later life, when Labour were in office, Diana and I both became ardent Conservatives.) Mentally lazy, I was unable to understand geometry until many years later when waking one morning I cried out triumphantly, 'At last I understand it!' 'Understand what?' asked my long-suffering husband. 'Geometry of course,' I shrieked. Did the mystery unravel in a dream? What else could have cleared a blockage of so many years? I'll never know.

But, returning to my school days, I must confess that although I was often miserable, I must have occasionally been happy too. I suspect that after every setback, and there were many, I simply shrugged my shoulders and returned to my usual exuberant self. I was still a very new soul, for though I wrote poems praising romantic love from an early age, it was many years before I knew anything of carnal desire. But I do remember Diana constantly pleading to be told what she called 'the facts of life': no one responded.

*

We waited a long time for war to be declared. We were issued with gas masks in cardboard boxes. A trickle of evacuees appeared and, it was said, cut up little birds with scissors. After much heart-searching a few parents began sending their children to safety abroad. The Waterhouses and the Kenningtons went and, like others, returned after the war with American or Canadian accents. Some wished that they had never gone, maybe feeling that without being consulted, they had been made to run away. But it was probably more distressing for their parents, who took the decision imagining that they might never see their offspring again. Cappy called a meeting in the drawing-room to discuss the matter. Josephine says it was a highly charged occasion. Eventually we decided that we would live and die together – a decision none of us ever regretted.

Amazingly on that historic day in September, which was to change all our lives, we were still without a radio. Ingenious as ever Cappy decided that we would hear the declaration of war on our tenant's radio. The cottages were now done up and had become one. The beanhole was the bathroom, with frosted glass replacing part of its old battered door. Our tenants were called Gittins and had come from Birmingham. Mrs Gittins was small and bustling, Mr Gittins was tall, thin and bespectacled. I cannot recall their Christian names, but they had two attractive daughters called Ursula and Honour. They all cared a great deal about appearance, and because of this could never have been our kindred spirits. Why Mr and Mrs Gittins wanted to live in Peppard I have no idea. They were not our friends for very long, but on that epoch-making day, we were still on speaking terms. Our parents sat and listened to their radio. I think I stood; maybe there were not enough chairs to go round. When the announcement came, in Neville Chamberlain's measured tones, it was almost an anti-climax; but we knew that with his words our lives had changed for ever. We were finally at war.

I think we walked home in silence. I believe that Mamma decided then that the war would not derail our lives as the previous one had derailed hers. Granny and Denis were still in France. The seas were already dangerous. Would Denis make it home? Would Granny return to England? It was the end of summer and in the orchard the trees were heavy with apples. But it did not feel like summer. In the bath that night, Diana smoked her first cigarette. Imagining Denis dying on some distant battlefield, I shed tears. Mamma quoted, not for the first time, 'God bless the narrow sea that keeps them off.' She had always insisted that we were lucky to be British, with the Channel to deter our foes, and lives unthreatened by earthquakes. Only recently she had told us about the Maginot Line, that wonderful defence the French had built which had miles of underground passages and even bathrooms, she said, a place where soldiers could live in safety and comfort, and an impregnable defence against the Germans for all time. None of us imagined that the Germans might simply go round it.

By now our ponies were steadily increasing in numbers. Before leaving, the Waterhouses had asked us to look after their black pony Susan, a rather dreary character with a white blaze, straight shoulder and low head carriage. We still had Milky and Rum and of course Shandy Gaff. Pennywise had been bought by that great expert, Glenda Spooner who, seeing her competing, at the Kidmore End show, announced that she was a pure-bred Dartmoor and must be registered at once. Knowing that she would now have a wonderful home, I did not mourn her going. Angus, a large-headed, short-legged black Shetland arrived at about this time, and a black and white cat called Magpie, who for some reason was mine, took to riding him bareback. Five or six ponies eat a lot of hay and when Mamma rang Ford and Sons of Hurst and was told that no hay had come into the docks, it was a devastating blow. It was only then that we realised just how much we had relied on food coming from the Commonwealth, English farms having gone to rack and ruin a long time ago.

After a traumatic journey Denis returned safely from France.

Granny, who loathed an English winter, refused to come home. Two days after his return, Denis enlisted in Cappy's old regiment, The Queen's Royal West Surrey Regiment; and since young men no longer needed career guidance, Cappy joined the Board of Trade.

I cannot remember exactly when Denis's cat Simon came to live with us. He had killed a family of kittens while living with Denis (who had been working in rep at a theatre in Bexhill at that time), and had subsequently been neutered. I don't think Simon took any interest in our outside cats. When it was cold he slept in the bottom oven of the Aga or in the airing cupboard in the bathroom. Like many Siamese cats, Simon was temperamental and when annoyed flung things off the kitchen or nursery chimney pieces. He also stole and on one terrible guilt-ridden day helped himself to our neighbours' joint – their entire ration for the week. We had only a pound of sausages to give them in return. The Platts did not complain. The only time I ever heard them complain was when they knocked on our front door and Mamma, who was typing and did not wish to be disturbed, hastily crawled across the room and hid under a table. The knocking continued for some time and afterwards they were to say, 'We knew you were there all the time, because we heard you typing and then it stopped!' But they were not offended, they never were. I cannot remember Mamma's response, but she did tell me that once when she had a visitor, Cappy crawled into the drawing room on all fours, before taking a wanted book out of the bookcase and crawling out again. What she said to the visitor I do not know – probably nothing. But I think it does show that we were an eccentric family!

From the beginning of the war our windows were blacked out. Petrol was rationed and we were reduced to one car. Hunting had resumed on horses that were thinner than a year ago. We tried to ignore the war. We were told it would be over by Christmas and, in the words of the popular song at that time, we would be 'hanging out our washing on the Siegfried Line' long before then. But there was no escape from the eerie feeling of waiting for something to happen. One of Cappy's friends, a schoolmaster I believe, shot himself and his young family rather than let them endure the horrors of the war. Later Cappy was to say that he would do the same if the Germans landed on British soil. None of us believed him.

It was a bitterly cold winter. The ponies grew still thinner. Oats, soon to be rationed, were hard to find. Bowley still worked in the garden. Joan continued to help in the house. But soon Moey (I never knew her real name) left. She came from a large family living nearby and Mamma had only employed her because she needed work. Moey was paid a mere ten shillings a week and was only supposed to come in the mornings but insisted on staying all day, and with Joan fetched wood from the spinney in the pony cart, with much merriment. Even so I felt that Moey hated us. She was only a few years older and when I took the nursery coal scuttle to her in the kitchen and requested coal from the cellar, I always felt uncomfortable. After Moey left, she never spoke to us again. I am sure she made much more money making ammunitions than she would ever have done as a domestic; so in a way war was a blessing for her.

Since we were still being educated at home, we had almost every afternoon free to ride. Food rationing began in January 1940. At last after a long hard winter spring finally arrived to cheer us up, the grass grew, the ponies lost their winter coats, their ribs disappeared and they became sleek and round again.

It was now that Cappy or maybe Mamma announced that they could no longer afford to keep so many ponies, and we started to give riding lessons in earnest – though some time would pass before we became The Grove Riding School, with a sign by the gate of a grey horse's head painted by Denis on a black board, and even longer before we became a limited company. (This was to placate Cappy, who because we were under age, feared that if we were declared bankrupt he would be liable for our debts.) So we became responsible for the ponies' food, shoes and any vet bills which occurred.

After Dunkirk, which was a great shock to us all, the Local Defence Volunteers were formed, later to be called the Home Guard. Cappy, like many ex-soldiers, was quick to join, and took command of the area around us. The garage filled up with bayonets on the end of metal tubes, belts of ammunition, and field dressings – which came in handy after the war for our horses.

Mr Gittins joined the Home Guard. Spurred on, I suspect, by his wife, he complained that when Cappy collected him for meetings he hooted his car horn – 'treating him like a little dog', his wife added furiously. (We of course were well-accustomed to being hooted at, and had never considered ourselves treated like dogs.) The Gittins could have taken into account that Cappy was lame and that by giving Mr Gittins a lift, he was doing him a favour. I am not sure whether the lifts continued after that, but from then on the Gittins were on our black list and must be cut dead by all of us. They were not the only ones on the list and we had long perfected the art, advancing on the proscribed person or persons with direct eye contact and then, at the very last minute, turning away with haughty expression and curled lip. We never questioned the list; for an order was an order in our house. Sometimes Cappy did not see eye to eye with his superior officer in the Home Guard, but fortunately it never reached the stage of a feud.

The Times and the Daily Graphic were delivered daily to The Grove so by this time we knew for certain that we would not be 'hanging out our washing on the Siegfried Line' in the foreseeable future.

I can no longer recall all the ponies which we bought or were lent during those early years of war. Certainly we bought Cocktail in April 1940. Dark brown, hogged, docked and cobby, he had bucked off his owner so frequently that the boy had given up riding. Cocktail cost us twelve pounds. He was not an easy ride. His trot was fast and unbalanced and the first time we cantered him, he bucked two of us off. We schooled him every day, setting an alarm clock which rang when one person's turn ended and the next began. At last, after many weeks of schooling and too many tosses to mention, Cocktail gave up bucking and we wrote a story about him called 'Cocktail Capitulates', which really began our literary careers. It was published in *Riding* and was soon followed by another called 'The Road to Ruin' which was about a spoilt pony we had failed to cure of rearing. He was based, I believe, on a Welsh pony called Brecon.

We bought more ponies in 1941. Bordeaux was one of them; rather long-backed and black, he bullied his owners and refused to leave the stable yard. He was also difficult to catch; but when he found we were not to be bullied, he gave in. Three days after we had bought him for five pounds he won rosettes at a local gymkhana. Subsequently he became one of the most useful ponies in the riding school.

Pablo, a tiny pony, was black too. He had been dying when his owners rescued him from gypsies. They nursed him back to health but, loving him too much, allowed him to become such a tyrant that they could not touch him without a titbit in their hands.

'Give me something to eat or else,' threatened Pablo with ears back, before attacking them with hoofs and teeth. One good thump from us and he stopped biting, a second thump and he stopped kicking. His owners had begged us to take Pablo for a mere five pounds. He was another bargain, in a long line of bargains which followed. It wasn't long before anyone who wanted to sell a difficult pony rang the Pullein-Thompsons. And it was surprising how many who came to us were simply misunderstood.

Melody was one of the few ponies we bought without a blemish on her character. A dear little Dartmoor, barely twelve hands high, she could not bear to be stabled, and, like Shandy Gaff, taught my children to ride in her old age. She grew rather fat and, several weeks after we bought her, presented us with an unexpected foal which we named Windfall.

As time passed, our pupils increased in number; there was little amusement for children at that time, so riding suddenly became fashionable. I remember one charming little girl from Pinner asking whether the pony she was riding took off his shoes when he went to bed at night!

Sometimes I am asked whether I was ever frightened in the war? I can honestly say no. So good was our propaganda, so certain were we of British superiority, that even the disappearance of signposts and the stacks of weapons in the garage failed to alarm me. So when one day an elderly member of the Home Guard arrived in our yard on his bike, carrying a gun, shaking with fear and crying out, 'They've come, they've come,' Josephine and I – the only people at home at the time – remained cool. Looking up at the clear summer sky above us, seeing no aeroplanes and hearing no guns, we told him to report to the assembly post in the builders' yard at the end of the road. To our surprise he left without arguing. Soon afterwards a farmer telephoned to say that someone had been tampering with his haystack. (I think he imagined a German had slept there.) Calmly Josephine told him to investigate it and then to report to the assembly point. A little later someone rang to ask whether they should ring the church bells. Josephine says now she had been instructed by Cappy that the bells were only to be rung if the invasion had truly begun. So we said no, not for the time being anyway. I do not know what actually happened at the assembly point that summer's day, but Peppard's church bells remained silent, though Nettlebed and other parishes rang theirs. Mamma and Diana eventually returned home from their ride complaining loudly that they had been stopped at every checkpoint and asked for their identity cards. 'Do we really look like the enemy?' Mamma asked, sounding both amused and bewildered. I cannot remember anyone complaining that at such a possibly crucial moment in the war, two teenage girls were actually in command of a contingent of the Home Guard.

One evening after the battle in the skies had been won and the Blitz had begun, we stood in the road and, looking at a sky red with flames, knew that more than thirty miles away London was burning. The Germans did not drop bombs on Peppard or Sonning Common. It was said that Hitler wanted to preserve Oxford for his seat of power, so had instructed his pilots to leave the area untouched. Whether this was true I do not know; but one night a plane, probably flown by a pilot who could not face the barrage around London, dropped its bombs nearby. We assembled in the kitchen and drank tea, waiting for more bombs to fall; but none did. Next morning we found shrapnel on the lawn and heard that windows were shattered in nearby Shiplake Bottom and there was a bomb crater at Gallowstree Common. Only poor Shandy, limping sadly, appeared to be injured. Our vet Miss Thomson was called, and announced that he had slipped his stifle. She pushed it back into place and instructed us to paint it with iodine and to be sure he rested, preferably on a tether.

A few days later, after a wet night, we woke to find the kitchen in chaos. Eggs lay smashed, the bread bin was empty, oatmeal was everywhere, mixed with tea-leaves from the caddy; and the floor was covered with small, muddy, unshod hoof prints. 'It must be Shandy,' we shrieked, rushing outside to find him. He was standing by his tethering stake looking calm and serene, but nothing could hide the fact that he was no longer attached to it. We knew then for certain that Shandy, as we had always suspected, was of unusual intelligence. (Of course, he would not have been able to invade the kitchen if Cappy had not returned late from a Home Guard meeting and left the back door ajar; and he would not have known about the kitchen at all if we had not taken him into it on numerous occasions when we enjoyed what was then called 'elevenses' by us, and by others 'lunch', a light snack taken at eleven o'clock with tea, coffee or milk if young.)

About this time, ignoring the Blitz, Cappy started to stay in London during the week, sleeping at his club and sometimes visiting The Players' Theatre. We were now expected to fill up forms from the Ministry of Agriculture stating, among many other things, how many lettuces we had growing in the garden. These forms were a great trial to Mamma as someone had to count the lettuces.

One dreadful night around midnight, the telephone rang. Always the quickest to wake, I leapt from my bed and rushed to pick up the receiver in Cappy's office. It was a totally unexpected call from a hospital in Lichfield to say that Denis was dying of a burst appendix. Silently Cappy and Mamma prepared to leave. Josephine, the old soul, handed them a thermos of coffee for the journey. It was a dark night and raining as they left, driving away into the blackout on a long, hazardous journey. The next day Nana, who must have been contacted by Mamma via Aunt Dot, arrived to look after us – though I'm sure we could have managed without her. Each night Mamma rang from Lichfield to tell us the depressing news that there was no change in Denis's condition. So as the doctor had said there was no hope, they sat waiting for Denis to die. To make things worse when Denis begged for ice and later for tomato soup, the nurses refused him, saying crossly that they had to keep the fridge shut ready for the air raid casualties. Mamma was to say later that it had been difficult to believe that Denis would die, when such wonderful witticisms were falling from his lips, but what they were I do not know. She was right, however, for he did survive.

Soon after Mamma and Cappy returned home, they were summoned back again by another call from the hospital, taken again by me in the small hours; but this time when they reached the hospital after driving through a blaze of falling bombs, Denis was out of danger once again.

As our pupils grew in number and older in years, many became our friends. I recall sitting under an apple tree with a group not much older than ourselves, with a book on fortune telling, given to Cappy as a farewell present by his London secretary. I think it must have been Josephine who was reading our hands; at times the results were embarrassing and frighteningly accurate, for the lines were strangely truthful, so that those who were selfish were decreed selfish and those who were greedy were described thus. It was then we discovered that Diana and I had heart and head lines woven in a continuous chain across the centre of our palms; this, according to the book, meant that our hearts and heads always worked together, making us strong, if sometimes uncaring, characters. My hands have remained the same while Diana's heart and head lines are now separate. Has she changed so much, while I have remained the same? I wish I knew. I have read somewhere that this peculiarity is often seen on the palms of children suffering from Down's Syndrome, though I cannot vouch for the truth of this.

By 1942 the buses from Reading to Peppard were filling up with children on their way to ride with us; they came on bikes too, often arriving before eight in the holidays and at the weekends to help us bring the ponies home from their scattered fields. Soon during the summer some stayed until six or seven in the evenings, and with many parents away all day doing war work the Grove Riding School became a second home.

It was about this time that we acquired two ancient upright bikes. We called them Victoria and Albert and rode them to the furthest field which was at Cane End. They had no lights and wonky brakes and often their chains came off, but it was still possible on a good day to lead two ponies tied to one another if you pedalled steadily and met nothing frightening on the way.

Quite early on, we made certain rules concerning the ponies working for us, and they were never changed; no pony was expected to work for more than three hours in one day without resting the following one. Every pony was to have at least two weeks holiday a year without shoes. And the stables were closed one day a week so that every pony had a day off.

Our classes in the holidays were at ten, eleven and two-thirty. When it was very hot the afternoon class was transferred to the evening. Sometimes we held a scholarship class for promising riders who could not afford lessons, and this was in the evening too. When the ground was hard, jumping and cantering were abandoned except in the woods where centuries of fallen leaves carpeted the ground. The first class in the morning was for the best riders, the second was for the not so good and the one in the afternoon was for beginners and generally took place in the paddock. Many of the ponies had to journey to their fields morning and evening, but they were all extremely fit. Illness among them was rare, lameness almost unknown and we never had a case of laminitis.

It was not long before we were also giving individual lessons, often to adults, for which we charged extra. I think Josephine was the most talented instructor, but I am told that I was the kindest.

Personally I felt then and I feel now that encouragement is the essence of good teaching. It is the same with horses: encouragement and praise, in my opinion, produce far better results than punishment. Diana combined both virtues and had her own devoted band of followers.

Most of the ponies seemed very happy with us; they liked the routine and the companionship of other ponies. Eventually Tarragona, having grown old, went to a new home. After a few days she jumped the hedge which fenced her field and appeared in the stable yard in time for the first ride, having covered three or more miles at breakneck speed – a sad reflection on growing old, and also confirmation of how happy she had been with us.

And now of course we were writing when we had time. Growing up with a mother who was an author, it seemed a natural thing to do, and with so many ponies and riders passing through our hands, we were not short of material – it was there in front of us all the time.

* * * *

Diana writes:-

When on the first day of war that air-raid siren wailed its message unforgettably across the blue skies of England, our parents had gone to the New Inn at Kidmore End, where they met their friends for a glass or two of beer every Sunday. We were still children, but for me the ominous siren stood for change, the end of an era. And the sunshine only increased the obscenity of impending bloodshed; for how could humans be so vile, so tiresome, when the world was at this moment so beautiful? The cigarette Mamma handed me in the bath (which I'm told I asked for), I smoked with bravado rather than pleasure, feeling it marked for me the end of childhood.

But the war itself? What do I remember of those first two and a half years which has not already been said by Christine – or is about to be told by Josephine, who likes to put everything into historical context? The claustrophobic smell of gas masks; identity cards which we usually forgot to carry; Dunkirk; searchlights sweeping the night sky, occasional ack-ack gunfire, and the roar of planes, coming and going, German and British. And no more joints of meat or mocha cakes. Darning socks, until they became more darns than anything else; sewing chamois leathers, which needed no coupons, on the inside legs of our jodhpurs. A stomach which always rumbled well before meal times, because we were still growing and working as hard as Land Girls, but without their extra rations.

Second-hand clothes. And a growing sense of achievement as the riding school grew, and difficult ponies, whose psychology we tried to understand, became rideable and obliging – for what is more rewarding than persuading a child or animal to change ways that have made their lives impossible, miserable or useless? There was one pony, Brown Sherry, who hated riders so much she tried to remove them by jumping sideways into thorn hedges, fences or gates. In comparison, backing young horses was easy, so long as no one had been there before us and made a mess of things. For if they trust you they are quite happy for you to sit astride them, especially if they have watched their companions being ridden. If they buck, it means you have moved too quickly. Fortunately we agreed totally about how ponies should be schooled and pupils instructed.

On very hot days we taught and rode only before ten in the mornings and after half-past-seven in the evenings. Between these times the ponies rested under trees in the yard; we covered our arms, legs and faces with olive oil, while it was still available and, wearing large straw hats, lay blissfully on the lawn under trees reading books. But whatever the weather, six times a week, we journeyed to rented fields up to two miles away to collect and return ponies; sometimes sitting very upright on Victoria or Albert, or jogging before jogging became fashionable, reciting poetry or singing on our way. The picture-postcard wells at Cane End and Gallowstree Common, now gone, provided us with water, which we carried to troughs or discarded baths. We bought an old yoke, which must have been made for men because it dug into our shoulders. At Kingwood Common, where we rented an orchard, we chucked buckets down a more primitive well and tugged them up three-quarters full. In winter we carried haynets to ponies on their day off, working, like all those who cared for animals, seven days a week.

Much of the time I revelled in feeling strong. Like Italian peasants, we used for hay every yard of spare unfenced grass we could lay our hands on, cutting it with a grass hook and bringing it back in a cart pulled by Susan. Dried nettles were useful, too, as they have a high proportion of protein. We mucked out stables, unloaded lorries of hay when we were lucky enough to get it, or cut it from our own stack. Often we rode up to six or seven hours a day, and cleaned tack late into the evenings in the kitchen to the sound of music on the gramophone.

Evacuees, left alone by their working 'aunties', brought sandwiches and spent their days during school holidays and at weekends in our yard. We gave them riding lessons when we had suitable ponies to spare. Sisters Cathy and Winnie, tense, pretty little girls, from, I think, Shepherd's Bush, would turn up at eight in the morning along with more privileged children to help us fetch up the ponies, riding bareback. It was a new life for me setting out with halters and a gang of children on sunlit mornings with the birds singing and the dew still wet on the grass, especially as I was at last *Diana*, not just one of the twins, and I found I liked being with children; in fact I liked having people of all ages around me all day, because I was, it turned out, very gregarious.

More and more pupils came, lured by word of mouth or the typed postcards we put in the saddlers' shops and elsewhere. A few lodged in the village in the holidays to ride with us every day. The Grove became then a meeting place and sometimes a refuge for children not happy at home. Mick, who didn't care for ponies, spent his spare time in our kitchen, running errands for Mamma, grinding coffee and fetching coke or anthracite up from the cellar. Mick's parents had not allowed him to take up a place at Henley Grammar School, because they were afraid he would get stuck up. So when his friend Val went, he was out on a limb. Afterwards, standing with his back against the Aga, he became almost as much a fixture as Simon on the chimney piece above.

We studied *Equitation* by Henry Wynmalen, and marked out a school with white-washed stones in the top meadow, where we had our jumps. Our riding lessons usually ended with races of one kind or another, to keep daredevils interested. Other times we took groups of riders hacking through the woods, over fields and commons and across Peppard Common, whose vivid green slopes and bunkers – it had once been a golf course – were tempered by the more muted shades of bushes and trees, until the yellow gorse set them ablaze. Burnt Platt, Witheridge Hill, Woodcote and Checkendon, Stoke Row, Dog Lane, Shepherd's Green, Highmoor and Nettlebed, Cray's Pond, Little Bottom Wood and Satwell, the Devil's Elbow and Hook End: these names, and many more, run through my head like never-to-be-forgotten songs, marking a moment of my life which was surely, despite the war, as happy as anyone's life can be.

With little hay around, we were always looking for more pasture. The sight of an empty field within two miles of us would send us running to the owner's doorstep. So when I saw an empty, overgrown paddock opposite the Greyhound on the Gallowstree Common Road I did not hesitate. And when a stricken, inaudible voice answered my knock at the open back door, I wandered inside and came upon a dying woman, whom I remember – surely wrongly – as Miss Mildew; a shrunken wreck alone on a dirty, dishevelled bed, all skin and bone, her neck tendons like rope, her hopeless eyes sunken berries in a grey face, her lips pale as paper. I had to go so close to hear the hoarse words dragged painfully from her defeated body that I could hardly bear to ask more than a single question. But she managed to say 'Yes'. We fixed a price and I walked home on leaden legs.

'What's the matter with her?' I asked Joan.

'Cancer of the throat,' she said.

'Does anyone look after her?'

'A neighbour goes in.'

It was my biggest shock since Mr Shea. The poor woman was, I suppose, a hopeless case and in those days before the National Health Service, there was perhaps no hospital place or hospice for her. Or did she want to die alone in her own bed? That question and the vision of her lonely misery haunt me still. And yet I never mentioned my shock at seeing Miss Mildew to my sisters. Deeply felt emotions were private and unspoken worries to be shut away in the subconscious and maybe brought out in gloomy moments for further thought.

We never saw bomb victims, but I remember staring in awed silence at the red glow behind the spinney, dramatic against the pines I loved, which was London burning. Then, naturally high-spirited, we buried the worry in work. Foxhunting around us was soon to stop; gymkhanas and horse shows continued as a pleasure for all those who had not left to fight. Bowley, now a soldier in the Pioneer Corps, came to see us, his uneven, brownish teeth replaced by a shining set of false ones. Miss Thomason arranged for a lorry-load of flyers (the husks of oats) to be delivered to us, because, dampened and sprinkled with salt, they helped fill our ponies' bellies.

Joan, now Mrs Chandler, left in 1940 a month or so before Jim, the eldest of her five children, was born. Not very long afterwards she nursed her mother until her death from cancer in 1942. Later, when family life allowed, she came back to work for us part-time. I look back on Joan now as a kind friend and often a mentor, too, for she seemed to know almost everyone in the village and was never afraid to tell us where we had gone wrong. She once advised me on how I should manage Cappy. She was not herself very put off by his temper, although she remembers revenging a slight by furiously tipping curry powder into a dish until the resulting meal was unbearably hot. The message got home and in later years, after I had left The Grove, Cappy would ask, when over-spiced meals were served, 'What have I done now to offend Joan?'

After Joan departed, help in the house became spasmodic. Mamma washed up, with our help, and cooked, but jibbed at heavy housework, so sometimes one of us scrubbed the lovely red flagstone floor in the dining room, where later we were all to write sitting round the same table. For although rather dark, this room was cool in summer and warm in winter; its open fire was fed with logs, which we were sent to saw in the scullery if we complained of being cold, sensibly killing two birds with one stone.

The winter of 1940 was bitter. There were weeks when the ground was too hard and icy for riding. In bed with 'flu, we passed round the thermometer, and then whoever had the lowest temperature got up and fed and watered the animals. I remember a day when Mamma and I trudged carrying haynets through the snow to Kingwood Common. On the way home our temperatures rose and we giggled rather hysterically over nothing. The next day we were worse and Mamma became delirious and saw fish on the wall, so Christine and Josephine braved the weather. Cappy was working in London and there was at this time no help in the house. The blue cupboard in the kitchen was almost empty of provisions, apart from packets of a chocolate pudding mix which we cooked over and over again, until no one wanted ever to eat a chocolate pudding again.

Every winter of the war we caught 'flu. Once when Joan turned up we welcomed her as a saviour; but she had come for glucose for Jim, who was ill, and was in no mood to help us. Another time Robert, a village boy, whom we taught to ride for nothing, rescued us and fed all the animals.

Worse than 'flu, because they were more insidious and unsightly, were our boils. My first ones appeared in late 1939 and resurfaced whenever I worked hard, until penicillin became widely available in the early nineteen-fifties. As they ripened, boils woke you at night and when the pain seemed almost unbearable you crept downstairs, boiled a needle or sterilised a knife and tried to lance them. When they finally burst you welcomed the revolting flow of greenish pus almost as a friend. The final moment arrived when the boil's root came out, leaving a small dark pit which I erroneously called the black hole of Calcutta. Dr Field gave us medicinal yellow powder, probably sulphonamide-based, which we mixed with water and painted on the boils without effect.

Surprisingly, German planes only once attacked Reading, a large railway junction, and dropped just two or three bombs, on the British Restaurant and the Heelas department store where, because it was early closing day, casualties were few. I only felt threatened much later when I heard the doodlebugs overhead and knew that if their engines cut off a rocket might drop on us.

By 1940 Christine was the healthiest and the tallest of us. She was up first in the mornings, mucked out stables most speedily, and, although she ran the highest temperatures (or perhaps because she ran them), made the quickest recoveries from flu.

The spring and summer weather of that year had been superb, which made the news of the fall of the Low Countries all the more distressing for me, because of my crazy idea that when the sun shone we should all rejoice.

> *Today I feel so happy, so happy,*
> *I don't know why I'm happy, I only know I am,*

we had sung for years. And:

> *The sun has got his hat on, hip, hip, hip, hurray,*
> *The sun has got his hat on and is coming out today.*

And now horrible, ranting Hitler was wrecking everything.

Our friendship with the Dutch inventor Henry Wynmalen, whom Josephine will describe, made us feel affectionately towards the Dutch and brought the awful tragedy closer to us. Yet, despite the dire news, there was the pleasure of ready money in our pockets for the first time. We could catch a bus into Reading whenever we wanted. When Mamma handed us the dentist's bill and suggested we pay it, we felt we were grown-up in responsibility if not in years.

We started our first book, *It Began with Picotee*, writing most of it on the ponies' days off, which were Sundays during the holidays and Mondays during term-time. The first few lines, written in pencil in a sixpenny exercise book from Woolworths, were prosaic:

> *We all were sitting at breakfast one morning at the beginning of the Christmas holidays, when Mummy showed us a letter from a woman we knew slightly, called Mrs Chantry, asking whether we would like to borrow a pony called Tony, which she had bought for her daughter, Jennifer, who couldn't manage him and had decided to give up riding.*

Several of the three girls' adventures in this book mirror ours; and Cocktail features as Bronx. We argued good-naturedly while writing *It Began with Picotee*, and giggled a lot, and, although the book was not to be published until after the war, the story was finished, apart from a little tidying up, by the spring of 1942 – without our parents' knowledge. By this time I had started writing my own book, *I Wanted A Pony*, which was influenced by Mamma's *A Pony for Jean*. This story, like many of my children's books, is as much about human relationships as ponies, perhaps because I was still trying to come to terms with my own failures.

Meanwhile, Mr Sworder brought us a temperamental, dark brown mare to school and sell, whom we called Tarragona. Tarragona was self-willed, hard-mouthed and traffic-shy. Her instinct was to flee when frightened, ignoring her rider's aids and jumping any obstacles in her way. The first time I rode her in a show she leapt out of the ring over three rows of chairs, which were fortunately empty. When I rode her down the Old Bath Road by Hare Hatch, she jumped into a restaurant's garden because she saw a lorry approaching. But her most dramatic escape happened as I rode her home from a field in a headcollar, bareback and leading a pony either side of me. The Home Guard had been busy the previous night making barbed-wire barriers to impede the enemy should they invade. One of these, which was decorated with white rags so local people could see it in the blackout, caught Tarragona's eye as we approached it on a patch of grass opposite Peppard post office.

'It's all right,' I patted her neck and urged her on, and we were almost safely past when a gust of wind set the white rags fluttering. And then Tarragona was away, hoofs clattering on the tarmac, and no amount of tugging at the headcollar would stop her. I let the other ponies go as The Grove came into sight; they turned up the drive and a few pupils dashed to the gate to see who was galloping by. Seconds later Tarragona and I passed the Kews' farm and turned right at the Butcher's Arms and down past the Bottomless Pond. Then my tugs at the headcollar grew more frantic because now we were heading for the main Reading-Peppard Road, which even in war took a good deal of traffic including buses. Supposing in her madness Tarragona crashed into some vehicle and we were both killed? But we were in luck, the road was empty and I managed to steer her straight across and up the hill beyond. (Hills are sometimes a rider's best friend.) Out of breath, we came to the fish shop, where Mamma sometimes sent us to buy whale meat when our meat ration was spent, and Tarragona broke into a walk; I jumped off and led her home. I was greeted by cries of 'John Gilpin!' and my gallop became a joke, but thereafter we always took a bridle when we fetched Tarragona up from the fields.

Tarragona became a great character and a good showjumper, although her dressage never reached Pony Club Inter-Branch Competition standard. So when Mr Sworder started to bring prospective buyers to see her, our hearts sank. He wanted twenty-five guineas for her, while we could only afford seventeen pounds. But fortunately for us she possessed one trait which made her unsuitable for many children – Tarragona could not bear to be laughed at. So when she was back in the stable after a trial ride we only had to stand in front of her door as she looked over, and laugh, and then, with ears back, she would bare her teeth and lunge at us viciously, unmistakable fury in her eyes. The prospective buyers would recoil and change their minds and Mr Sworder would agree that she wasn't quite suitable for *kiddies* after all.

The day came when Mr Sworder asked if by any chance we would like to buy Tarragona. 'She'd be handy in your school,' he said. We offered him fifteen pounds and he said, 'Twenty,' and there followed one of those pauses which come about when two people are trying to strike a bargain, before we said 'Seventeen?' And he agreed. We shook hands. Mr Sworder watched me writing the cheque.

'Not like that,' he said. 'Never leave a gap there. Someone could put a one in front of the seventeen, and make it one hundred and seventeen. And don't leave a gap there either or a sharp customer could add nineteen shillings.' Tarragona *was* useful in the school. She won lots of prizes, but lacking patience, would tread on the feet of any children who spent too long grooming her. Yet she loved being with us, and when at last our school shut down, she escaped from her new home at Stoke Row and returned to The Grove's now empty yard.

Much earlier, Denis, looking pale and thin, had been home during the first stage of his recovery from his acute peritonitis, but he left quite soon to stay in an army convalescent home, after Cappy, whose leg was probably hurting, quarrelled with him. Apart from Josephine, Cappy didn't like his children around him. He would fight our causes, be proud if we enjoyed success – although we only heard this second-hand from Mamma – but would have been happier if he had been an upper-class father with his children behind a green baize door. Mamma said all men were like bulls, difficult when they reached middle age. And, of course, at this time he was also suffering from the Blitz.

Cappy, who had come out top of his course at the Staff College at the end of the First World War and believed himself to be a good tactician, was soon at odds with his Home Guard commanding officer, Colonel Ogilvie, who had seen less active service. Cappy's hip had locked, fixing his leg at the wrong angle, but, although near mental collapse, he never complained. Then an orthopaedic surgeon, who was a member of Cappy's club, offered to break the leg and straighten it out. So Cappy went into the Royal Orthopaedic Hospital, Stanmore, where we all visited him; afterwards he said his operation and convalescence had saved him from a nervous breakdown.

Waiting for Denis to die and the other unspoken anxieties of war had taken their toll of Mamma, too. Although *Idle Apprentice* and *Death at the Dog* (set at the New Inn) came out in 1940 and *Blind Messenger* the following year, there was an uncharacteristic gap before *More Ponies for Jean* (which was inspired by our school) appeared in 1943. When food was scarce, Mamma always insisted she didn't want a second helping. She began to cough at night and when we suggested she went to the doctor, she said, it was nothing, just smoker's cough. There is a moment I shall not forget when she stood, hands in hot washing-up water, and said flatly and wearily, 'Granny's gone.' And none of us comforted her, for at that stage in our lives we only knew how to comfort animals and children. Anyway, if we had, Mamma might well have been embarrassed.

Granny had refused to come home when war broke out, although all her three daughters had offered to accompany her, saying firmly that she would rather face Hitler than the English climate. As the war went on her financial returns from stocks and shares had come increasingly slowly through Portugal and Switzerland. And Mme Darde, hating the British for leaving the French in the lurch – as she saw it – did not like waiting for money. Granny sold her car and boat to pay Mme Darde and then gave her some of her belongings including a fur coat in lieu of payment. But when Granny died, it was Silvio, now working against his will as a chauffeur for the Germans, who found money for a burial and temporary grave and an English chaplain, still resident in the South of France, who wrote to Mamma.

In 1941 or thereabouts, I lost a top front tooth, when an abscess developed and my face swelled. The French dentist who had replaced Mr Bruce stopped root canal work when he began to fear cellulitis. I was riding Tarragona, my temperature rising, when Mamma told me I had to go back and have it out under gas. The gap never closed, which is why – as photographs show – I smiled with my mouth shut for almost twenty years, until a dentist filled the gap. Yet that summer I decided naïvely that the jumping prize Tarragona and I won soon afterwards was meant to cancel out my loss, proving that bad luck could sometimes be an advance payment for success.

Parties were few and far between. Most of our clothes coupons went on riding gear. Riding, writing and books became our life. With no radio of our own – the parents' was strictly for their own use – we were at a loss when contemporaries talked of ITMA, Much-Binding-in-the-Marsh or other popular wartime programmes. In bad weather we resorted to the gramophone and, when Cappy was in London, Mamma would come to the nursery and urge us, if we were listening to songs, to slow the turntable down so that she could hear the words, which always meant more to her than the music. We played 'South of the Border', The Chocolate Soldier, The Merry Widow, the 'Barcarolle' from The Tales of Hoffmann, Madam Butterfly, Strauss waltzes and much more in the same vein. Christine and I liked Richard Tauber and later discovered Gigli and Edith Piaf. Mamma sang 'Abide With Me' and 'You are my Heart's Delight,' and 'Just a Song at Twilight', and none of us was musical enough to know she was out of tune.

We became a team which survived another decade and, after the war, ran a second riding school at Wolvercote, Oxford. We gave each other riding lessons, competed in practice sessions against one another and in shows, and so long as a Pullein-Thompson won a competition, no one minded being beaten by a sister. Later it was the same with our books – surprisingly we were not then jealous of each other. Fortunately the pupils appeared to show no preference for any one of us.

Ironically, we who had disliked teachers loved teaching. Josephine was the most systematic, Christine the most easy-going and I was, as usual, somewhere in the middle, although I liked to think, perhaps wrongly, that I specialised more than the others in explaining *why* we rode in a certain way. We were all asked, while still in our teens, to judge at shows and gymkhanas; and eventually we each possessed our own grey horse. When Christine and I left the field, Josephine went on to become a well-known riding instructress and one-day-eventer on Rosebay, who was sired by Henry Wynmalen's Hungarian Arab, Basa.

So we grew up belonging to no outside group, no teenage craze, no movement, learning what we wanted to learn from books. We grew accustomed to being with all sorts of people, and over the years countless children and ponies provided, without knowing it, material for our stories. But I always felt and still feel that however conventionally we might dress or behave we were never quite like other people, neither superior nor inferior, just different.

* * * *

Josephine writes:

When war was declared I think everyone expected instant horror; we braced ourselves for gas attacks, for bombs to rain down on us, and, as Cappy had put it, to die together. Some people, who remembered the 1914–18 war and were convinced that this one would be even worse, fled to the United States or committed suicide. When Cappy's friend killed his wife and then put his head in a gas oven – my version is different from Christine's, and I don't think they had children – the executors sent Cappy his wrist watch (a half-hunter) and he gave it to me. I displayed it proudly and heartlessly, telling everyone that it had belonged to a murderer.

The Gollans, who lived on the west side of Peppard Common, had never forgotten the terrible sufferings of the horses in the last war and, sending for the vet, they had their beloved hunters shot. Later it transpired that gun-horses and officers' chargers were no longer needed; the army was fully mechanized, and only the occasional pack pony or mule was used for carrying supplies in mountainous terrain.

As the months of the 'phoney' war passed, our fear faded and life became boring. The parents remained apprehensive, and Mamma hated it when Joan and Moey sang the triumphant songs of the period: 'We're Going to Hang out the Washing on the Siegfried Line' and 'Run Rabbit Run'. CLOSED FOR THE DURATION notices appeared on the doors of clubs and non-essential businesses; it became unpatriotic to give parties, and the Pony Clubs, which had lost their organizers to the war effort, ceased to function.

Before our education had been totally abandoned Cappy had written round the veterinary colleges trying to find me a place, but it seemed that women were not wanted and the small number of places allotted to us were filled for many years ahead. When the parents had worked out that I would not qualify until my late twenties, Mamma explained apologetically that, as they couldn't support me until then, I must choose another profession. I think I was only mildly disappointed and I promptly decided to become an equitation expert.

Horsemanship in Britain was at a very low ebb. Throughout the 'twenties and 'thirties our riders had been hopelessly out-classed in international jumping competitions, and dressage was unknown or mockingly referred to as 'that dressage and massage stuff'. Becoming aware of this, the twins and I turned away from the hearty but unscientific works by English cavalry officers to read foreign writers. Fillis was interesting, but too abstruse; there was no point in teaching horses to canter backwards on three legs. But we discovered a very lucid work on the forward seat, by Piero Santini of the Italian cavalry; and *Equitation* by the Dutchman, Henry Wynmalen, instantly became our bible. The photographs in both books convinced us that horses were far happier ridden over fences and downhill with the forward seat, so we adopted it immediately, despite our unsuitable saddles: all were straight cut and some had knee rolls, which made riding with short stirrups impossible. Gazing at photographs of the permanent course at Geneva, I began to dream of the day when British shows would have solid fences instead of flimsy poles topped with lathes, that earned you half a fault if your horse swished one off with his tail.

Henry Wynmalen's book introduced us to dressage, and schooling a pony assumed new dimensions. Kicking with the heels became barbaric; the rider's legs and seat had to create impulsion invisibly. Every corner became interesting when, instead of swinging round in polo-pony style, you had to bend your pony in the direction of the movement, and make sure his hindlegs followed the same track as his forelegs. We became proficient at turns on the forehand, could announce airily that the rein-back was a forward movement in two-time, and were soon attempting shoulder-in.

It seemed an extraordinary piece of good fortune when we learned that Henry Wynmalen had come to live at Hare Hatch – only twelve miles away – and was to share the mastership of the Woodland with Colonel Hill. Our first meeting with our new hero was inauspicious. We were out hunting – two of us on rough borrowed ponies – and when a longed-for fence appeared we all raced for it at once. H.W., as we were soon to call him, gave a furious roar, followed by a lecture on the dangers of jumping on another rider's 'tail'. Used to Cappy's roars we were not too cast down. We had observed that H.W. rode beautifully, that his splendid horse was better schooled than any we had seen before, and, while we tried to placate him by hurrying to open recalcitrant gates, we were already plotting.

H.W. had retained the charisma of his youth. He had been an early and intrepid aviator, winning the Paris-to-Brussels race and the Grand Prix for altitude flying; and with his first wife, a well-known singer until she was struck down by illness he had been fêted all over Europe. Now it was rumoured he was in the construction business and erecting aircraft hangars for the Government. Obviously we couldn't ask him to give us riding lessons, but perhaps if we formed a riding club . . .

I appointed myself secretary of the Woodland Riding Club, which was to be restricted to experienced riders, and telephoned round our horsey contemporaries. Deprived of holiday amusements, they were delighted to join, and we agreed to meet to jump each other's jumps, and for occasional instruction. When the membership reached ten, each paying a subscription of 2/6d, it was plainly my duty to telephone H.W. and persuade him that, in the interests of horsemanship, it was *his* duty to instruct us. I had great difficulty in screwing up the courage, and when I had explained about the riding club, he didn't help me at all, demanding in his then very guttural accent, 'Well, what have you got to say for yourself?' I stuttered nervously how keen we all were to improve our horsemanship, how we had read his book and how much we would appreciate it if he could spare the time to instruct us. At last, reluctantly, he agreed to a date and place.

As the day approached, we put an enormous amount of energy into grooming and tack-cleaning; but when it came, more urgent business had demanded H.W.'s presence and he sent a substitute. The friend was a pleasant man, but he lacked H.W.'s charisma and knowledge, and we were all deeply disappointed.

Later H.W. found time to come himself, but his ferocity with bad riders scared away some of the members. In those days, in moments of stress, his Ws had a habit of becoming Vs; so he said, 'This is vot you are doing to your pony's mouth,' as he took Edward's ear and gave it several sharp tweaks. And, after a particularly fierce roar at Patricia, he demanded, 'Vy are you veeping?' He seemed to have no idea of how ferocious he sounded, but fortunately, as the riding club members faded away and the club was abandoned, he became our friend and mentor. Even Cappy admired him, though they had nothing in common, and Mamma was thrilled that one of the fantasy Masters of Foxhounds of her youth had actually materialised. Later, seeing that I had grown to love H.W., she told me that she and I both liked difficult and dangerous men.

H.W. would tell stories of his wartime journeys round Britain, trying to find airfields. Endlessly lost in a land from which all road signs and finger-posts had been removed and maps taken out of circulation, stopping to ask the way was a waste of time; his Dutch accent meant he was invariably taken for a German spy, or parachutist, and the locals, filled with patriotic cunning, would send him in the opposite direction. At the Wynmalens' Kingswood House there was the sort of stableyard we had always longed for, and it was bliss to be invited there. At first we rode Holly, a pony belonging to Julia – H.W.'s vivacious second wife, whom we were invited to call Juanita. Later we graduated to riding the horses. Basa, the grey, Hungarian-bred Arab stallion, was my favourite. Highly intelligent and lovely to look at, he was almost house-trained. It was as though he had an inherited memory of sharing an Arab master's tent. He used one corner of his loose box as a lavatory, and when I rode him in the outdoor school I was disconcerted by his refusal to sully the peat track; he would suddenly turn and leave his droppings neatly in the grass alongside. We were also allowed to drive the high-stepping hackney horse in the elegant phaeton, which was a thrilling exercise in the control of energy, and quite unlike driving a pony and cart. In the garage at Kingswood hung fascinating evidence of H.W.'s previous life – a collection of framed photographs, depicting youthful helmeted aviators standing beside tiny aircraft, which appeared to be tied up with string.

It was largely through H.W.'s instruction and interest that we were in the vanguard when, after the war, British riders began to adopt the continental style of horsemanship. We dutifully passed on all we had learned to our pupils and ponies which enabled them – representing the South Berkshire Pony Club – to win the first nationally-held Pony Club Inter-branch Competition in 1949.

It was also fortunate for budding equitation experts to have so many human and equine pupils on which to experiment. A single rider with one horse could not have made the mistakes, or had the successes, which increased our knowledge in such enormous bounds. I enjoyed teaching and found it deeply fulfilling, especially as time passed and our pupils became more advanced. I also loved schooling horses and knew the poetry of perfect harmony between horse and rider, not only when jumping and riding cross-country, but also in the well-executed dressage movement: half-passes at the canter, shoulder-in at the trot. I was not so keen on the housework of horses; mucking out was heavy and boring work, grooming was a chore that had to be done. Tack-cleaning, though dreary on one's own, became a social occasion at The Grove when a large number of the older pupils – including boys, those well-known haters of tack-cleaning – would stay on to help us.

Mamma enjoyed the riding school. She never interfered, though she would help in emergencies, and she shamelessly collected copy for More Ponies for Jean. Cappy didn't show much interest, and guarded his remaining territory of house and garden against the hordes of pupils, but I think he was pleased that we were doing something profitable and constructive and making a large contribution towards the telephone bill. In Bowley's absence, we tried to keep the place up; as well as clipping hedges, mending fences and mixing concrete, we picked the apples and, obeying the constant exhortations to 'Dig for Victory', attempted to grow soft fruit and vegetables.

Firewatching teams were recruited in every street and village and in Peppard this seemed to be a female preserve; all the able-bodied men had joined the Home Guard. Mamma and I attended a training session at which Marjorie (the dominant Miss Platt) and Babs, the Doctor's sister, were demonstrating the use of the stirrup pump. The water source was a bucket and, while Babs pumped, Marjorie directed the jet on the imaginary incendiary bomb. They took it extremely seriously, and their commanding cries of 'Ready, Babs?' and 'Water on!' 'Water off!' gave Mamma and me the giggles. Marjorie and Babs organized a rota and a route round the scattered village, and we were enrolled. At first we rode and the ponies seemed to enjoy a nocturnal expedition, but there were soon complaints about the clatter of hoofs waking the inhabitants and we had to walk our beat, gazing up at the rooftops to see if some unnoticed plane had dropped an incendiary.

The phoney war ended, and, with terrifying rapidity, the Germans occupied Denmark and Norway and in May launched their long-awaited attack on Belgium and France. The news was always bad and when the much-vaunted Maginot line fell and the out-flanked allies fell back, our hearts sank and sank. Only the fact that Winston Churchill had become Prime Minister, and we had a leader at last, saved us from despair. Our parents, though deeply gloomy, normally preserved stiff upper lips, but I remember Mamma hiding tears as she listened to Duff Cooper, the Minister for Information, speaking from Paris and she knew that her beloved France was about to fall. There was also the worry about Granny who had obstinately refused her last chance to come home, as the remaining English residents – including the novelist Somerset Maugham – were evacuated on a coal boat.

Then, on Mamma's birthday, May 27th, abject defeat became elevated into a kind of victory, when the Navy and a flotilla of little ships and boats chugged across the Channel to fetch home the soldiers trapped on the beaches of Dunkirk. We listened avidly to every news bulletin, and the courage of the crews of tugs, fishing and pleasure-boats, making trip after trip, filled us all with pride. Then came Churchill's famous speech about defending our island whatever the cost:

'We shall fight on the beaches and the landing grounds, we shall fight in the fields and in the streets, we shall fight in the hills; we shall never surrender . . .' And, as with all his wartime speeches, he lifted our spirits and we believed him implicitly.

As the twins have written, the Battle of Britain went on all that beautiful summer. The Germans had taken over the French and Belgian airfields and were now on our doorstep. We watched the aircraft streaking cross the brilliant blue sky, there were vapour trails and smoke trails, but one never knew whether the planes were ours or theirs. Below, the garden bloomed with careless indifference, the herbaceous borders were a bee-loud dream and Mamma swore she would never like phlox again. In September there were heavy attacks on the airfields near London and then on September 7th the Blitz began. In November it was the turn of the Midlands to be bombed and the German planes would fly over The Grove every night. At first they were heavy-laden and then, as they returned in the early hours, their engines had a different note, and you knew they had dropped their bombs. Christine has described how Denis lay dying of peritonitis. I have never forgotten the night the parents came home and our relief that Denis was out of danger was muted by their grey faces and look of exhaustion. They had spent their days at his bedside, the nights at a hotel in the midst of the bombing, and they had economised on food. We gave them dinner and hurried them to bed, and then, as Christine has told, the hospital rang to say Denis was haemorrhaging and asked them to return at once. They set off into the night, with the tiny amount of light that the blackout shutters on headlights allowed, Cappy reassuring us that he more or less knew the way.

We went to bed. Later, when the telephone rang again, I answered. A voice asked if the parents had started and, when I said 'Yes', rang off. The twins were asleep; Nana called out to know who it was. I told her and went back to my room convinced that Denis was dead. It was a terrible night. All the week before I had been praying for Denis, now suddenly I found myself praying for Mamma. I hardly slept at all for I knew how much she loved Denis and I felt that his death would destroy her.

Nana did not seem perturbed and next morning began her

daily quarrel with Joan, who still came in for a few hours to cook for us. When I burst into tears, too miserable to arbitrate, it was Joan, not Nana, who tried to comfort me. At lunchtime Mamma telephoned. She was horrified to learn that we had been left in suspense, for the nurses had told her we had been reassured that Denis was not in danger.

The parents had suffered unnecessary horrors, too, for on reaching the hospital – it was one of those hastily converted from lunatic asylums – they had found the impregnable gates locked. They had banged and shouted frantically, as they imagined Denis dying, and, after an age, had wakened the gatekeeper and been let in. The surgeon had also been locked out, but being young he had climbed the gates – and then found that the haemorrhage was not from a vital area; it was a false alarm. Denis recovered slowly, but was never to be graded A1 again. We became regular blood donors as we waited in vain for his character to change, expecting that, full of Birmingham blood, he would develop a taste for begonias and the shiny cushions with tassels which we believed decorated every Midland home. Indignant at missing active service, he later volunteered as a glider pilot, but was fortunately turned down for being colour-blind.

Of the dogs, Darkie died during the war, and Mamma took on Sarah, a deerhound belonging to a young RAF officer who had been posted overseas. Sarah was slightly smaller than a wolfhound, and had even less brain. Later when Denis was sent overseas with an Infantry Method of Instruction Team, another dog joined us – a golden cocker spaniel jointly owned by Denis and his girl friend Joan, who was also posted abroad. Rufus was an enthusiastic dog, who showed extremes of excitement when walks or dinners were mentioned; but his vocabulary was small and, using the same voice, you could invoke equal joy by offering to have him painlessly destroyed. Initiated by Denis, we all used this as Rufie's party piece.

Life would have been very drear without the riding and writing. No adolescent amusements were provided in the winter and long journeys in blacked-out buses to blacked-out towns were not lightly undertaken. There was no opportunity for adolescent rebellion, for how could you rebel, or even complain, when other people were being bombed or shot down by German planes? Adults were in short supply and we found ourselves called upon to help with running gymkhanas and building show-jumping courses for local shows, all run to raise money for the Red Cross or some other worthy cause. We were asked to provide pony rides, which were extremely popular, at charity fêtes. But it was purgatory for ponies to have endless children scrambling on and off their backs and, by the end of the day, they longed to savage every child in sight. The riders were often insatiable, running to rejoin the queue after every turn. I remember a police fête in Reading where the long queues for each pony never grew less and, when evening fell and we insisted on going home, the waiting mothers were furious.

In the winter evenings we settled down to write. Now we had proved that we could get our stories published without adult help, it became permissible to consult Mamma on literary matters. To split an infinitive was definitely a sin, and she vowed to turn in her grave if we ever sold our copyrights. But when I asked how to punctuate – I seem to have missed that lesson at Wychwood – she answered, 'By inspiration' which I found unhelpful.

Mostly we were referred to Quiller-Couch's *On the Art of Writing*. He taught us not to use 'case', 'Jargon's favourite child', to prefer the concrete word to the abstract and the direct expression to circumlocution, while the advice contained in *The King's English* – to prefer the short word to the long, the Saxon word to the Romance – soon had us in conflict with horse show committees determined to use 'commence' and 'terminate' on their schedules.

In conversation one could commit endless sins. Cappy had always banned horse-talk at meals, except for tea, on the grounds that we must not become horsey bores. His other constant cry was '*Think* before you speak', but I think this had less influence, for most of us still belong to the 'How do I know what I think until I see what I say?' school of thought. Another of his injunctions was that we must learn to drink beer and *always* ask for it when taken out by impecunious young men. This last was delivered with feeling, for apparently Mamma had always asked for champagne when they were courting. Saying 'Pardon?' instead of 'What?' was the worst sin of all, and young men using the dreaded word were never welcomed to the house.

Mamma had added children talking about school to her list of sins. Veronica in *Blind Messenger* is much afflicted by her children's endless accounts of school and their use of peer group words, and a boy in *More Ponies for Jean* is said to be 'all right, except that he will talk about school'. Now that our Wychwood days were over, we found that profitless speculation and all sentences beginning with 'I wonder' were also sinful. Dithering and saying 'I don't mind' had never been allowed, and women who bought dresses and then spent the day wondering if they 'should have taken the blue' were beyond the pale. If you did wish to make a banal remark it had to be addressed to a fictitious Mrs Snooks. 'It never rains, but it pours, Mrs Snooks,' was perfectly acceptable.

As I grew older and voiced alien opinions, Mamma was inclined to dismiss them with 'Claptrap!' She believed in evil and free will and her other retort, when I tried to excuse delinquent behaviour on the grounds of a difficult childhood or chemical imbalance, was a mocking 'Glands!'

Though the parents' censoriousness did not inhibit our conversation or prevent us holding our own views, it did limit our friendships. There were so many people you could not ask to the house; or if they turned up, you waited on tenterhooks for them to commit one of the many deadly sins. I think my only teenage rebellion took place quietly inside myself; I began to feel that the parents' feuds were absurd and most of the sins were nonsense.

Physically, I was an extremely late developer. At seventeen I was still a year away from puberty, and it was only by growing until I was twenty-two that I finally matched the twins in height. I struggled to become adult. I smoked for a whole week and then decided that, as I still hated it, cigarettes must be a waste of money. I took to lipstick and, in the absence of hairdressers, put my hair in rollers every night to produce a fashionable pageboy style. Most women had given up and, tying a greasy ribbon round their heads, turned their hair outwards and then tucked the ends behind the band, making a very unbecoming roll. We all three tried to look older than we were and, finding that felt hacking hats were still in the shops and needed no coupons, we wore them in our roles as riding instructors, convinced that they gave us an air of authority and sophistication.

Being stunted had its uses. As I still weighted less than seven stone, I could break and school the small ponies. Mr Sworder had produced a charming little skewbald called Sunstar, who became so accomplished that to keep her in the 'family' we arranged to sell her at a loss to one of our pupils. Later, when outgrown, she was sold to the small daughter of a show-jumping family at a vast profit, and we learned not to expect a return on generosity. We tried to persuade Mr Sworder to buy horses for the twins to school, but this was not a success, for he wasn't prepared to put up the extra money needed. I remember only a huge gawky chestnut, which couldn't bring itself to jump and finally fell spectacularly flat, crushing a long section of the paddock hedge.

In June the Germans invaded the Soviet Union and, though we were used to Hitler breaking his treaties and overpowering his erstwhile friends, this time there was a general feeling that he had made a mistake – the bully had picked on someone his own size – and there was quiet jubilation that we were no longer fighting alone.

Our expectation of invasion had faded, but Cappy was still fiercely territorial about his defences. When white lines were painted over the camouflage of a small concrete pillbox placed strategically at the Gravel Hill crossroads, he roared, raged and then painted 'What fool did this?' across the offending lines. The culprit was an official, I think the District Surveyor, who had hoped to save the populace from colliding with the emplacement in the dark. The whole village read the message and laughed. The Surveyor was deeply humiliated, and his son came to The Grove to protest. I never knew what he said, but Cappy decided that I must make a return visit. I was to tell the District Surveyor that I had come as my brother was in the army, and then point out the absurdity of endangering the lives of the Home Guard by painting white marks on their defences. I was far from willing, but Cappy seemed to think it was my duty to support him, so I set off with my feelings lurching between trepidation and disgust. When, in the Surveyor's office, I announced the reason for my visit, his reply was, 'I think you are a very brave little girl', which I found both unexpected and deflating. I struggled on with my next piece, and he answered that he didn't feel fathers should involve children in their disputes. I wanted to say that I agreed with him and, if it had been my quarrel, I would have made it up there and then, but I had to depart on frosty terms. And afterwards there was the embarrassment of meeting him in the road and having to look away; I hated feuds.

I was pale, suffered from summer nose-bleeds, and became spotty. Christine teased me, saying I had a bovine temperament and little sunken eyes. I taunted her with 'codfish eyes' in return and complained that while I followed the middle way, she soared and plunged from trough to peak. Then Cappy said that I had acne, and that his sister Muriel had suffered from it. Mamma, outraged, drew herself up to her full height and observed, in Granny's voice, 'No daughter of mine has acne' – but I *was* provided with vitamin B. The problem, I discovered later, was that I didn't have the Cannan dry skin and while Mamma, Denis and the twins thrived on a policy of never letting soap touch their faces, mine cried out for it.

Mamma had decided that the twins, with their Dresden shepherdess complexions and their Scottish noses, were more marriageable than I was – Denis and I had inherited the squashy Pulleyn nose. Once she looked at me sadly and said, paraphrasing Yeats, 'You'll have to find someone to love the pilgrim soul in you.' I quite liked the idea of having a pilgrim soul, it seemed even more desirable than a Dresden shepherdess complexion.

As Diana and Christine have written, ponies usually loved living at The Grove, but I remember one, Mingo, who was miserable. She hated the noise and bustle, and when we sold her to an introverted teenager it was soon apparent that the solitary life suited her, and the change in her expression told us she was happy.

Physically and emotionally horses vary so much that they can never be fed or handled in a completely uniform way. There are also huge variations in their intelligence. Later, when Diana owned one of Basa's daughters, Favorita, she showed her how to undo the bolt on her stable door, and rewarded her when she pulled it back with her teeth. The clever horses and ponies watched with interest and then copied Favorita. Suddenly the yard was full of loose horses and barking dogs, and we had to hurry into Reading to buy a bolt for the bottom of every door. The less intelligent horses and ponies never learned the trick, but their very lack of brain was useful as it made them more suitable mounts for novice riders. It was always difficult to persuade non-riding parents to buy old ponies for their children. They hankered after three- and four-year-olds, convinced that it would be 'nice for them to grow up together', and ignored our warnings that, while older horses are consistent in their faults, young ones try out some new rebellion every day. Leaving an inexperienced and solitary child to cope with a young pony was akin to landing him or her with a juvenile delinquent. We learned never to take young horses out on their own when we had an important appointment, because, like small children, they sense that you are in a hurry and play up. We also learned that it was better to miss a train than to lose a battle. Of course we made mistakes. When Shandy, at his very first show, jumped a clear round, we allowed him to jump off. He jumped clear again; and then the injudicious judge had the triple raised to an enormous height for a twelve-two pony. We should have withdrawn, but we foolishly took a chance – and Shandy went in and refused three times. After that he never jumped in a show again. He had learned his lesson: if he jumped well he would be asked for more and more, if he refused three times he could leave the ring. So, though he would jump at home or at the pony club, at shows he invariably came out at the first fence.

We learned a lot about the children too. Some of our pupils were brought by nannies and at different times Berrys, Guinesses and Clores were having lessons, and the present Aga Khan, aged three. We always tried to persuade parents that seven was the perfect age to start. We felt that when children began too early, they became bored on the leading rein, before they had developed the brain and muscle to control a pony on their own. But, if parents insisted, the very small ones would be led out for half an hour with the instructor on foot. We found that it was important not to let small boys have frights or falls as, under twelve, they were much more nervous than girls. At puberty this seemed to change; the boys who had kept up their riding would grow in daring while some of the girls became more cautious. Boys invariably gave up if they were unsuccessful; they had to be taught well and provided with accomplished ponies. Some girls were equally ambitious, but for others the actual riding was not so important, it was loving and looking after the ponies that mattered and presumably satisfied their budding maternal instincts.

My childhood was over and, as I approached the age for war work, we began to discuss what I should do. Cappy had discovered that the Royal Army Veterinary Corps ran a remount depot at Melton Mowbray and was looking for women over eighteen to groom and exercise its horses. Half of me hankered to join something more adventurous and to wear a uniform; but it was rumoured that, with no need for further expansion and very few casualties, the Women's Services had grown top-heavy and new recruits were condemned to years of scrubbing floors. At least the Remount Depot seemed more exciting than that, or than the Land Army, which Aunt May suggested – I had had my fill of picking brussels sprouts with the frost on them and haymaking with a bleeding nose. Leaving the sixteen-year-old twins in charge, I settled for horse housework and set off for Melton Mowbray. In my suitcase was the typescript of *It Began With Picotee*, which still needed a tidy-up and an illustrator; I was soon to find one, Rosemary Robertson, among my fellow-workers.

Epilogue

Diana writes:-

My sisters say some of my contributions are too gloomy. Yet I remember my childhood at home as extremely happy, so is it this very happiness that causes the cruelties of humans, nature and chance to stand out in my mind? And was I more conscious of my failures than my sisters were of theirs?

I have forgotten to mention much: the joy of waking to cocks crowing and a dawn chorus which was surely one of the finest in the country; the pleasure of running early across dew-wet grass to let out my bantams, to watch them tripping one by one down the little ladder from their hatch-door. Or the excitement of helping wet chicks break from their egg shells before handing them to a clucking mother to tuck under her wing. Nor have I described the sheer, unforgettable physical pleasure of being one with a pony, of jumping a difficult fence or, better still, a double in perfect unison; and the contentment which steals over me even now when I sit in the grass with ponies around me. And the scent of flowers wild on the Oxfordshire banks or splendid in The Grove's garden, and the smell of new-mown hay and apples freshly picked. And I only have to see whiteheart cherries for sale to be back in those golden days in our own tree, legs astride a branch, eating as many as I wanted.

Of course there was a down side too: bleak mornings when you fought the rain or snow to reach your bantams, or, soaked through, rode ponies bareback from the fields. Above all there was the endless circle of birth and death: the burial of a little bantam one day and the chick breaking from the egg the next, a good preparation perhaps for life itself.

People, particularly academics, ask me whether I was handicapped by a mismanaged education. I don't know. We began adult life more literate than most, thanks mainly to Mamma, but embarrassingly ill-informed on many subjects and with no pieces of paper to help us get jobs. But when TB ended my career with horses, I had no difficulty in finding work with a literary agent, on the strength of a letter and an interview, and subsequently better-paid part-time work with other agencies and with publishers. Later, level pegging with graduate contemporaries, I turned down further opportunities, because I wanted more time for my addiction to writing. Would a conventional education have turned me into a better writer or would it have crushed the small talent I possess? These are, I think, unanswerable questions, and I do not resent my parents' decision, although reading Josephine's last piece I am staggered to think that the continuation of Christine's and my education, which ended when we were fourteen, may well have depended on whether or not there was a place for Josephine at a veterinary college.

Sometimes, if I wake in the early hours, I wonder whether I should have made more effort to understand Cappy. We were brought up to be brave, stoical, merry-hearted and physically tough, but not to be especially sensitive to others' feelings. The Pullein-Thompsons said what they meant and expected everyone to do the same. 'Don't hint,' was my mother's frequent cry. So I grew up without realising that not everyone is capable of saying what they mean first time round, without grasping that hints can signify a wish, a longing or a commitment which needs encouragement if it is to be voiced. Cappy, who suffered so many disappointments, didn't hint, but some of his actions were, I suspect, unheard cries for help. 'Stress' and 'counselling' were not words in our vocabulary. The stiff upper lip, although mocked in theory, was in practice expected of us all. And so it's quite possible that Cappy would have been insulted and infuriated by any attempt of mine to understand him. As I grew older I did try to breach the gulf between us. 'Have a good time,' I would foolishly say as he set off to shop in Reading and, hating what he saw as condescension, he would tell me how utterly stupid my remark was.

The stiff upper lip had seen our parents through two world wars and one of the worst financial slumps England has known. they only went abroad together once – in 1946, to re-inter Granny, repay Silvio and holiday in the south of France – but they believed in enjoying life. Henley Regatta, Wimbledon, riding, foxhunting, golf, films, plays, books, drinks with friends at the pub, cocktail parties, gardening – their life was far from dull; they never got up late or rested in the afternoons. Mamma was nearly always in the process of writing her next book. Cappy was looking for more challenges. He restarted the Kenton Theatre in Henley, organised fêtes and celebrations for VE day, ran the local cadets and more. After retirement he became a County Councillor and, when infirmity ended his golfing days, he learned croquet and played in a tournament in Oxford shortly before his death, a hard example to follow.

There were two older girls I admired immensely for their style and sophistication when I saw them once or twice at children's parties. The first, Anthea Hodgson, married the publisher Michael Joseph; the second, Amaryllis Fleming, became a famous cellist. Gauche and untidy, I coveted their clothes, their hair and what I saw as their self-confidence. Nearly half a century later, I had reason to write to Anthea, who was by now a widow. 'You may just remember me,' I began by way of introduction, 'as one of three rather scruffy girls.' And writing back Mrs Joseph said she *did* remember us, but 'on the contrary, how we envied you your Bohemian way of life'. That I suppose sums up the normal longing of almost every child at some stage to lead a different life. I think I loved Mamma, The Grove and the animals far too much to want to swap places with anyone, but sometimes I simply longed to be a different me.

* * * *

Josephine writes:-

It is fascinating, but probably a waste of time, to speculate on what one might have been like if the circumstances of childhood had been different. I always assumed that perfect parents were an impossibility, as each generation is either repeating, or reacting against, the imperfections of its own parents – 'Glands!' I hear Mamma's voice mocking – and, consequently, no childhood could ever be perfect.

We were lucky to have a lively and witty mother who, though often critical, was never boring and never nagged. I believe poor Cappy wanted to be a good and jolly father, but his upbringing, his innate jealousy, and the five years spent in the trenches, followed by years of almost constant pain, seemed to have filled him with anger. It was, I think, our awareness of this volcano waiting to erupt that made a trusting relationship with him impossible. His physical disabilities also influenced us, but in a constructive way. Having a father who could not fetch and carry for you and occasionally needed your help – if Denis wasn't at home I would be stood on top of the refrigerator to fix the electrical fuses – encouraged self-reliance. Growing up in the war, with all the able-bodied men away in the services, called for yet more self-reliance, and Mamma's admiration for those who were 'good' on a desert island ennobled it into a virtue.

Without the twins my childhood would have been very different and I suspect that I would have been more of a bookworm, less of a doer. The challenges of two very enterprising younger sisters forced me to compete, and I had to learn to lead by stealth; this has proved very useful in later life when chairing committees. There is no doubt that numbers generate courage and as a three we did much more than any one of us would have attempted on her own.

With so much space we enjoyed the advantages of growing up in a family without too many of the disadvantages. Meals could be claustrophobic, but otherwise it was easy to escape to solitude or to commune with the animals. The presence of Bowley and then Joan as part of the extended family was important, as we were sadly deprived of grandparents.

Though we were encouraged to be endlessly active, contemplation was permitted. 'A poor life this, if full of care, we have no time to stand and stare' was an unanswerable retort to anyone complaining of your sloth or procrastination. As we grew older, Mamma's 'I don't care what you do as long as you're not non-entities' acted as a spur, partly because the shame of failure or of making a fool of yourself was rated so low. Her 'Well, it's not the end of the world,' or 'Where's your sense of proportion?' helped one to accept trivial defeats and go on trying.

Possibly we would have been better writers if we had had less happy childhoods. The loneliness of the remittance child, or the inhibitory rule of the convent school, seem to offer more fertile breeding-grounds for imagination than bucolic happiness. But there was always a pony-book flavour about The Grove: Cinderella, Ugly Duckling, Rags-to-Riches themes abounded. Beginning without skill, wearing the wrong clothes and riding untrained ponies, we failed for a time and then succeeded beyond all expectations. We bought ponies with bad names which became prizewinners, and in the role of the hard-up scruffy child, we managed to beat the richer, well-dressed children on their expensive ponies. We became convinced that skill, courage and determination could triumph over almost anything and we tried to pass this on in our books.

In a television programme a psychiatrist spoke of our influence on the girls of the 'fifties and 'sixties and the feeling we gave them that they *could* succeed. Certainly our heroines were always equal and sometimes superior to the boys; they might suffer from doubts and indecision but by the last page their courage, patience and talent were rewarded. We have boy readers too – they often complain that the book jackets invariably depict a girl – and at a comprehensive school I was introduced to a male fan. Aged thirteen, he had read one of my books eleven times: it was *Showjumping Secret*, a story told by its hero, who is recovering from polio.

I think our lack of education would have been a disaster if we had not learned to read and write fluently, if we had not lived in a house full of books and been taught that all knowledge was accessible to those prepared to look things up.

Of course the final report from Wychwood was right, 'gaiety and high spirits would not find us jobs in life'. But I think they equipped us to deal with life itself and certainly we all grew up feeling that we were the Captains of our Fate and the Masters of our Souls.

* * * *

Christine writes:-

So with time we did become 'Fair girls on grey horses,' for we each had a grey – the Grove Greys, we called them. We whipped in to the Woodland Foxhounds and Henry Wynmalen was heard to say once that he had never seen anyone cross country like the Pullein-Thompson sisters. We bought ourselves the right clothes: boots from Peal & Co, breeches from Savile Row, coats from Moss Bros. While we had grown up, old grooms had faded away and girl grooms had taken over. And riding had ceased to be a pastime for a few and – how ugly it sounds – a leisure industry. I have been told that our books changed the way people treated horses. I hope so. Certainly we considered horses individuals and friends rather than animals to be exploited. Perhaps that is why we were so successful with supposedly wicked and ruined horses.

By the 'fifties we had two stables and forty-two horses, but life without crippling business rates was easier then. Clients demanded less; they happily rode quietly when the ground was hard, and dismounted and led their mounts when the roads were slippery with ice and hard-packed snow. I think we were lucky to have spent our childhood so free from fear, free from child-snatchers and cars travelling at ninety miles an hour; so free that as we grew older we could ride ponies bareback a mile along the road to Peppard Common twice a day in headcollars, two on each side of the one we rode in the middle. Who would dare to do that now?

On the whole there was little acrimony at The Grove. Returning, I would hurry from the bus stop at Gravel Hill, past the Chapel; and then, seeing the tree at the corner and knowing I was almost there, a great sense of joy would sweep over me, and I would run the last few precious yards home. Of course loving it so much I stayed too long, and kept returning.

Sadly Diana and I have never really escaped from the trauma of being twins. Too often we have heard each other at different ends of a room saying the same thing at the same time. Somehow it diminishes one. I do not know what the answer is. We were alike, we looked alike, and often we were dressed alike. I think we were alluded to as 'the twins' for far too long. But really I cannot blame anyone; maybe it's just the fate of identical twins. And I wish Cappy and Mamma had discussed things more with us. So often I was guessing how they wanted me to be, and what they wanted me to do – Diana too. Sometimes we got it wrong and they said nothing. I cannot tell you why. Maybe it was to do with being free spirits.

I have never been back to The Grove, not even when I lived within easy riding distance. Too much of me is still there, and I know that without the people who made it what it was, it would feel desolate and full of ghosts. Besides I could not bear to see the house in the paddock now, and the damson trees, where we once hung our dental braces, long gone. But I sometimes wonder if the weather vane still turns with the wind on the old stable roof. And is the Blenheim tree still standing in the orchard? And the spinney full of bluebells in the spring? And is the brick flagged floor still there in the dining room? And the beech tree we could see from our bedroom window where squirrels chattered? And are there horses in the top meadow? And who sits now where Mamma sat writing her novels in the bay window in the drawing room?

No, I shall not go back, for it was a time and an era which has gone; a time of endeavour and hope, when right was right and wrong was wrong and there was nothing in between. Besides, I want to remember it just as it was, for in spite of the drawbacks of being a twin, for me it was, and will for ever remain, a child's paradise.